Using German

A guide to contemporary usage

MARTIN DURRELL

Henry Simon Professor of German, University of Manchester

CAMBRIDGE UNIVERSITY PRESS

Companion titles to *Using German*

A guide to contemporary French usage
R. E. Batchelor and M. H Offord
[ISBN 0 521 28037 0]

Using Spanish
A guide to contemporary usage
R. E. Batchelor and C. J. Pountain
[ISBN 0 521 42123 3 hardback]
[ISBN 0 521 26987 3 paperback]

Using French synonyms
R. E. Batchelor and M. H. Offord
[ISBN 0 521 37277 1 hardback]
[ISBN 0 521 37878 8 paperback]

Published by the Press Syndicate of the University of Cambridge
The Pitt Building, Trumpington Street, Cambridge CB2 1RP
40 West 20th Street, New York, NY 10011–4211, USA
10 Stamford Road, Oakleigh, Victoria 3166, Australia

© Cambridge University Press 1992

First published 1992

Printed in Great Britain at the University Press, Cambridge

A catalogue record for this book is available from the British Library

Library of Congress cataloguing in publication data

Durrell, Martin.
Using German: a guide to contemporary usage / Martin Durrell.
    p.   cm.
Includes index.
ISBN 0 521 42077 6 hardback.   ISBN 0 521 31556 5 paperback
1. German language – Grammar – 1950– 2. German language –
Textbooks for foreign speakers – English.   I. Title.
PF3112.D78   1992
438.2′421 – dc20   91–20949   CIP

ISBN 0 521 42077 6 hardback
ISBN 0 521 31556 5 paperback

Contents

Abbreviations used in this book are given in full on page 258

Introduction

This book is directed at the student who has mastered the basics of German and is venturing into the complexities and subtleties of the language. It is not a comprehensive grammar, but it deals with those aspects of German grammar and usage which the advanced learner may find difficult.

The areas of difficulty which are treated in this book can be grouped under two headings. First, there are those which result from variation within the German language itself. The learner may often be confused because everyday and conversational German is often quite different from written German and from what he or she has been taught. German, just like English, has many alternatives and varieties – in pronunciation, grammar and vocabulary. One purpose of this book is to explain for the English-speaking learner how modern German usage can differ widely, depending, for instance, on the formality or informality of the situation or on where the speaker or writer comes from. This kind of variation in usage can be unsettling for the foreign learner, and standard reference works often give insufficient detail or contradictory information. In this book, the most common variations in current usage which stem from regional differences or differences depending on the degree of formality are shown as fully as possible. It will be made clear, for example, that the use of the present subjunctive is not a matter of grammatical rule, but of register (see section **4.5**). Chapter **1** provides an introduction, with examples and commented texts, to the range of variation in modern German. The reader is advised to study this chapter closely before consulting the other chapters, which are intended to be used for reference and give extensive detail on selected points concerning vocabulary (chapter **2**), declensions (chapter **3**), grammar (chapter **4**) and syntax and word order (chapter **5**).

Secondly, the book covers those aspects of German which for one reason or another cause particular difficulty for English speakers. This may be because German expresses things in a different way to English, as when English uses present participles and German does not (see section **5.3**), where there is a lack of one-to-one correspondence between the vocabulary of the two languages (see section **2.1**) or in the various uses of prepositions (see section **2.5**). In such cases the differences between the languages are shown in as much detail as possible. There are other aspects of German, such as gender and plural of nouns (see section **3.1**), which have to be coped with in their own terms, as there is little comparable in English.

The prime intention of this book is to provide information on German as it is actually used nowadays, especially on points where conventional grammars and surveys of vocabulary are silent. It aims to help the English-speaking learner to communicate effectively and accurately by developing an awareness of the subtleties of the language.

Acknowledgements

No book such as this can be the unaided work of a single individual, and I must acknowledge a debt of gratitude to Wini Davies, Dr Karen Herrmann, Professor R. E. Keller and Paul Webster for their many helpful suggestions which have been incorporated in the text. The remaining inadequacies are my own, especially where I have been foolish enough to ignore their sound advice. I am also grateful for much information, advice and encouragement to Stephen Barbour, Friedrich Dehmel, Julie Flynn, Anna Hochsieder, Derek McCulloch, Herbert Meyer, Manfred Prokop, Margaret Rogers, Jon West and Ellen Wilhelmi, all of whom provided me with data or were kind enough to read particular chapters. My thanks are due, too, to all colleagues at the Institut für deutsche Sprache in Mannheim, especially Dr Karl-Heinz Bausch, Tobias Bruckner, Professor Alan Kirkness, Professor Gerhard Stickel and Eva Teubert. I was able to collect or check much of the material in the book during a stay in Mannheim which was generously funded by the Deutscher Akademischer Austauschdienst. The great bulk of the initial work was completed in the academic year 1983/84, which I spent as an exchange professor at the University of Alberta, and I must give special thanks to all my colleagues in Edmonton for their help and encouragement during a thoroughly enjoyable and productive stay in Canada. Particular mention must be made of the superb library facilities at the University of Alberta. I should also like to thank Rosemary Davidson, Amanda Ogden, Annie Cave and Julia Harding for their invaluable editorial advice and much encouragement, Debbie Carlisle for her skill in coping with a difficult manuscript and, last but not least, all my past and present students in London, Manchester and Edmonton, whose queries and problems furnished much of the raw material.

General reference books

The following reference works were consulted at all stages of preparing the manuscript.

E. Agricola *et al.* (eds.), *Wörter und Wendungen. Wörterbuch zum deutschen Sprachgebrauch*, 8th edn, Leipzig 1977.

M. Clyne, *Language and Society in the German-speaking Countries*, Cambridge 1984.

J. Dückert and G. Kempcke (eds.), *Wörterbuch der Sprachschwierigkeiten. Zweifelsfälle, Normen und Varianten*, Leipzig 1984.

DUDEN, *Das große Wörterbuch der deutschen Sprache*, 6 vols., Mannheim 1976ff.

DUDEN, *Grammatik der deutschen Gegenwartssprache*, 4th edn, Mannheim 1984.

DUDEN, *Rechtschreibung der deutschen Sprache und der Fremdwörter*, 17th edn, Mannheim 1973.

R. B. Farrell, *Dictionary of German Synonyms*, 3rd edn, Cambridge 1977.

A. E. Hammer, *German Grammar and Usage*, revised edn, London 1983.

K. E. Heidolph *et al.* (eds.), *Grundzüge einer deutschen Grammatik*, Berlin 1981.

G. Helbig and J. Buscha, *Deutsche Grammatik. Ein Handbuch für den Ausländerunterricht*, 3rd edn, Leipzig 1975.

G. Helbig and W. Schenkel, *Wörterbuch zur Valenz und Distribution deutscher Verben*, 4th edn, Leipzig 1978.

R. E. Keller, *The German Language*, London 1978.

A. Lamprecht, *Grammatik der englischen Sprache*, 5th edn, Berlin 1977.

R. Quirk *et al.*, *A Comprehensive Grammar of the English Language*. London and New York 1985.

P. Terrell *et al.* (eds.), *Collins German–English English–German Dictionary*, London and Glasgow 1980.

G. Wahrig, *Deutsches Wörterbuch*, Gütersloh 1968.

G. Wahrig (ed.), *dtv-Wörterbuch der deutschen Sprache*. Munich 1978.

Specific references

Where the books listed above give more information than could be encompassed in this book, or where I have made particular use of their material or presentation, they are listed below in abbreviated form, giving the author and the year of publication. Specialized works relevant to individual sections are also listed below.

1.3 Examples of variation: pronunciation

For this section the following standard works of reference were consulted. Both give details on acceptable (and unacceptable) colloquial and regional usage as well as on the received standard pronunciation of German. DUDEN, *Band 6: Aussprachewörterbuch*, 2nd edn, Mannheim 1974; and T. Siebs, *Reine und gemäßigte Hochlautung mit Aussprachewörterbuch*, 19th edn, revised by H. de Boor, H. Moser and C. Winkler, Berlin 1969.

1.5.1 Regional variation in vocabulary

The major sources for the material in this section were: J. Eichhoff, *Wortatlas der deutschen Umgangssprachen*, 2 vols., Bern/Munich 1977; and W. Seibicke, *Wie sagt man anderswo? Landschaftliche Unterschiede im deutschen Wortgebrauch* (DUDEN-Taschenbücher, vol. 15), Mannheim 1972.

1.5.2 Austrian and Swiss words

This section was compiled with assistance from the following works, which give much more detail on Austrian and Swiss lexical peculiarities: J. Ebner, *Wie sagt man in Österreich? Wörterbuch der österreichischen Besonderheiten* (DUDEN-Taschenbücher, vol. 8), Mannheim 1969; S. Kaiser, *Die Besonderheiten der deutschen Schriftsprache in der Schweiz*, 2 vols., Mannheim 1969–70; and H. Rizzo-Baur, *Die Besonderheiten der deutschen Schriftsprache in Österreich und Südtirol*, Mannheim 1962.

2.1 Problems of meaning

Much more detail on English–German lexical correspondences is to be found in Farrell (1977), to which this section is indebted at many points. I have also consulted E. Leisi, *Der Wortinhalt. Seine Struktur im Deutschen und Englischen*, 5th edn, Heidelberg 1975, which is still unequalled as a comparative study of the vocabulary of the two languages.

2.3 Word formation

For this section I have consulted W. Fleischer, *Wortbildung der deutschen Gegenwartssprache*, 3rd edn, Leipzig 1974, and the relevant sections in DUDEN (1984), pp 386–501.

2.5 Prepositions

The compilation of this section was particularly assisted by reference to Hammer (1983), chapter 13; Lamprecht (1977), pp 309–31; and to W. Schmitz, *Der Gebrauch der deutschen Präpositionen*, 9th edn, Munich 1981.

2.6 Modal particles

This section has benefited greatly from the account of the German particles in Hammer (1983), chapter 9; Helbig and Buscha (1975), pp 434–45; and H. Weydt *et al.* (eds.), *Kleine deutsche Partikellehre*, Stuttgart 1983.

3.1 Nouns: genders and plurals

The statistics in sections **3.1.1** and **3.1.2** are taken from G. Augst, *Untersuchungen zum Morpheminventar der deutschen Gegenwartssprache*, Tübingen 1975, pp 5–70.

4.1 Verbs and cases

DUDEN (1984), pp 602–33; Helbig and Buscha (1975), pp 51–68; and Helbig and Schenkel (1978) give extensive surveys of verb government and sentence patterns in German. These works were of great assistance in the compilation of this chapter. In addition, mention must be made of Wahrig (1978), which is particularly useful in that it indicates very clearly the construction found with each verb in all its meanings.

4.3.2 Past and perfect

The use of the past and perfect in modern German is comprehensively documented in S. Latzel, *Die deutschen Tempora Perfekt und Präteritum*, Munich 1977.

4.4 The passive

This section draws on the excellent accounts of German passive constructions in Helbig and Buscha (1975) and G. Helbig, *Probleme der deutschen Grammatik für Ausländer*, Leipzig 1976, pp 42–54.

4.5 The subjunctive

This account of the subjunctive in modern German is based largely on the survey by K.-H. Bausch, *Modalität und Konjunktivgebrauch in der gesprochenen deutschen Standardsprache*, Teil I, Munich 1979. I am most grateful to Dr Bausch for allowing me to consult the unpublished second part of his work.

4.6 The modal auxiliaries

The following works were particularly valuable in the compilation of this section: Hammer (1983), pp 227–33; Helbig and Buscha (1975), pp 109–14; Lamprecht (1977), pp 163–75; and F. R. Palmer, *Modality and the English Modals*, London 1979.

5.1 Word order

This explanation of German word order draws in particular on the accounts in U. Engel, *Syntax der deutschen Gegenwartssprache*, Berlin 1977; Heidolph *et al.* (1981), pp 702–64; U. Hoberg, *Die Wortstellung in der geschriebenen deutschen Gegenwartssprache*, Munich 1981; and H. W. Kirkwood, 'Aspects of Word Order and its Communicative Function in English and German', *Journal of Linguistics* 5 (1969), pp 85–106.

In addition, occasional examples and data were drawn from many sources, in particular from the Mannheim corpus of modern spoken and written German at the Institut für deutsche Sprache, from the works of Alfred Andersch, Thomas Bernhard, Heinrich Böll, Friedrich Dürrenmatt, Max Frisch, Max von der Grün, Herrmann Kant, Siegfried Lenz and Erwin Strittmatter and from the following newspapers and periodicals: *Bild, Frankfurter Allgemeine Zeitung, Frankfurter Rundschau, Neues Deutschland, Neue Zürcher Zeitung, Die Presse, Der Spiegel, Süddeutsche Zeitung, Die Zeit.* In order not to overburden the text unnecessarily, specific sources for such occasional data are only given where the source is particularly relevant or in the case of longer extracts.

Glossary of linguistic terms

In order to talk about language we need to use some special terms. Although we have tried in this book not to introduce a large number of technical terms, some are necessary both for the sake of clarity and to avoid lengthy and tedious repetitions. As far as possible, we have kept to the more usual grammatical terms. Some, such as 'noun', 'verb' and 'adjective', need no explanation but the less familiar ones commonly used for German and English are explained below. Not all of them are found in this book, but are included to help the reader consult other works, and for similar reasons German equivalents are given where they exist. Terms used in these definitions which are themselves explained in the glossary have been given an asterisk.

Ablaut   The vowel changes in the *past tense and *past participle of German *strong verbs, eg *singen, sang, gesungen*, see **3.3**.

accusative (*der Akkusativ*)   see **case**.

adverb (*das Adverb*)   A word or phrase used to indicate, for instance, how, where, why or when something happens or is done, eg *heute, aus diesem Grunde, in der Stadt*, see **5.1.5(c)**.

antecedent (*das Bezugswort*)   see **relative pronoun**.

apposition (*die Apposition*)   A descriptive phrase or word added to a noun phrase without any connecting preposition, eg *Kaiser Wilhelm II, **der letzte deutsche Kaiser**, starb im Exil in Holland*.

article (*der Artikel*)   *Determiners which give a noun specific reference. German has a 'definite' article (*der, die, das*, etc) and an 'indefinite' article (*ein, eine, einem*, etc), see **3.4**.

assimilation (*die Assimilation*)   The pronunciation of a particular sound may be affected by ('assimilated to') neighbouring sounds, eg in colloquial German *gebm, er hap mir* (for *geben, er hat mir*).

Ausklammerung   Excluding a phrase from the verbal *bracket, ie putting it after the *past participle, *separable prefix, etc, which is usually last in the clause, eg **Ich rufe an *aus London***, see **5.1.6**.

auxiliary verb (*das Hilfsverb*)   A verb used with another verb to make tenses, the passive voice, etc. The main German auxiliaries are *haben, sein, werden* and the *modal auxiliaries *dürfen, müssen*, etc.

(verbal) bracket (*die Klammer*)   The characteristic sentence construction of German whereby most elements of the sentence (or clause) are enclosed between the two parts of the verb, eg *Ich **habe** sie gestern in Ulm **gesehen***, see **5.1.1**.

case (*der Fall*)   The indication of the role played by a noun or pronoun in the sentence by *inflection, ie by changing its form or the form of the *determiners or adjectives used with it. German has four cases: the nominative (mainly for the *subject of the verb), the accusative (mainly for the *direct object), the dative (mainly for the *indirect object) and the genitive (mainly to show possession or to link nouns together), see **3.2**, **4.1** and **4.2**.

cleft sentence   A typically English construction, little used in German, by which part of the sentence is emphasized by placing it at the beginning in a clause introduced by *it*, eg *It was **yesterday** that she came*, see **5.1.4(d)**.

(adjective) comparison (*die Steigerung*)   The relative qualities of persons or things may be compared by using the comparative or superlative 'degree' of adjectives, usually formed in German by the suffixes *-er* and *-(e)st* respectively, eg *schnell – schneller* (comparative degree) *– (der) schnellste* (superlative degree).

complement (*die Ergänzung*)   A part of the sentence which is closely linked to the verb and 'completes' its meaning in some way, eg the *direct and *indirect objects, *prepositional objects, direction phrases with verbs of motion, etc, see **5.1.5(e)**.

compound (*die Zusammensetzung*)   A word formed by joining two (or more) words together, eg *das Rathaus, die Aktiengesellschaft, brustschwimmen*.

conditional   A conditional sentence (*der Konditionalsatz*) is one which contains or implies a condition. In German, they often contain the conjunctions *wenn* or *falls* and the verb is often in the past or pluperfect *subjunctive (*Konjunktiv II*, see **4.5**), eg *Wenn ich das Fenster aufmachte, würden wir alle frieren*. The *würde* form of *Konjunktiv II* is often called 'the conditional tense' in English grammars of German.

conjugation (*die Konjugation*)   see **inflection**.

conjunction (*die Konjunktion*)   A word used to join clauses together, eg *und, aber, wenn, nachdem*.

dative (*der Dativ*)   see **case**.

declension (*die Deklination*)   see **inflection**.

demonstrative (*das Demonstrativum*)   A word used to point to something specific, eg English *this, that*, German *dieser, jener*. Demonstratives may appear as *determiners or pronouns, see **3.5.1**.

determiner (*das Artikelwort, das Determinativ*)   One of a small group of function words used at the beginning of a noun phrase. They include the definite and indefinite *articles, *demonstrative adjectives, possessive adjectives (*mein, sein*, etc), the indefinites (*einige, jeder, mancher*, etc), and so on; see **3.4** and **3.5**. With a few exceptions, only one determiner can be used at a time, see **3.4.3**.

derivation (*die Wortbildung*)   Forming a word on the basis of another, usually with the help of *prefixes and/or *suffixes, eg *verbessern* ('derived' from *besser*), *Bildung* ('derived' from *bilden*), see **2.3**.

dialect (*der Dialekt, die Mundart*)   A language *variety restricted to a particular geographical area, see **1.2**. In the German speech-area they are often strikingly different from *Hochdeutsch* in phonetics and grammar. Compare Zurich German *Er isch i mys Huus choo*, Westphalian (Münster) *He is in mien Huus kuemmen* for standard German *Er ist in mein Haus gekommen*.

direct object (*das direkte Objekt*)   The person or thing directly affected by the action of the verb. In German it is in the accusative case, eg *Er stellte* **den Stuhl** *in die Ecke*.

doublet (*die Dublette, die Formvariante*)   An alternative form of the same word, eg *benutzen/benützen*, see **2.2.4**.

elision (*die Elision*)   The omission of a sound, as characteristically occurs in rapid colloquial speech. For example, in a word like *Hauptbahnhof* the *t* is often 'elided' in spoken German so that it sounds like *Haupbahnhof*.

ellipsis (*die Ellipse*)   Omitting words, typically in colloquial speech where their meaning can be deduced from the context. In spoken German, for instance, we often find ellipsis of pronouns, eg *Geht nicht* for *Das geht nicht*, or *Komm gleich* for *Ich komme gleich*.

extended epithet (*das erweiterte Attribut*)   An adjective, particularly a *participle, which is expanded into a clause-like construction, eg *die* **in dem Park spielenden** *Kinder*. Such constructions are characteristic of formal written German.

figurative meaning (*die übertragene Bedeutung*)   A word may have an 'extended' or 'figurative' meaning besides its 'literal' meaning. For example, *blaß*, besides its literal meaning 'pale', can have a figurative sense 'vague, faint', eg *eine blasse Ahnung*, 'a vague suspicion'.

filler   A conventionalized word or phrase used in conversation to give the speaker time to think or express a reaction, eg *selbstverständlich, das gibt's doch gar nicht*.

finite verb (*das finite Verb*)   A verb form used with a subject and agreeing with it through the ending, eg *er* **machte**, *ihr* **kommt** *an, er* **hat** *es gesagt*. Finite forms of the verb are distinguished in this way from the 'non-finite' forms, ie the *participles and the *infinitive.

gender (*das Genus*)   A grammatical classification system of nouns indicated in German by the different forms of the *determiners used with a particular noun, eg **der** *Tisch*, **die** *Luft*, **das** *Heft*. German has three genders: masculine, feminine and neuter, see **3.1**.

genitive (*der Genitiv*)   see **case**.

government (*die Rektion*)   The requirement that a particular verb or preposition should be followed by a noun in a particular case. Thus, in German, we say that *ohne* 'governs' a noun in the accusative and *helfen* 'governs' a noun in the dative.

Hochdeutsch   The standardized, official *variety of German as used in all the German-speaking countries, see **1.2**.

idiom (*die Redewendung*)   A set phrase with a special meaning which cannot be understood by taking the words individually, eg *schwer auf Draht* ('on the ball'), see **2.4**.

imperative mood (*der Imperativ*)   The form of the verb used to give commands, eg **Bleib** *da!* **Stellen Sie** *sich das vor!*

imperfect tense   see **past tense**.

indicative mood (*der Indikativ*)   The form of the verb used to make statements, ask questions, etc, eg *Sie* **kam** *aus dem Haus*, **Bringen** *Sie es mir morgen?*

indirect object (*das indirekte Objekt*)   A verb *complement which typically refers to a person indirectly affected by the action of the verb in some way, for instance by receiving the direct object, eg *Ich gab* **ihrem Bruder** *das Geld*. In German the indirect object is in the dative case, whilst in English it either precedes the direct object or is in a phrase introduced by *to*, eg *I gave **her brother** the money* or *I gave the money **to her brother***.

indirect speech (*die indirekte Rede*)   Also called 'reported speech': a construction in which what someone said is incorporated into our own sentence rather than quoted directly. Compare 'direct speech' *Er sagte: ,,Ich bin krank"* with 'indirect speech' *Er sagte, daß er krank sei*, see **4.5.2**.

infinitive (*der Infinitiv*)   The base form of a verb. In German it ends in *-en* or *-n*, eg *schlag**en**, zieh**en**, verhandel**n***. When used with another verb it is usually preceded by *zu* in the so–called 'infinitive phrase' (*der Infinitivsatz*), eg *Er hat mir empfohlen, **den Wagen in die Werkstatt zu bringen***.

inflection (*die Flexion*)   Changing the form of a word to show different grammatical categories, eg for case and plural with nouns, or tense, mood, person and number with verbs. Traditionally the 'inflection' of nouns and adjectives is referred to as 'declension', the 'inflection' of verbs as 'conjugation'.

inseparable verb (*das untrennbare Verb*)   A prefixed verb whose *prefix is not stressed and remains attached to the verb in all types of sentence construction. The main inseparable verb prefixes of German are: *be-, emp-, ent-, er-, ge-, ver-* and *zer-*, see **2.3.3**.

interjection (*die Interjektion*)   A part of speech such as *ah! oh! ach!* etc expressing a reaction or response.

inversion (*die Inversion*)   We speak of 'inversion' or 'inverted word order' in German if the verb precedes the subject, for instance in a question, or in a statement where something other than the subject occupies the initial position, eg *Gestern **habe ich** ihn nicht gesehen*, see **5.1**.

intransitive verb (*das intransitive Verb*)   A verb which does not govern a *direct object in the accusative case, eg *bleiben, fallen*, see **4.1**.

Konjunktiv   see **subjunctive**.

modal auxiliary verb (*das Modalverb*)   In German, the six verbs *dürfen, können, mögen, müssen, sollen* and *wollen* are known as 'modal auxiliary verbs'. They are used to express possibility, permission and obligation, see **4.6**.

modal particle (*die Modalpartikel*)   Short words such as *aber, auch, doch, ja, nur*, etc, which are very characteristic of spoken German and express the speaker's attitude to what is being said, see **2.6**.

nominative (*der Nominativ*)   see **case**.

number (*der Numerus*)   A grammatical category for indicating the difference between singular and plural. The difference between *Haus* and *Häuser* or between *ich komme* and *wir kommen* is one of 'number'.

object (*das Objekt*)   see **direct object** and **indirect object**.

participle (*das Partizip*)   see **past participle** and **present participle**.

partitive (*der Partitiv*)   An expression of measurement or quantity, eg ***ein Stück** Brot, **zwei Flaschen** Wein*, see **4.2.4**.

passive voice (*das Passiv*)   A verb form using the *auxiliary verbs *werden* or *sein* with the *past participle. The subject of the verb in the passive voice is normally the *direct object of the equivalent active construction, eg active *Sie lobte mich*, passive *Ich wurde (von ihr) gelobt*, see **4.4**.

past participle (*das zweite Partizip*)   A non-*finite verb form used as an adjective or with an *auxiliary verb to form the *perfect tense and the *passive, eg *gemacht, gestanden, zerbrochen*.

past tense (*das Präteritum*)   A simple tense (ie one formed without an *auxiliary verb) mainly used to relate events which occurred before the present moment, eg *machte, brach, zerfiel*, see **4.3.2**. This tense is sometimes called the 'imperfect tense' in English grammars of German, but this is a misleading term which is best avoided.

perfect tense (*das Perfekt*)   A tense formed with the present tense of the *auxiliary verbs *haben* or *sein* and the *past participle, eg *Ich habe gegessen, Sie ist angekommen*. It is used to relate past events to the moment of speaking and, especially in spoken German, to report past events, see **4.3.2**.

person (*die Person*)   A grammatical category of the verb by which we show the difference between the person(s) speaking ('first' person, ie *ich, wir*), the person(s) spoken to ('second' person, ie *du, ihr, Sie*) and other person(s) or thing(s) spoken about ('third' person, ie *er, sie, es*).

personal pronoun (*das Personalpronomen*)   Words such as *ich, du, ihm*.

phrasal verb (*das Funktionsverbgefüge*)   A combination of a noun derived from a verb and a common verb such as *bringen, kommen* or *nehmen*, eg *etw zum Abschluß bringen* ('to finish sth'), *in Betracht kommen* ('to be considered').

pluperfect tense (*das Plusquamperfekt*)   A tense formed with the *past tense of the *auxiliaries *haben* or *sein* and the *past participle, eg *Ich hatte geschlafen, Ich war gegangen*.

prefix (*das Präfix*)   An element added to the beginning of a word or root, eg **An***fall*, **ge***standen*, **un***glaublich*.

prepositional adverb (*das Präpositionaladverb*)   Words formed by the combination of *da(r)-* with a preposition, eg *dabei, darin, damit*, see **4.1.5**.

prepositional object (*das Präpositionalobjekt*)   A *complement of the verb, linked to it by means of a preposition, eg *Ich warte **auf** dich, Er glaubt **an** Wunder*, see **4.1.4**.

present participle (*das erste Partizip*)   A non-*finite verb form made by suffixing *–d* to the form of the *infinitive, eg *spielend, verbessernd*. Unlike the corresponding English *ing*-form (eg *playing*) the German present participle is mainly used as an adjective, see **5.3**.

principal parts (*die Stammformen des Verbs*)   The three main inflectional forms of each verb, ie the form of the *infinitive, the *past tense (first person singular) and the *past participle, eg *machen – machte – gemacht, sinken – sank – gesunken*, see **3.3**.

progressive tenses   In English, the tenses formed with the *auxiliary verb *to be* and the *ing*-form of the verb, eg *She is going, We shall be sailing*.

reflexive verb (*das reflexive Verb*)   A verb which is used in combination with the reflexive pronoun, ie *sich* in the third person and the pronoun corresponding to the subject in the first and second persons, eg *sich verabreden*.

register (*die Textsorte*)   A language *variety determined by use and influenced by such factors as medium (ie speech or writing), subject matter and situation, see **1.1**.

relative pronoun (*das Relativpronomen*)   A word which introduces a subordinate clause describing a noun, for instance English *who, which, that*, German *der, die, das*, etc. Eg *Die Frau, **die** einen Hut trägt, kenne ich nicht*, see **3.5.2**. The noun on which such a relative clause depends is called the 'antecedent'.

rhetorical question (*die rhetorische Frage*)   A question which is really a statement, as the answer is assumed to be obvious, eg *Wer kennt ihn nicht?*

Schachtelsatz   A German sentence construction where a number of clauses are contained within each other, eg *Der Autor, der ein Buch, das dieses Problem behandelt, geschrieben hat, hat in der Nazizeit sehr gelitten*. As such sentences may be confusing, they tend to be avoided in modern German, see **5.1.6**.

semantic (*semantisch*)   Having to do with meaning.

separable verb (*das trennbare Verb*)   A verb with a stressed *prefix which is detached from the verb in some sentence types (eg in statements) and forms the second part of the verbal *bracket, eg *ankommen: Wir **kommen** heute um fünf Uhr **an***.

stress (*die Betonung*)   In all words of more than one syllable in English and German, one syllable, known as the 'stressed' syllable, is pronounced with more force than the others. This is indicated in this book by the symbol ' before the stressed syllable, eg *Be'tonung, 'Anfang, le'bendig*.

strong verb (*das starke Verb*)   A verb whose *principal parts are made by altering the vowel (ie by *Ablaut*) and which has the suffix –*en* in the *past participle, eg *schwimmen – schwamm – geschwommen*.

subject (*das Subjekt*)   The noun or pronoun (in the nominative case) which determines the ending of the verb, ie with which the verb 'agrees' in *person and *number. In statements in the active voice the subject will typically be the person or thing performing the action, eg *Der **Stein** fiel mir auf den Kopf*.

subjunctive mood (*der Konjunktiv*)   A verb form mainly used in German to show *indirect speech or in *conditional sentences, see **4.5**.

subordinate clause (*der Nebensatz*)   Also called 'dependent clause'. A clause, usually introduced by a *conjunction, which functions as part of another clause (eg as subject, object, adjective, adverb) on which it depends. In German subordinate clauses the *finite verb is typically found as the second part of the verbal *bracket, eg *Die Frau, **die sehr klein war**, konnte es nicht erreichen* (the subordinate clause has the function of an adjective qualifying *Frau*), ***Als er ankam**, waren die Brüder schon fort* (the subordinate clause plays the role of an *adverb of time).

suffix (*das Suffix*)   An element added to the end of a word or root, eg *Bedeutung, gelblich, machte*. A grammatical suffix, as in *machte*, is often termed an 'ending'.

superlative (*der Superlativ*)   see **comparison**.

tag question   In English, the short questions with an auxiliary verb at the end of the sentence, eg *He's coming, **isn't he?***

topic (*das Thema*)   Also called 'theme'. The first stressed element in a sentence typically refers to something 'given' (having been mentioned previously) or 'known' to both speaker and listener. This is the 'topic' of the sentence and some 'new' or 'unknown' information (known as the 'comment' or 'rheme') is given about it. In German main clauses the topic typically occurs in first position before the *finite verb, see **5.1**. Thus the sentence *Dieses Buch hat sie in Ulm gekauft* starts with an element (*dieses Buch*) which has presumably just been referred to (the 'topic') and says something about it.

transitive verb (*das transitive Verb*)   A verb *governing a *direct object (in the accusative case), eg *schlagen, verbessern*, see **4.1**.

Umgangssprache   The *register of everyday speech in modern German, often coloured with regionalisms, see **1.1** and **1.2**.

variant (*die Variante*)   A word, sound or grammatical form typical of a particular *variety, see **chapter 1**.

variety (*die Varietät*)   A particular form of language with differences characteristic of a particular region, social group, speech situation or medium, etc. *Hochdeutsch, *dialects, *Umgangssprache, *registers are all 'varieties' of German, see **chapter 1**.

valency (*die Valenz*)   A term often used in modern German grammars to refer to the types of *complement found with a particular verb or the kinds of object it *governs.

verbal noun (*das Verbalsubstantiv*)   A noun formed from a verb, either the *infinitive used as a noun, eg *das Kommen*, or some other form of *derivation, eg *die Bedeutung* (from *bedeuten*) or *der Bruch* (from *brechen*).

weak masculine noun (*das schwache Maskulinum*)   A masculine noun which forms its genitive case with the ending *–en*, eg *des Menschen, des Franzosen*, see **3.2.1**.

weak verb (*das schwache Verb*)   A verb which forms its *past tense and *past participle with the ending *–t*, eg *machen – machte – gemacht*, see **3.3**.

1 Varieties of language

German is spoken as a native language by about 92 million people in 15 countries, the largest speech community in Western and Central Europe. It is an official state language in Germany, Austria, Switzerland (with Liechtenstein) and Luxembourg. It also has recognized regional status in areas of Belgium, Denmark, Italy and Romania and accounts for sizeable minorities in France, Hungary and the Soviet Union. It is used in many ways: for everyday conversation, formal speech, technical writing, journalism, literature (in the widest sense), and so on.

Given this broad geographic range and the number of uses to which it is put, it is quite natural that there are many variations. Different words, grammatical constructions and sentence types are used depending on who is speaking or writing, to whom, on what topic, in what circumstances, in what region. Most people can choose to speak formally or informally as they feel appropriate in a given situation. A student, for instance, will express himself or herself in different ways when discussing politics or sport with friends in a café, talking to his or her parents or a lecturer, writing a seminar paper or a letter of application for a job. The spoken language will also differ markedly from Berlin to Munich, Zürich or Vienna. There may be substantial differences between the written German of a modern novel, a serious newspaper, a history book and a travel guide. All these different forms are *varieties* of German, and we can identify those characteristic features, the *variants*, which go to make up each variety. In the process of learning their own language native speakers develop an awareness of the variants available to them and a degree of competence in using those which are appropriate to a given situation. They also develop a keen sensitivity towards such variation, so that when they hear or read a particular variant in an inappropriate context it will sound at best out of place, and, as often as not, comical, affected, pompous, slipshod – or even rude. Clearly, this presents problems, and potential traps, for the foreign learner. In order to communicate effectively in German he or she has to go through a much more conscious process of acquiring the ability to recognize and use those forms which are right for each particular situation. This is not always straightforward because there are no hard and fast rules, and yet the language is most frequently presented in a rather artificially uniform variety in the early stages of learning. Initial confrontation with variation can be confusing or frustrating – for example when a student finds that laboriously learnt grammatical constructions amuse native speakers if they are used in everyday conversation, or when he or she is told that a particular expression is not said 'here', often with the implication that it is not very good German. But developing competence in handling varieties appropriately is an essential aspect of mastering the

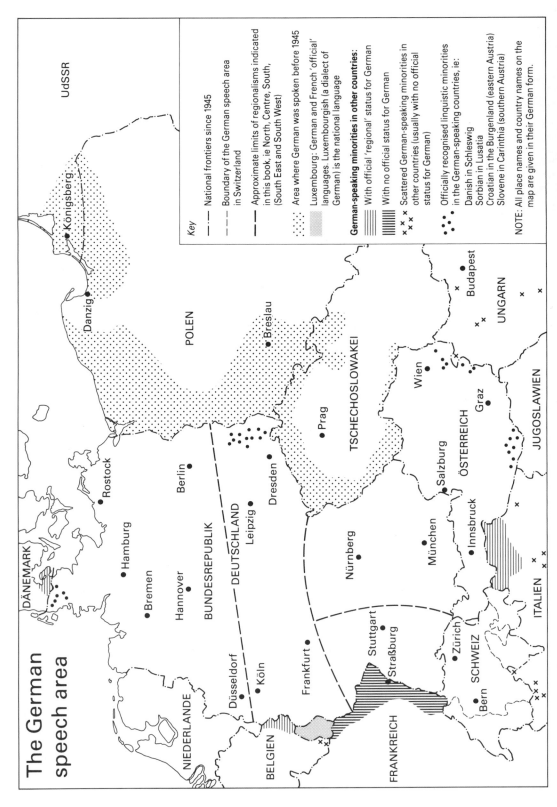

The German
speech area

Key

— National frontiers since 1945

– – – Boundary of the German speech area
in Switzerland

– · – Approximate limits of regionalisms indicated
in this book, ie North, Centre, South,
(South East and South West)

Area where German was spoken before 1945

Luxembourg: German and French 'official'
languages. Luxembourgish (a dialect of
German) is the national language

German-speaking minorities in other countries:

‖ With official 'regional' status for German

‖‖ With no official status for German

x x x Scattered German-speaking minorities in
other countries (usually with no official
status for German)

Officially recognised linguistic minorities
in the German-speaking countries, ie:
Danish in Schleswig
Sorbian in Lusatia
Croatian in the Burgenland (eastern Austria)
Slovene in Carinthia (southern Austria)

NOTE: All place names and country names on the
map are given in their German form.

UdSSR

Königsberg

Danzig

POLEN

Breslau

Prag

TSCHECHOSLOWAKEI

Rostock

Berlin

Dresden

Leipzig

Wien

Salzburg

ÖSTERREICH

Graz

DÄNEMARK

Hamburg

BUNDESREPUBLIK

DEUTSCHLAND

Nürnberg

München

Innsbruck

JUGOSLAWIEN

Bremen

Hannover

Budapest

UNGARN

NIEDERLANDE

Düsseldorf

Köln

Frankfurt

Stuttgart

Straßburg

Zürich

SCHWEIZ

Bern

ITALIEN

BELGIEN

FRANKREICH

2

language fully, as much for the foreign learner as for the native speaker.

Within the scope of this book it is impossible to describe in detail all the varieties of modern German. There is in fact no agreement on how many there are, as distinctions between them are not clear-cut and each one tends to shade into the next. This book identifies some of the most frequent variants which the native speaker has at his or her command and which the advanced foreign learner is most likely to encounter. This is done by explaining in detail the major factors which affect choice between the variants. Such factors can be usefully divided into two categories: those relating to the *uses* which the language serves and those relating to the *users* of the language, in particular to the social groups to which they belong.

NOTE: More extensive information on variation in German may be found in Clyne (1984) and Keller (1978), chapter 7. The account here draws on these works and has also benefited from the analysis of register in French in Batchelor and Offord, *A Guide to Contemporary French Usage* (Cambridge 1982), on which the numbering in **1.1.5** is based.

1.1   Varieties according to use: register

The forms used by a native speaker are influenced by such factors as subject matter, medium and situation. Variation of this kind, which depends on the use to which the language is being put, is commonly known as *register variation*. A *register* is a type, or stylistic level of language (eg colloquial, formal), which is influenced by these factors.

1.1.1   Medium

The first crucial distinction affecting register is that between spoken and written language. In writing there is more time to consider, to be precise in expression, to formulate more carefully than in the flow of speech, and as a result written language tends to be more elaborate and complex than spoken. And because there is no direct contact with the person being addressed, more detailed explanation and a greater degree of formal coherence are necessary than, for example, in a conversation with a close friend. Consequently, written language exhibits more formal structure and a greater degree of organization in every aspect. It has a more extensive vocabulary, with distinctions of meaning which are often ignored in the spoken language. There are grammatical forms, such as the present subjunctive, the genitive case and the past tense, which are used more sparingly in everyday spoken German than in writing. Sentences tend to be longer and structured in a more complex fashion. On the other hand, regionalisms are more limited and are largely restricted to a few items of vocabulary, in the main those characteristic of the different German-speaking countries.

The spoken register, by contrast, although subject to considerable variation according to situation (see **1.1.3**), is characterized in general by grammatical carelessness, with incomplete sentences, broken or elliptical constructions, repetitions, and phrases added or inserted as afterthoughts without proper syntactic links. There are fewer subordinate clauses; main–clause constructions are the rule. Filler words, such as the modal particles (*aber, doch, denn*, etc, see **2.6**), hesitation markers (*öh, mhm*, etc), interjections, and comment clauses (*sehen Sie, weißt du*, etc) are prevalent. Regionalisms are almost inevitably present to some extent and they become more noticeable the further South one goes (see **1.2.2**).

Finally, not all writing is in the 'written' register as described above, and not all speech is in the 'spoken'. One may imitate natural speech in writing, and many modern novelists and the popular press cultivate a register close to it. However, in practice this is restricted to certain characteristic words and expressions, and possibly some phonetic contractions such as *sehense* for *sehen Sie*. The lax grammar which is typical of spontaneous informal speech (see the examples in **1.4.2**) is rarely found in any written form. Similarly, characteristic written forms may be spoken, often in the most formal situations, eg a sermon, a public lecture, a parliamentary speech or a news broadcast; as often as not these are given from a prepared text.

1.1.2   Subject matter

What is being talked or written about can influence the way it is expressed. A discussion of politics calls on a whole range of vocabulary and forms which would be inappropriate in other areas. Every activity and field of study has its own special terminology and expressions, and these are used irrespective of situation: the same characteristic forms may be used by a politician in a television interview, in a newspaper article or between friends. But this is not always so: an electric light bulb is, in the everyday spoken register of German, *die (Glüh)birne*, but in the special register of electricians it is *die (Glüh)lampe*. Similarly, doctors regularly use different terms for diseases or conditions when talking to other doctors from those they use to their patients. Although subject matter most obviously influences the choice of vocabulary, it is important to realize that, in modern German, it also affects grammar and sentence construction. Much non–literary writing in German favours forms and constructions which are found less often, for instance, in a modern novel. The passage in section **1.6.5** gives many characteristic examples of these. Thus, there are *forms* which are regarded as more appropriate for a particular range of subject matter.

1.1.3   Situation

The term *situation* is used here to refer to the whole context of speech or writing. It is perhaps the most important of the factors underlying register variation, and its characteristic manifestation is in the degree of formality in the words, expressions and constructions used.

This may depend, first, on the context in which people are

speaking, in that some contexts are inherently more structured and formal than others and may be taken as requiring a corresponding register level. Some typical cases were mentioned at the end of the last section. We may also, for instance, find colleagues in an office using a greater degree of formality in their speech in a meeting with set procedures than they would employ in the normal course of everyday business.

However, the notion of speech situation is usually defined rather more widely, to include the relationship between the people talking, and this plays a crucial part in the selection of a particular register. We should first note, though, that variation in language which is due to differences in situation is more typical of speech than writing. With a few exceptions, of which letter-writing is the most obvious, a writer has no personal relationship to the reader, and it follows that the most formal register variants are normally chosen. In this respect variation according to the medium may be seen as a sub-type of situation variation.

By and large, in speech, the use of a more formal register may be considered a mark of deference to the person addressed, as part of social conventions of politeness. Conversely, the use of an inappropriately casual form may be interpreted as showing a lack of due respect. Most of the factors which affect the choice of register are linked to accepted norms of social behaviour in this way. This is certainly the case with sex differences. For example, many German men feel it appropriate to adopt a more formal mode of speech when addressing a woman than a man. Although this is perhaps less true than formerly, it is by no means unusual, particularly in the higher social classes, when the woman is not known personally, among older people or in certain areas, as in Austria. Nevertheless, at the very least, there are numerous forms (eg vulgarisms such as *Arschloch, Scheiße, vögeln*, see **1.1.5**) which are widely avoided by most Germans in mixed company, though used fairly freely in exclusively male gatherings.

The role of age is quite similar; it is still taken as a mark of respect to use a more formal register to people older than oneself. This is even more widely expected in the German-speaking countries by adults from children and young people, and failure to do so may be resented. On the other hand, a different form of speech, with simpler grammar and special words, is often used towards younger children. In general, too, a less formal tone is adopted towards all children up to the age of 14 or so, with the universal use of *du* towards them, although this may be less determined by their age *per se* than by their social status as dependants.

In conversations between adults, the relative social status of the participants is often the crucial factor in setting the register level. People in a subordinate social situation, such as a shopkeeper to a customer, an employee to a boss, a student to a professor, can signal this relationship by the use of a more formal speech style than is normal between equals. Failure to do so may indeed have serious social consequences, eg *Ich kaufe nicht mehr bei Meyer, der redet einen so grob an*, as with the transgression of any other social conventions.

How someone wishes to be seen by the person he or she is addressing is also relevant here. The people in a subordinate position just mentioned may express themselves in a particular manner in order to confirm their position to the listener. Alternatively, by using different, more casual forms, they may assert a measure of equality, as an employee to a boss in the course of an industrial dispute. We can thus adopt roles and present ourselves in a particular way through our speech. It has been noticed that some German politicians choose an especially earthy or racy casual register, very marked by regionalisms, when talking to rural constituents in order to appeal to them as an equal. This is likely to be very different from the one they habitually use in the Bundestag. Some people signal their contempt for all social conventions by ignoring linguistic ones as well. They deliberately use the least formal register to everybody, including those who might be seen as their superiors. This attitude was particularly noticeable after 1968 among radical student groups in West Germany, and it may still be encountered.

However, the use of a less formal register most often marks a measure of equality and intimacy with the person addressed. One clear indicator of this in German is the switch from *Sie* to *du*.

1.1.4   Register and regionalism

Finally, in this analysis of register in modern German, we must note that there is a strong correlation between varieties according to use and varieties according to user, to be dealt with in **1.2**. In general, the degree of regionalism in a person's speech will increase in proportion to the degree of informality in the register. The most formal register, especially when written, will be relatively uniform over the whole of the German speech-area, with regional variation limited to a few items of vocabulary. The casual register of everyday speech, on the other hand, is widely characterized by regionalisms in pronunciation, grammar and vocabulary.

1.1.5   The indication of register in this book

There are no really clear-cut divisions between the registers of German, but for practical purposes it is useful to identify three main register types. To start with, we can roughly label these as 'informal colloquial', 'neutral' and 'formal', though the latter will have to be subdivided into 'literary' and 'non-literary'. In the rest of the book, words and forms which can be seen as typical of one of these registers will be marked by the symbols R1, R2 and R3 (if necessary split into R3a and R3b) as follows:

R1: The most casual register of everyday colloquial speech. It is used between equals in informal situations to discuss relatively mundane topics and is the natural mode of speech for most people. Articulation is rather careless and unstressed syllables and words tend to be reduced or elided. Sentence construction is often rather loose compared with the formal structures of writing. In spontaneous speech we hesitate, correct ourselves, have afterthoughts, repeat ourselves and break off sentences to go off along another track. Sentences are very often incomplete because much is understood by implication. In matters of vocabulary there is a fondness for exaggeration, and many words are effectively restricted to this register because they are considered too 'casual' for writing. There may also be a lack of precision in the vocabulary, with all-purpose words being used when the speaker cannot think of an exact term. Informal speech usually has substantial regional colouring. In its characteristic form it is seldom written, although some writing (eg modern novels, the popular press) may imitate certain features of it.

R2: A neutral register bridging more formal speech and some less formal types of writing. Indeed, it is less clearly a distinct variety than a kind of mid-point between the extremes of R1 and R3. Its major characteristics are therefore best described in negative terms: the carelessness in pronunciation and grammar typical of R1 is avoided, as is the familiar vocabulary; and regionalisms are less prevalent if not entirely absent. Equally, one does not find the degree of elaboration and complexity in sentence constructions, grammar and vocabulary which characterizes R3. Most R2 items are acceptable in both R1 and R3, whereas there are quite definitely words, forms, constructions and pronunciations which are restricted entirely to R1 and R3 and scarcely found in any other register. Most introductory material for foreign learners will nowadays be in R2.

R3: Essentially the register of modern written German, with the typical complex and extensive vocabulary of the written medium. Regionalism is minimal and is usually limited to a few items of vocabulary. It is spoken only in the most formal situations, and then typically from a prepared text. In this case, the pronunciation is much more careful and clear than in R2 or R1. It is useful to distinguish two major types of this register, basically differentiated in terms of subject matter, as follows.

R3a: The literary language as established and laid down from the late 18th century on, and still used in much creative writing, especially fiction. It may have a rather archaic or scholarly ring to it, but it enjoys great prestige through formal education, and many still regard it as the only 'good' form of German, considering deviation from it in other registers (including R3b) as deficiencies.

R3b: Modern non-literary prose of all kinds, as found in the serious press, business letters, official documents, instruction manuals, popular scholarship (the German equivalent of Pelican books), writing in science, philosophy, economics, etc. Its most striking feature is the preference for noun constructions over verb constructions; main clauses prevail as contrasted to the complex sentences with dependent clauses characteristic of R3a. Such features of R3b have been widely criticized by purists – proponents of R3a – as *Papierdeutsch* or *Beamtendeutsch*, and at its worst this register can be ludicrously pompous. However, at its best it has a notable conciseness, and most Germans will consider it appropriate for non-fictional writing of all kinds.

It must be stressed that these categories are something of a simplification. The scale of register is continuous, and there are no natural divisions. Each of the categories above will cover a fair range of often very different types of German. R1, for example, ranges from a socially perfectly acceptable conversational language, as used every day by most German speakers, to gross vulgarisms, which are avoided except in very special cases and which foreign learners would be best advised not to use (indicated by R1* in this book). The other registers have no less a range: R3b would include, for instance, the very precise and considered expression of an editorial in *Die Zeit* and the unnecessary verbosity of an official pronouncement. But there is still enough similarity in some essential features to make this broad categorization useful. A larger number of categories could be confusing.

It would also be true to say that most speech or writing cannot be assigned as a whole to one of the above categories. More than anything it is a question of greater or lesser use of variants characteristic of one register or another. For example, a political discussion between friends in a café might drift between R2 and R1 (with more of the latter as the evening wears on), but with certain features of R3b if they use words and phrasing typical of the way their subject matter is treated in newspapers and in television broadcasts by practising politicians. Some modern novelists (eg Günther Grass) use lexical and syntactic elaborateness typical of R3a, but with a fair leavening of R1, often vulgar, variants. Other recent writers try to avoid the complexity of R3a and aim at a more informal register level, close to R2.

1.2 Varieties according to user: regionalism

We shall deal here with those varieties of language which relate to the social group(s) to which people belong. We can frequently observe people, quite unconsciously, using forms and expressions which indicate their membership of a particular group. Small groups of young people, say, at a particular school or college, will often have a range of slang forms and expressions which are peculiar to the group; the use of these excludes outsiders and signals membership of this 'in' group.

Variation according to user is equally typical of very much larger groups. Within the German speech–area we come across variation related to the social class of a speaker and to the region which he or she comes from. Sometimes the two factors are linked, as is regularly the case in England: Eliza Doolittle, in George Bernard Shaw's *Pygmalion*, is marked by her speech as a lower–class Londoner. This is not so frequent in Germany, where, especially in the South, regional variants are used by members of *all* social classes. In fact, in Germany the influence of social class is most often seen in the ability (or willingness) to use a particular register, as we saw earlier. Less educated speakers may not be as competent in less casual registers. Given the correlation between more colloquial register and degree of regionalism, this may have the secondary effect that such speakers use more regional varieties.

However, it is important for English learners of German to be aware that, as a general rule, such local varieties, accents or dialects may be widely accepted and used by all sections of society. Rarely do

R1* = vulgar
R1 = informal
colloquial
R2 = neutral
R3 = formal
R3a = literary
R3b = non-literary
(see 1.1.5)

we find anywhere in the German speech-area the kind of social stigmatism which in England is commonly attached to broad accents like Eliza Doolittle's.

1.2.1 Regionalism and standard German

Regional variation is an important feature of German and the learner will encounter it at a much earlier stage and to a much greater degree than, say, in French. We need first to look at it in relation to the standard German as taught to foreigners. This variety (*Hochdeutsch, die deutsche Hochsprache*) arose from the time of Luther onwards as a *written* standard language for the whole of the German speech-area. In the terms we are using, it was restricted to R3; even nowadays, it is still frequently referred to as *Schriftdeutsch*. In its modern form, R3, it has a uniform spelling, as prescribed by the *DUDEN-Rechtschreibung* (1973), and a uniform grammar, for which the *DUDEN-Grammatik* (1984) is usually taken as the standard authority. In these aspects of language, regional variation is limited. There is more in the realm of vocabulary, where there is no universally recognized authority. In particular there is considerable variation here between the various German-speaking countries, with different words being in current use in Austria and Switzerland from those in Germany. The most important of these are given in **1.5.2**. Divergences also emerged between the DDR and the other German-speaking countries, though these were mainly in the field of political and state institutions. But even within Germany itself, there are many instances where no single word has ever gained full acceptance over the whole area. The case of Northern *Sonnabend* and Southern *Samstag* is well known, but there are numerous others, although it is noticeable that they are more prevalent in areas of everyday life, such as food and drink and traditional trades, where the influence of the standard language may have made itself felt less strongly.

1.2.2 Regionalism and spoken German

Certainly until 1800, and in many parts of Germany until 1900, standard German was used for *writing* only. What people *spoke* was their *dialect*, a language variety peculiar to a particular locality only. In German this often differs from the standard language in so many respects – in pronunciation and grammar as well as in vocabulary – as to be all but incomprehensible to a speaker from another region, and certainly to the foreigner who has learnt only standard German.

By the end of the 18th century, though, a spoken form of *Hochdeutsch* had arisen, based on a North German pronunciation of the written language, primarily for the very formal speech of stage declamation rather than for everyday purposes. This came to be used more widely in the course of the 19th century and it was eventually accepted for teaching in schools in all the German-speaking countries. Largely because of its use in education, some form of this spoken standard has been adopted in the present century by most Germans, even in colloquial registers, but the extent to which this is the case varies considerably. However, the foreign learner is still most likely to encounter in R1 anywhere a variety of German coloured to a greater or lesser degree by regional features in pronunciation, grammar and vocabulary.

As a general, if not invariable rule, such regionalism becomes stronger and the difference from standard German more marked as one proceeds from North to South. Indeed, from Saxony, Hesse and the Rhineland southwards, and especially in Swabia, Bavaria and Austria, much natural R1 speech will be in dialect, especially in rural areas. In Switzerland, dialect is still used by *all* social classes in *all* speech situations except the most formal. Standard German is used almost only in writing or when talking to non-Swiss.

In conclusion the close link between the degree of regionalism and the degree of formality in register must be stressed again. This means that an individual's speech often shows more local features in more casual speech, for instance at home or in the pub, than in formal situations. Many speakers have command over a considerable range in this way, from broad dialect to a slightly accented form of standard German.

1.2.3   The indication of regionalism in this book

Regionalisms can be extremely confusing for foreign learners, who may, for instance, encounter three or four apparently synonymous equivalents for a single English word and be uncertain which one to use through not knowing that they are dealing with regional variants. In the main they need merely to be aware which words and forms are regionally restricted and which are standard. In practice, learners are probably best advised to avoid regionalisms in their own usage, given the associations which might be evoked: outside the area in which such regionalisms are used they can sound comical, whilst inside it they might sound patronizing or condescending if used by a stranger or a foreigner.

Regional forms will be specified in terms of the following large areas (see map on p 2). These are intended mainly to give a rough general indication of where a particular form is current, rather than be absolutely precise:

N   North of a line running East–West through Düsseldorf.
C   A central area from there to a line running East–West through Frankfurt/Main.
S   South of Frankfurt/Main. Sometimes it will be necessary to split this area into **SW** and **SE** along the Bavarian border.

Forms specified as S, SW, SE are also current in Switzerland and/or Austria unless a separate form is given, indicated as follows:

AU   Austria
CH   Switzerland

1.3 Examples of variation: pronunciation

As will be clear from the preceding sections, regional variation is often inextricably linked to register variation. In this section we have attempted to disentangle them, though with some reservations.

As far as possible, spoken regional or R1 forms are given below in an adapted version of standard German spelling rather than in phonetic transcription. This is merely for the sake of convenience; such spellings will not normally be encountered.

Phonetic alphabet

By and large, the spelling of standard German gives a clear guide to pronunciation (unlike English), at least for careful, standard speech. However, at times we need to indicate the sometimes very different sounds of colloquial or regional speech. As far as possible, this has been done by adapting the usual spelling conventions of German, eg standard *kommenden* is often heard as *kommdn* in fast colloquial speech. These spellings are of course never usually found in print, but they are used here for convenience and ease of recognition. However, there are times when we have had to use the special alphabet of the International Phonetic Association (IPA) to make it quite clear exactly what sounds we are dealing with. The following table gives all the IPA symbols used in this section; English or French examples are given in illustration if the sounds are similar to those of German.

VOWELS

iː	Ger **bieten**, Engl **beat**
ɪ	Ger **bitten**, Engl **bit**
eː	Ger **beten**, Fr *écouter*
ɛ	Ger **Bett**, Engl **bed**
ɛː	Ger **wäre**, Fr **scène**
a	Ger **Band**, Fr **passer**
aː	Ger **Vater**, Engl **father**
ɔ	Ger **kommen**, Engl *caught*
oː	Ger **Boot**, Fr *eau*
ʊ	Ger **Butter**, Engl **butcher**
uː	Ger **Kuh**, Fr **trou**
yː	Ger **Mühle**, Fr **mur**
ʏ	Ger **Fülle**
øː	Ger **Höhle**, Fr **peux**
œ	Ger **Hölle**
aɪ	Ger **fein**, Engl **fine**
aʊ	Ger **Maus**, Engl **mouse**
œʏ	Ger **Mäuse**
ʌ	Ger **bitter**, Engl **but**

R1* = vulgar
R1 = informal
    colloquial
R2 = neutral
R3 = formal
R3a = literary
R3b = non-literary
(see 1.1.5)

⟫⟫→

ə	Ger **bitt***e*, Engl **chin***a*
ã	Ger **Restaur***ant*, Fr *en*
ɔ̃	Ger **Balk***on*, Fr *on*
ɛ̃	Ger **P***en***sion**, Fr p*ain*

CONSONANTS

p	Ger **p***assen*, Engl **p***ass*
b	Ger **b***itte*, Engl **b***it*
t	Ger **t***un*, Engl **t***on*
d	Ger **d***umm*, Engl **d***umb*
k	Ger **k***ommen*, Engl **c***ome*
g	Ger **g***ut*, Engl **g***ood*
f	Ger **f***aul*, Engl **f***oul*
v	Ger **w***ann*, Engl **v***an*
s	Ger **l***ass***en**, Engl **s***at*
z	Ger **s***aß*, Engl **z***ero*
ʃ	Ger **sch***ießen*, Engl **sh***eet*
ʒ	Ger **G***enie*, Engl **lei***s***ure**
x	Ger **Bu***ch*, Scots **lo***ch*
ç	Ger **mi***ch*
h	Ger **h***olen*, Engl **h***ole*
m	Ger **m***ich*, Engl **m***ine*
n	Ger **n***eun*, Engl **n***ine*
ŋ	Ger **hi***ng*, Engl **hu***ng*
l	Ger **l***aut*, Engl **l***oud*
ʀ	Ger **r***ot*, Fr **r***ouge*
j	Ger **j***a*, Engl **y***ear*
ɣ	A sound between [x] and [g], the voiced *ch* often heard in the North German pronunciation of **Wagen**.

NOTE: a subscript dot, eg [m̩], [n̩], indicates that the consonant forms a syllable, eg in Ger **bitten** [bɪtn̩], **geben** [geːbm̩], Engl **button** [bʌtn̩].

1.3.1 Regional variation in pronunciation

(a) The following pronunciations are used almost universally in the areas indicated, irrespective of register:

Area		Regional	Hochdeutsch
NORTH	-*g*- pron as voiced -*ch*- between vowels	**Waghen** [vaːɣən]	Wagen
	pf pron as *f*	**Fund**	Pfund
	-*ung* pron as -*unk*	**Hoffnunk**	Hoffnung
	long vowels pron short in words of one syllable	**Rătt, grŏpp, Tăch**	Rat, grob, Tag
NORTH + CENTRE	-*g* pron as -*ch*	**taucht, Zeuch**	taugt, Zeug
	long *ä* /ɛː/ pron as *eh* /eː/	**wehre, speht**	wäre, spät
SOUTH	-*ig* pron as -*ik*	**dreißik**	dreißig [draɪsɪç]
	ch- pron as *k*-	**Kina**	China [çiːna]
	some long vowels pron short, esp before *r* + cons	**Art, wird** [art, vɪrt]	Art, wird [aːrt, viːrt]
	nasal vowels pron as simple vowel + *n*	**Balkon, Pension** [balkoːn, pɛnsjoːn]	Balkon, Pension [balkɔ̃, pãsjɔ̃]
	unstressed -*e* pron as [e]	**guté** [guːte]	gute [guːtə]
	different stress in some words	**Tunˈnel, Kafˈfee, Taˈbak**	ˈTunnel, ˈKaffee, ˈTabak

---

ˈ stressed syllables are preceded by a stress mark

(b)   The following pronunciations are mainly confined to R1:

Area		Regional	Hochdeutsch
NORTH	*sp-*, *st-* pron with [s]	**S-tein, S-prung** [staɪn, spruŋ]	Stein, Sprung [ʃtaɪn, ʃpruŋ]
	g- pron as *j-* (esp Berlin, Cologne)	**jeht, jemacht**	geht, gemacht
	pron of *nicht*	**nich**	nicht
	-nd- pron as *-nn-* (also Rhineland)	**anners, Kinner**	anders, Kinder
CENTRE	*ich-Laut* [ç] pron with *sch*	**misch, dreißisch**	mich, dreißig
	-en pron as *-e* (also SW)	**komme, lasse**	kommen, lassen
CENTRE + SOUTH	*p, t, k* pron as *b, d, g*	**Abodehge, dodal**	Apotheke, total
	ü, ö pron as *i, e*	**Brieder, scheen**	Brüder, schön
	a pron as *o*	**Wosser, schlofen**	Wasser, schlafen
	unstressed *-e* dropped in all words	**heut, Leut**	heute, Leute
	pron of *nicht*	**net/nit**	nicht
SOUTH	*ge-, be-*, pron as *g-, b-*	**gmacht, bstellt**	gemacht, bestellt
	-sp-, -st- pron with *sch* (mainly SW)	**beschte, Weschpe**	beste, Wespe

1.3.2   Register variation in pronunciation

R1 speech is characterized by imprecise and less careful articulation. However, even rather more formal spoken language tends to simplification, especially of unstressed syllables. There is thus a gradual progression from the most casual speech style, R1, to the most formal, R3, where every letter is given its full value. R3 is, of course, primarily a written register, and the extremely precise and distinct articulation it represents will be found only in rather special situations, eg reading aloud in public. Some German speakers may insist that foreign learners ought only to use and be taught this style of speech, as only it is 'correct'. But it can sound very stilted and artificial in any but the most formal situations.

```
R1* = vulgar
R1 = informal
        colloquial
R2 = neutral
R3 = formal
R3a = literary
R3b = non-literary
(see 1.1.5)
```

	R1	**R3**
unstressed -*en* reduced and assimilated	**gebm** [geːbm̩] **kommdn** [kɔmdn̩] **gehn** [geːn] **eign'n** [aɪgnn̩]	geben kommenden gehen eigenen
simplification and assimilation of consonant groups, esp at the beginnings and ends of words	**Norpol** [nɔʌpoːl] **Herbsflanze** [hɛʌpsflantsə] **sons nix** [zɔns nɪks] **scho ma** [ʃoma] **ma'tudoch** [matudɔx] **fuffzig** [fuftsɪç] **dabbich** [dabɪç] **garbeit** [gaːbaɪt] **un a is** [ʊn ʌ ɪs] **er hap mir…** [ʌ hap miʌ]	Nordpol Herbstpflanze sonst nichts schon einmal man tut doch fünfzig da habe ich gearbeitet und er ist er hat mir…
reduction of pronouns	**hammer** [hamʌ] **simmer** [zɪmʌ] **wissnse** [vɪsnzə] **kommste** [kɔmstə] **isse** [ɪsə] **mussich** [mʊsɪç]	haben wir sind wir wissen Sie kommst du ist sie muß sich
reduction of articles and pronouns	**da** [dʌ], **di** [dɪ], **s** **n, m** **n, ne, n'n** [nn̩] **nem/eim, ner** **meim, unsem**	der, die, das den, dem ein, eine, einen einem, einer meinem, unserem

articles fused with almost any preposition	**bein, ausn**
	mim, mitn
	minnem, minner
	durchn, durchn'n
	
	von'n, in'n
	nachm, hinnem
		bei den, aus den
		mit dem, mit den
		mit einem, mit einer
		durch den, durch
		  einen
		von den, in den
		nach dem, hinter
		  dem

unstressed -*e* dropped in verb endings	**ich komm** **ich könnt** **geh**	ich komme ich könnte gehe
unstressed -*e* dropped in basic form of some adjectives	**blöd, feig, irr, mild, trüb, zäh**	blöde, feige, irre, milde, trübe, zähe
unstressed -*e* added in some numerals and other words	**fünfe, sechse, neune, elfe, alleine, vorne**	fünf, sechs, neun, elf, allein, vorn

≫→

	R1 *contd*	**R3** *contd*
foreign words given German pronunciation	**Schenie** [ʃɛniː] **Restaurang** [rɛstoraŋ]	Genie [ʒɛniː] Restaurant [rɛstorã]
denn reduced and suffixed to verb	**Was machs'n du hier in Hamburg?**	Was machst du denn hier in Hamburg?
r pronounced as [ʌ] (ie like the vowel of English *but*)	[viʌ] [ɛʌdə] [bɛsʌ]	wir [viːʀ] Erde [ɛʀdə] besser [bɛsəʀ]

1.4 Examples of variation: grammar

The following examples illustrate grammar variation. The cross-references indicate where further detail is given elsewhere in the book.

1.4.1 Regional variation in grammar

Regionalism is less significant in grammar than in pronunciation and vocabulary. However, the following variant uses are widespread and are sometimes found in writing, although the foreign learner is advised to keep to standard forms.

Area		**Regional**	**Hochdeutsch**
NORTH	*sein* in perfect of *beginnen, anfangen*	**Ich bin begonnen** **Ich bin angefangen**	Ich habe begonnen Ich habe angefangen
	splitting *da* + preposition	**Da weiß ich nichts von**	Davon weiß ich nichts
	confusion of accusative and dative	**Er hat mir gesehen**	Er hat mich gesehen
	am + verbal noun to express continual action	**Mein Vater ist am Schreiben**	Mein Vater schreibt gerade
	more nouns with plural in *-s* (see **3.1.3**), eg:	**die Doktors, Onkels, Wagens**	die Doktoren, Onkel, Wagen
	nach used for *zu*	**Ich fahre nach dem Bahnhof**	Ich fahre zum Bahnhof

CENTRE + SOUTH	*wo* for relative pronoun	**das Auto, wo da steht**	das Auto, das da steht
	deviant verb forms	**gedenkt** **bräuchte**	gedacht brauchte/würde brauchen
		gewunken	gewinkt
SOUTH	*sein* in perfect of *liegen, sitzen, stehen* (see **4.3.3**)	**Ich bin gelegen** **Ich bin gesessen** **Ich bin gestanden**	Ich habe gelegen Ich habe gesessen Ich habe gestanden
	no *-n* in dative plural	**mit den Bücher** (SE: **mit die Bücher**)	mit den Büchern
	deviant plural formation, eg:	**die Wägen** **die Stücker** **die Stiefeln**	die Wagen die Stücke die Stiefel
	variation in gender, eg:	**der Butter** **der Radio** **der Gewalt** **die Bach** (also C) **der Schokolad** **der Kartoffel**	die Butter das Radio die Gewalt der Bach die Schokolade die Kartoffel
	no *Umlaut* in present	**er schlaft, laßt**	er schläft, läßt
	dative used for possessive	**Das ist mir**	Das ist meines
	double auxiliary in pluperfect	**Ich habe ihn gesehen gehabt**	Ich hatte ihn gesehen
	es gibt	**es hat** (SW)	es gibt
	variation in preposition used with verbs (see **4.1.4**), eg:	**etw um DM4 verkaufen** (SE) **auf etw denken**	etw für DM4 verkaufen an etw denken

N = North
C = Central
S = South
SW = South West
SE = South East
AU = Austria
CH = Switzerland
(see 1.2.3)

1.4.2 Register variation in grammar

Usage is fairly flexible with a number of these variants, but most German speakers would avoid specifically R1 forms in writing. In the great majority of cases, the rather less casual spoken R2 tends to follow R3 usage and so the table below gives the two extremes of R1 and R3 with exceptions indicated.

	R1	R3
singular of weak masculine nouns (see **3.2.1**)	den Bär, dem Bär, des Bärs	den Bären, dem Bären, des Bären
genitive case rare in R1 (see **4.2.2**)	meinem Vater sein Hut der Hut von meinem Vater (also R2) wegen dem Regen im Oktober voriges Jahr sich an den Vorfall erinnern (also R2)	der Hut meines Vaters wegen des Regens im Oktober vorigen Jahres sich des Vorfalls erinnern
no vowel change in imperative of strong verbs	Eß deine Möhren! Nehm's doch! Geb's her!	Iß deine Möhren! Nimm es doch! Gib es her!
demonstrative used for personal pronoun	Ich habe den gesehen Die kommt heute nicht Deren Mann kann ich nicht leiden	Ich habe ihn gesehen Sie kommt heute nicht Ihren Mann kann ich nicht leiden
demonstratives replaced	das hier der da, das da	dies(es) jener, jenes
wer for jemand	Es hat wer angerufen Die hat wieder wen angelächelt	Es hat jemand angerufen Sie hat wieder jemanden angelächelt
replacement of solch (see **3.5.6**)	so 'ne Farbe so Ansichten	eine solche Farbe solche Ansichten
was with prepositions, etc	An was denkst du? Von was lebt er?	Woran denkst du? Wovon lebt er?
definite article used with names	Der Thomas kommt mit der Angelika Hast du den Rainer gesehen?	Thomas kommt mit Angelika Hast du Rainer gesehen?
confusion of wie and als	Der ist größer wie ich Der ist anders wie die Petra	Er ist größer als ich Er ist anders als Petra
double negatives	Der hat nie nix gesagt Die haben nirgends kein Haus gebaut	Er hat nie etwas gesagt Sie haben nirgends ein Haus gebaut

	R1	**R3**
tun used as auxiliary verb	Sie tut gerade schreiben Ich tät's nicht machen	Sie schreibt gerade Ich würde es nicht machen
omission of *zu* after *brauchen*	Wir brauchen nicht so schwer arbeiten	Wir brauchen nicht so schwer zu arbeiten
weil followed by main clause word order	weil der kann eben kein richtiges Deutsch sprechen	weil er eben kein richtiges Deutsch sprechen kann
extended epithets (restricted to R3)	die Sitzung, die auf Januar verschoben wurde (R2) die Zahlung, die vor Monatsende geleistet werden muß (R2)	die auf Januar verschobene Sitzung (R3) die vor Monatsende zu leistende Zahlung (R3)
main clause used rather than relative	Es gibt Leute, die reden im Schlaf	Es gibt Leute, die im Schlaf reden
wo plus prepositional adverb used instead of preposition and relative pronoun	der Tisch, wo die Blumen drauf stehen	der Tisch, auf dem die Blumen stehen
extensive use of *da* to start sentences	Da kann man in dem Fall einfach nix machen	In diesem Fall kann man einfach nichts machen
elements placed after final verb, etc (so-called *Ausklammerung*, see **5.1.6**)	Er hat Post bekommen von zu Hause	Er hat Post von zu Hause bekommen
omissions, esp of pronouns and auxiliaries	Hab' ich ihm schon gesagt Mal schauen, was da los ist Noch keinen Bericht gehört drüber	Das habe ich ihm schon gesagt Wir wollen mal schauen, was da los ist Ich habe noch keinen Bericht darüber gehört
repetition for emphasis or clarification	Der Peter, den kann sie nicht leiden Den hatt' ich schon, den Wunsch	Peter kann sie doch nicht leiden Den Wunsch hatte ich schon
use of present subjunctive	see **4.5.2**	
use of past tense	see **4.3.2**	

1.5 Examples of variation: vocabulary

1.5.1 Regional variation in vocabulary

As with pronunciation, it is not always simple to disentangle regionalism from register, and many regional words are limited to R1. Others, including the familiar case of *Sonnabend* and *Samstag* mentioned earlier, are used freely in all registers. This is especially true of Austria and Switzerland, where a South German (SE or SW) variant is often used even in written R3.

The tables below give some of the most frequently encountered regional variants together with their usually accepted equivalent(s) in the *Hochsprache*. None are wholly restricted to R1, although some are commoner there than in more formal registers; it is difficult to give hard and fast rules. One point to remember is that standard German has sometimes adopted more than one regional variant, sometimes without any significant meaning difference, as with *sehen* and *schauen*, but often creating a distinction in meaning. For example, *Pferd*, *Gaul* and *Roß* were originally all local words for 'horse' in various areas. But in the standard German *Hochsprache* the general word is *Pferd*, whilst *Gaul* and *Roß* have the more specific meanings 'nag' and 'steed'. There can also be register differences; for example, in the standard, *sieden* 'to boil' is an R3 word compared with R2 *kochen*. But in South German, especially in Austria, it is the everyday word.

R1* = vulgar
R1 = informal
colloquial
R2 = neutral
R3 = formal
R3a = literary
R3b = non-literary
(see 1.1.5)

N = North
C = Central
S = South
SW = South West
SE = South East
AU = Austria
CH = Switzerland
(see 1.2.3)

Area	Regional	Hochdeutsch
NORTH	**das Abendbrot**	das Abendessen
	belemmern	belästigen
	buddeln	graben
	denn	dann
	doof (R1 – also C)	dumm
	flöten	pfeifen
	die Gören	die Kinder
	die Hacke	die Ferse
	der Kasten	die Schublade
	klönen	plaudern
	kloppen	schlagen
	kucken, kieken	sehen
	langskommen	vorbeikommen *to drop in*
	plätten	bügeln
	der Pott	der Topf
	der Schlachter	der Fleischer
	der Schlips (R1 – also C)	die Krawatte
	Sonnabend	Samstag, Sonnabend
	die Stulle	das Butterbrot
	der Tornister	der Schulranzen
	der Trecker (also C)	der Traktor
	die Wurzel	die Mohrrübe, die Karotte

Area	Regional	Hochdeutsch
CENTRE + **SOUTH**	**ackern**	pflügen
	daheim	zu Hause
	der Gaul (C + SW)	das Pferd
	gell (R1)	nicht wahr
	heim	nach Hause
	kehren	fegen
	der Metzger	der Fleischer
	der Rechen	die Harke
	das Rotkraut (C), **das Blaukraut** (S)	der Rotkohl
	es schellt	es klingelt
	der Schreiner	der Tischler
SOUTH	**alleweil** (SE)	immer
	arg	sehr
	aufdrehen	anmachen *to switch on*
	Brosamen (SW), **Brösel** (SE)	Brotkrümel
	eh (SE)	ohnehin
	der Erdapfel (SE)	die Kartoffel
	feist	fett
	die Gasse (SE)	die Straße
	der Gehweg (SW) ⎫ **der Gehsteig** (SE) ⎭	der Bürgersteig
	die Geiß	die Ziege
	die gelbe Rübe	die Mohrrübe, die Karotte
	geschwind	schnell
	gschert (SE)	dumm
	der Hafen	der Topf
	die Hetz (SE)	der Spaß
	heuer (SE)	dieses Jahr
	hocken	(lange) sitzen
	hüpfen	springen
	der Kamin	der Schornstein
	der Karfiol (SE)	der Blumenkohl
	der Kasten	der Schrank
	der Knödel (SE)	der Kloß
	langen	fassen, greifen
	es läutet	es klingelt
	lugen (SW)	gucken (R1)
	das Mädel, Mädle	das Mädchen
	der Mietzins	die Miete
	das Nachtessen (SW)	das Abendessen
	nimmer	nicht mehr
	die Orange	die Apfelsine
	pressieren	Eile haben
	der Rahm	die Sahne
	reden	sprechen
	das Roß (SE + CH)	das Pferd
	schaffen (SW)	arbeiten
	schauen	sehen

⟫→

Area *contd*	Regional *contd*	Hochdeutsch *contd*
[SOUTH]	die Scheuer (SW)	die Scheune
	schmecken (SW)	riechen
	die Schnake	die (Stech)mücke
	die Schnur	der Bindfaden
	der Schwamm	der Pilz
	die Semmel (SE)	das Brötchen
	sieden	kochen *to boil*
	der Spatz	der Sperling
	sperren (SE)	schließen
	springen (SW)	laufen
	stad (SE)	still
	der Stadel	die Scheune
	das Trottoir (SW)	der Bürgersteig
	sich verkälten (not AU)	sich erkälten
	der Wecken (SW)	das Brötchen

1.5.2   Austrian and Swiss words

Lexical usage in Austria and Switzerland is a rather special case. In the spoken register, dialect is widely used – in Switzerland exclusively, in Austria still predominantly, at least in informal R1. In writing, standard German is used, but over the centuries of political separation from Germany independent traditions have grown up in these two countries, especially in matters of vocabulary. Thus, regional words (see **1.5.1**) are commonly used in writing, and in addition, each country has a stock of words peculiar to itself which are almost always used in writing within the country and are not always familiar even to Germans. The following tables give a list of some of the most common:

AUSTRIA

Austria	Germany	Austria	Germany
abgängig	vermißt	fesch	schick
die Abwasch	das Spülbecken	der Fleischhauer	der Fleischer
der Advokat	der Rechtsanwalt	Gefrornes	das (Speise)eis
albern	dumm	der Gendarm	der Landpolizist
allfällig	eventuell	Geröstete	Bratkartoffeln
der Anrainer	der Anlieger	das Goal	das Tor
aufscheinen	vorkommen	der Hausherr	der Hausbesitzer
die Auslage	das Schaufenster	in Hinkunft	in Zunkunft
der Beistrich	das Komma	inskribieren	immatrikulieren
der Corner	der Eckball	Herr Inspektor	Herr Wachtmeister
da	hier	Jänner	Januar
das Dirndl	das Mädchen	die Jause	der Imbiß
entlehnen	entleihen	der Kapuziner	der Milchkaffee
zu ebener Erde	im Erdgeschoß	die Kassa	die Kasse
fad	langweilig	der Kerker	das Zuchthaus
färbig	farbig	komplett	besetzt
der Fauteuil	der Sessel	der Kondukteur	der Schaffner

Austria	Germany	Austria	Germany
der Kren	der Meerrettich	**das Ringelspiel**	das Karussell
das Kuvert	der (Brief)umschlag	**die Rodel**	der Schlitten
die Matura	das Abitur	**rückwärts**	hinten einsteigen
die Maut	der Straßenzoll	**einsteigen**	
die Mehlspeise	der Nachtisch	**die Schale**	die Tasse
der Mistkübel	der Abfalleimer	**die Schnalle**	die Klinke
das Nachtmahl	das Abendessen	**der Sessel**	der Stuhl
nächtigen	übernachten	**der Spezi** (R1)	der Kumpel (R1)
das Obers	die Sahne	**das Spital**	das Krankenhaus
der Paradeiser	die Tomate	**die Stellage**	das Regal
Parteienverkehr	Bürostunden	**die Stiege**	die Treppe
der Plafond	die Decke	**der Turnus**	die Arbeitsschicht
der Polster	das Kissen	**die Umfahrung**	die Umleitung
pragmatisieren	fest anstellen	**sich verkühlen**	sich erkälten
der Probelehrer	der Referendar	**im vorhinein**	im voraus
der Professor	der Studienrat	**der Zuname**	der Nachname
der Rauchfang	der Schornstein	**die Zwetschke**	die Pflaume
raunzen	jammern		
die Retourfahrkarte	die Rückfahrkarte		

SWITZERLAND

NOTE: in Switzerland, unlike Germany or Austria, the letter *ß* is not used, only *ss*, see **5.4.2**.

Switzerland	Germany	Switzerland	Germany
der Abwart	der Hausmeister	**der Car**	der Reisebus
allfällig	eventuell	**der Chauffeur**	der Fahrer
allwo	wo	**der Coiffeur**	der Friseur
das Altersasyl	das Altersheim	**einläßlich**	eingehend
anmit	hiermit	**ennet**	jenseits
anmuten	zumuten	**erst noch**	(noch) obendrein
ansonst	andernfalls	**erträglich**	einträglich
der Anstösser	der Anlieger	**es macht kalt**	es ist kalt
aufbehalten	aufbewahren	**etwelche**	einige
äufnen	mehren	**der Führer**	der Autofahrer
ausserorts	auswärts	**der Fürsprech**	der Rechtsanwalt
der Automobilist	der Autofahrer	**garagieren**	in die Garage stellen
die Base	die Tante	**der Geschlechtsname**	der Nachname
beiderseitig	beiderseits		
beiläufig	ungefähr	**glätten**	bügeln
berichten	unterrichten	**das Grosskind**	das Enkelkind
beschlagen	betreffen	**die Halde**	der Hang
das Billett	die (Fahr)karte	**hässig**	verdrießlich
bis anhin	bisher	**der Hausmeister**	der Hausbesitzer
bis und mit	bis einschließlich	**hinfort**	fortwährend
die Busse	die Geldstrafe	**die Identitätskarte**	der Personalausweis
der Camion	der Lastwagen	**innert**	innerhalb »»→

Switzerland *contd*	Germany *contd*	Switzerland *contd*	Germany *contd*
inskünftig	zukünftig	**das Salär**	das Gehalt
das Kleid	der Anzug	**die Schiesswaffe**	die Schußwaffe
der Kondukteur	der Schaffner	**schlimm**	schlau
die Konfitüre	die Marmelade	**die Serviertochter**	die Kellnerin
köstlich	kostspielig	**spenden**	spendieren
lärmig	lärmend	**der Spital**	das Krankenhaus
das Lavabo	das Waschbecken	**der Spörtler**	der Sportler
leid	unlieb	**die Ständerlampe**	die Stehlampe
letztendlich	letzten Endes	**streng**	anstrengend
mangelbar	mangelhaft	**das Tram**	die Straßenbahn
die Maturität	das Abitur	**die Türfalle**	die Türklinke
merci (R1)	danke	**der Turnus**	die Arbeitsschicht
das Morgenessen	das Frühstück	**Überzeit**	Überstunden
das Motorfahrzeug	das Kraftfahrzeug	**unanschaulich**	unansehnlich
nachten	Nacht werden	**urchig**	bodenständig
nächsthin	demnächst	**das Velo**	das Fahrrad
nebstdem	außerdem	**verdanken**	danken
parkieren	parken	**der Verunfallte(r)**	der Verunglückte(r)
der Perron	der Bahnsteig	**von . . . abhin**	ab…
der Pneu	der Reifen	**zum vornherein**	von vornherein
die Primarschule	die Grundschule	**der Vortritt**	die Vorfahrt
der Radio	der Rundfunk	**währschaft**	dauerhaft
rauh	roh	**der Wartsaal**	der Wartesaal
der Redaktor	der Redakteur	**weisseln**	tünchen
regulieren	regeln	**wüst**	häßlich
das Retourbillett	die Rückfahrkarte	**zügeln**	umziehen
Rösti	Bratkartoffeln		

1.5.3 Register variation in vocabulary

The effect of register is perhaps most marked in the area of vocabulary. Many words are restricted to informal R1 or formal written R3. On the other hand, there is a large core vocabulary of neutral (R2) words which may be used in either of the extreme registers as well, even where a specific R1 or R3 alternative is available. The following lists give some common examples of this register variation. It should be realized, though, that there is not always complete semantic identity between the variants. For example, the R1 word *pumpen* is used for 'to lend, to borrow' (ie = *leihen* (R2) or *borgen* (R3)) only in the context of money. This brief survey cannot cover all such details.

The list is arranged in alphabetical order of the R2 words, which will be the most familiar.

R1	R2	R3
das Abi	**das Abitur**	die Hochschulreife
pfuschen, mogeln, schummeln	**abschreiben**	
protzen	**angeben**	prahlen, sich rühmen
Schiß haben	**Angst haben**	sich fürchten
schuften	**(schwer) arbeiten**	
fuchsen	**ärgern**	verstimmen
pleite	**arm**	mittellos, bedürftig
die Puste	**der Atem**	der Odem (poetic R3a)
	sich aufhalten	verweilen
Fisimatenten	**Ausreden**	
hinhauen, langen (S)	**ausreichen**	genügen
unheimlich	**äußerst**	extrem
	die Backe	die Wange
losgehen	**beginnen, anfangen**	anheben (R3a)
verscharren	**begraben**	bestatten
kriegen	**bekommen**	empfangen, erhalten
eingeschnappt	**beleidigt**	gekränkt
der Sprit	**das Benzin**	der Treibstoff
anstänkern	**beschimpfen**	schmähen
meckern, maulen	**sich beschweren**	sich beklagen
schmieren	**bestechen**	
bescheißen (R1*), einseifen, hereinlegen	**betrügen**	
blau, besoffen	**betrunken**	
der Kahn, die Klappe	**das Bett**	
	die Bitte	das Gesuch
	bitten	ersuchen
pusten	**blasen**	
	blaß	bleich
	bleiben	verweilen
	brauchen	benötigen
	dauern	währen (R3a)
blöd, doof (N + C)	**dumm**	einfältig, töricht
der Dussel, der Depp (SE), der Blödmann	**der Dummkopf**	der Tor
	die Dunkelheit	die Finsternis
miserabel	**dürftig**	armselig
eine Schnapsidee	**ein dummer Einfall**	

$\ggg\!\!\rightarrow$

R1 *contd*	**R2** *contd*	**R3** *contd*
	erfrischen	erquicken
	erlauben	gestatten, zulassen
fressen, futtern, mampfen, naschen	**essen**	speisen
	die Fahrkarte	der Fahrausweis
die Pulle (N + C)	**die Flasche**	
türmen	**flüchten**	(ent)fliehen
	der Flügel	die Schwinge, der Fittich
der Kumpel	**der Freund**	
	das Frühjahr	der Frühling
die Kneipe, die Pinte (N + C), das Beisel (SE)	**die Gaststätte, das Wirtshaus**	
das Kittchen, der Knast	**das Gefängnis**	das Zuchthaus
	gehen *go*	sich begeben
latschen, laufen	**gehen** *walk*	
übergeschnappt, bekloppt, meschugge	**geisteskrank**	geistig umnachtet
die Moneten, der Kies, der Zaster	**das Geld**	
klappen	**gelingen**	
die Fratze, die Fresse, die Visage	**das Gesicht**	das Angesicht (R3a), das Antlitz (R3a)
der Mief	**der Gestank**	der üble Geruch
egal	**gleich**	
Schwein haben	**Glück haben**	
enorm, prima, klasse, toll	**großartig**	hervorragend
die Pfote	**die Hand**	
mulmig	**heikel, unangenehm**	
der Arsch (R1*)	**der Hintern**	das Gesäß
die Klamotten	**die Kleider**	
die Birne, der Deez	**der Kopf**	das Haupt
der Krach	**der Lärm**	
der Pauker	**der Lehrer**	der Studienrat *(secondary school)*
pumpen (Geld)	**leihen**	borgen
büffeln, pauken	**lernen**	
geil auf etw sein	**Lust zu etw (dat) haben**	
die Biene	**das Mädchen**	
der Alte	**der Mann** *husband*	der Ehemann, der Gatte, der Gemahl

R1 *contd*	R2 *contd*	R3 *contd*
schiefgehen	**mißlingen**	
auf jdn/etw stehen	**jdn/etw mögen, gern haben**	
erschossen, fertig	**müde**	ermattet
das Maul (R1*), die Klappe, die Schnauze	**der Mund**	
bloß	**nur**	lediglich
der Löffel	**das Ohr**	
jdm eine kleben, knallen, verpassen	**jdm eine Ohrfeige/ Schläge geben**	
zünftig	**ordentlich**	
die Polente	**die Polizei**	
piesacken	**quälen**	peinigen
heimzahlen	**rächen**	ahnden
	schicken	senden
	jdn schimpfen	jdn schelten
pennen	**schlafen**	
hauen	**schlagen**	
miese	**schlecht**	übel
ätzend	**sehr schlecht**	
	schmecken	munden
dreckig	**schmutzig**	
fix	**schnell**	flink
die Penne	**die Schule**	
irre, schwer	**sehr**	
klauen	**stehlen**	entwenden
krepieren, abkratzen, verrecken	**sterben**	ableben, verscheiden, entschlafen
den Mund, das Maul (R1*) halten	**still sein**	schweigen
herunterputzen	**tadeln**	zurechtweisen, maßregeln
der Schwof	**der Tanz**	
saufen	**(Alkohol) trinken**	
	trotzdem, dennoch	gleichwohl, nichtsdestoweniger
kotzen (R1*)	**sich übergeben, brechen**	sich erbrechen
	überlegen	erwägen
schofel, fies	**unangenehm, gemein**	
das Pech	**das Unglück**	
der Quatsch, der Käse	**der Unsinn**	der Nonsens

≫→

R1 *contd*	**R2** *contd*	**R3** *contd*
spinnen	**Unsinn reden**	
	verbieten	untersagen
platt	**verblüfft**	
verhunzen, verpatzen, verpfuschen, versauen	**verderben**	
verschwitzen	**vergessen**	entfallen
versohlen	**verprügeln**	züchtigen
	verschwenden	vergeuden
kapieren, mitkriegen (tr), mitkommen (itr)	**verstehen**	
lauern (N + C), passen (S)	**warten**	harren
wieso	**warum**	weshalb
futsch	**weg**	verschwunden
abhauen	**weggehen**	sich entfernen
	wehtun	schmerzen
schmeißen	**werfen**	
	zeigen	weisen
fackeln	**zögern**	zaudern

R1* = vulgar
R1 = informal colloquial
R2 = neutral
R3 = formal
R3a = literary
R3b = non-literary
(see 1.1.5)

N = North
C = Central
S = South
SW = South West
SE = South East
AU = Austria
CH = Switzerland
(see 1.2.3)

1.6 Passages illustrating levels of register

In this section a selection of passages is given to show the reader how the differences in register outlined in earlier sections are reflected in longer texts. The progression is broadly from least formal to most formal and the most characteristic features are indicated after each passage.

1.6.1 Telephone conversation (R1)

This passage illustrates characteristic features of spontaneous informal speech in private conversation between friends.

Frau A: Ach so! Und die Wohnung, em. Der Typ hat sich no nich entschieden, morgen ru/ ruft wohl noch jemand an, an dem er noch mehr Interesse hat als als an uns, ne.

Frau B: Ah so.

Frau A: Aber wir sind ziemlich…, weil…

Frau B: Naja, immerhin etwas.

Frau A: Ich nehm auch an, wenn en Typ so auf morgen verschiebt, ne, hat der au nich so'n großes Interesse, oder?

Frau B: Wenn er das auf morgen ver/ ja, kann sein!

Frau A: Guck ma, wenn ich ne Wohnung unheimig gut finde, dann/ da geh ich doch das Risiko nich ein, daß der die Wohnung jemand anders gibt, ne?

Frau B: Jaja.

Frau A: Naja, jedenfalls isses 110 Quadratmeter.

Frau B: 110! Is ja irre! Wir ham nur 90!

Frau A: In nem gepflegten . . . Altbau, ganz toll. Müssen wer allerdings selber renovieren, ne, aber sie is nich in nem scheußlichen Zustand, sondern zwar nich/ also die is bewohnt, ne. Alles scheußliche Tapeten und so, aber sauber, ne, nich irgendwie in nem ekeligen Zustand. Naja, bin ma gespannt! Also, den Quadratmeterpreis, den gibts überhaupt nich ansonsten, ne.

Frau B: Toll, ja! Un das immerhin . . . doch direkt in der Innenstadt, ne?

Frau A: Hm, günstig!

Frau B: Na schön, ja!

Frau A: Un es is, wie gesagt, für mich auch günstig nach Gummersbach, ne. Muß ja ab 1.2. nach Gummersbach.

Frau B: Ja. Freust dich drauf, oder findsdes schlimm?

Frau A: Och, hab ich jetzt noch keine Meinung zu.

Frau B: Ja.

Frau A: Ich mein, die erzählen immer viel von dieser Referendarzeit, ne. Am Anfang solls wohl gemütlich sein, hinterher sehr anstrengend, ich mach mir da jetzt keine Gedanken.

Frau B: Naja.

(Ruth Brons-Albert, *Gesprochenes Standarddeutsch: Telefondialoge*, Narr, Tübingen 1984, pp. 59–60)

Pronunciation	much ellipsis and elision	**no nich** **ich nehm** **en Typ** **au nich** **ne Wohnung** **isses** **is**	**wir ham** **in nem** **bin ma** **un** **findsdes** **jetz** **solls**
Grammar	verb forms	only present and perfect tenses; no subjunctive	
	case	no genitive	
	demonstratives for pronouns	hat **der** au nich **die** is bewohnt	
Sentence construction	repetitions	mehr Interesse hat **als als** an uns	
	highlighting	**den** Quadratmeterpreis, **den** gibts überhaupt nich ansonsten	
	subordination	Over 80% of clauses are main clauses.	
	initial *da*	**da** geh ich doch das Risiko nich ein	
	sentences beginning with *und*	**Und** die Wohnung, em	
	ellipsis of pronouns, etc	(**das**) Müssen wer allerdings freust (**du**) dich drauf... (**ich**) bin ma gespannt	
	In general, sentence units are brief and emotive in tone.		
Vocabulary	**der Typ** bloke **ziemlich** fairly **so'n** like that **guck ma** look **unheimig** very, very **irre** fantastic **toll** fantastic	**scheußlich** awful **irgendwie** somehow **ekelig** awful **bin ma gespannt** I can't wait **ansonsten** anywhere else **gemütlich** relaxed	
Interjections, fillers and particles	Extensive use of these is very typical of this register.		

ach so	wohl noch	kann sein
em	immerhin	guck ma
ne	auch	jedenfalls
naja	au nich	und so
oder?	doch	günstig
also	allerdings	schön
hm	zwar	wie gesagt
och	überhaupt	ich mein
	immer	
	wohl	

Regionalisms	The speakers are from Cologne, which is on the border between N and C.	
nich (N)	cf: *net, nit* (C + S)
guck (C + SW)	cf: *kuck* (N), *schau* (SE)
und so	very typical filler in the Rhineland
wir, wer (N)	cf: *mir* (C + S)
(da) hab ich noch keine Meinung zu	splitting *da* + prep (N)
jemand anders (N + C)	cf: *jemand anderer* (S)

1.6.2   In a travel agency (R1/2)

This is a more formal conversation between people who do not know one another. There are still some typical features of unprepared speech, though fewer clear R1 elements than in **1.6.1**.

Herr A: Guten Tag!

Frau B: Tag!

Herr A: Ich wollte gern mal einen Reiseprospekt haben.

Frau B: Können Sie, bitte.

Herr A: Dann wollt ich auch noch was fragen.

Frau B: Ja.

Herr A: Äh, was macht man, wenn man eine schnelle Bestellung machen möchte noch für für März?

Frau B: Ja. Habe mer noch auf obe, Frau . . . ?

Frau C: Nein, morgen früh wieder.

Herr A: Morgen früh.

Frau B: Ja.

Frau C: Das Reisebüro is vormittags immer öh immer geöffnet.

Herr A: Ja. Gut. Mhm.

Frau C: Ja, nicht? Gucken Sie dann morgen früh mal rein.

Herr A: Ja.

Frau C: Sie können auch Ihre Reise telephonisch vorbestellen,

Herr A: Ach, toll.

Frau C: damit sie nicht vergeben ist.

Herr A: Ja, ja.

Frau C: Jaja, können Sie öh morgen früh noch mal anrufen? Lassen Sie sich mit Frau Westermann verbinden.

Herr A: Ja. Mhm.

Frau C: Die macht solche Reisen unter sich.

Herr A: Und was muß man äh normalerweise so an Reiseunterlagen mitbringen, wenn man ins Ausland geht?

Frau C: An Reiseunterlagen brauchen Sie gar nichts mitzubringen. Sie können sich das äh Sie können hier buchen. Sie können äh das schon telephonisch vorbestellen. Sie kommen hierher und bezahlen äh zahlen auch, ja? In dem Moment,

                                                      ⟫→

wo Sie bezahlen, dann buchen Sie eben für dies, nicht? Ich kenn mich da nicht so genau aus.

Herr A: Hm.

Frau C: Nicht? Aber Sie kriegen hier Ihre Unterlagen. Das wird von hier aus nach Fürth geschickt, und ich glaube . . . und dann finden wir Bescheid, daß wir s Geld einschicken, ne?

Herr A: Gut. Ja.

Frau C: Am besten ist äh, rufen Sie morgen mal bei uns an, und sprechen Sie mal mit der Dame, die das mit den Reisen macht. Frau Westermann ist das, ne. Kommen Sie, ich schreib s Ihnen hier mal auf.

Herr A: Danke schön.

(Harald P. Fuchs and Gerd Schank (eds),
Texte gesprochener deutscher Standardsprache, vol. 3,
Hueber, Munich, and Schwann, Düsseldorf, 1975, pp. 159–60)

Pronunciation	comparatively little ellipsis and elision	**ich wollt** **was** **is**	**ich kenn** **s Geld** **ich schreib s**
Grammar	verb forms	only present tense used subjunctive restricted to **möchte**	
	case	no genitives used	
	demonstratives for pronouns	**die** macht solche Reisen	
Sentence construction	repetition	vormittags **immer öh immer** geöffnet noch **für für** März	
	elements placed after final verb or prefix	machen möchte noch **für für** März habe mer noch auf obe	
	subordination	Over 80% of clauses are main clauses.	
	ellipsis of pronouns, etc	(**das**) können Sie (only one example)	
	broken sentences (fairly few)	Sie können sich das **äh Sie können hier buchen** ich glaube . . . **und dann finden wir Bescheid**	

In general, sentences are relatively complete and longer than in **1.6.1**, especially when information is being given.

Vocabulary	Some typical R1 elements, but other more formal and official phrasing, as if from a brochure.
R1:	**gucken, toll, rein, kriegen** **die das mit den Reisen macht** has the typical lack of precision of R1
R2/3:	**vormittags geöffnet** **telephonisch vorbestellen** **damit . . . vergeben ist** **lassen Sie sich verbinden** **Reiseunterlagen**

Interjections, fillers and particles	These are still very apparent in this register.		
	äh	**nicht?**	**mal**
	öh	**ich glaube**	**auch**
	mhm	**kommen Sie**	**ja**
	ach		**schon**
	hm		**aber**
	ne		

Regionalisms	The passage is from Freiburg, but aside from **gucken** (C + SW), the only distinctive regionalisms characteristically occur when one lady addresses her colleague, ie someone familiar to her.	
	-e for **-en** (SW)	**habe , obe**
	mer for **wir** (C + S)	**mer noch auf obe**

1.6.3   Dürrenmatt: *Der Richter und sein Henker* (R2/R3)

A relatively straightforward narrative from one of Dürrenmatt's detective stories; the register is neutral, with few elements wholly characteristic of informal colloquial or of formal literary style.

Er ergriff den Revolver und entsicherte ihn. Da machte auch der andere im Korridor Licht. Bärlach, der durch die halboffene Türe die brennende Lampe erblickte, war überrascht; denn er sah in dieser Handlung des Unbekannten keinen Sinn. Er begriff erst, als es zu spät war. Er sah die Silhouette eines Arms und einer Hand, die in die Lampe griff, dann leuchtete eine blaue Flamme auf, es wurde finster: der Unbekannte hatte die Lampe herausgerissen und einen Kurzschluß herbeigeführt. Bärlach stand in vollkommener Dunkelheit, der andere hatte den Kampf aufgenommen und die Bedingungen gestellt: Bärlach mußte im Finstern kämpfen. Der Alte umklammerte die Waffe und öffnete vorsichtig die Türe zum Schlafzimmer. Er betrat den Raum. Durch die Fenster fiel ungewisses Licht, zuerst kaum wahrnehmbar, das sich jedoch, wie sich das Auge daran gewöhnt hatte, verstärkte. Bärlach lehnte sich zwischen dem Bett und Fenster, das gegen den Fluß ging,

⤕→

an die Wand; das andere Fenster war rechts von ihm, es
ging gegen das Nebenhaus. So stand er in undurch-
dringlichem Schatten, zwar benachteiligt, da er nicht
ausweichen konnte, doch hoffte er, daß seine Unsicht-
barkeit dies aufwöge. Die Türe zur Bibliothek lag im
schwachen Licht der Fenster. Er mußte den Umriß des
Unbekannten erblicken, wenn er sie durchschritt.

(Rowohlt, Hamburg 1955, p. 92)

Grammar	tense	past (with a few pluperfects) throughout, as is normal in written narrative
	conditional	one one–word form only: **aufwöge**
	case	genitive used freely, eg: **des** Unbekannten, **eines** Armes
Sentence construction	subordination	Over 70% of clauses are main clauses.
	a few complex constructions	**das sich jedoch, wie sich das Auge daran gewöhnt hatte, verstärkte**
		As is suited to a narrative building to a climax, there is a sequence of fairly short sentences.

Vocabulary

Almost exclusively words in general use, with no R1 items,
although there are a few which are largely restricted to written
registers, eg:

finster	**betreten**	**benachteiligt**
herbeiführen	**wahrnehmbar**	**aufwiegen**
öffnen	**undurchdringlich**	**durchschreiten**

Regionalisms

Limited, even though the author is Swiss.

die Türe is a typically Swiss written form
wie (for *als*) is a S feature

1.6.4   Grass: *Die Blechtrommel* (R3a)

Fräulein Dr. Hornstetter, die fast jeden Tag auf eine
Zigarettenlänge in mein Zimmer kommt, als Ärztin mich
behandeln sollte, doch jedesmal von mir behandelt weniger nervös das Zimmer verläßt, sie, die so scheu ist und
eigentlich nur mit ihren Zigaretten näheren Umgang
pflegt, behauptet immer wieder: ich sei in meiner Jugend
kontaktarm gewesen, habe zu wenig mit anderen Kindern
gespielt.

Nun, was die anderen Kinder betrifft, mag sie nicht ganz
unrecht haben. War ich doch so durch Gretchen Schefflers
Lehrbetrieb beansprucht, so zwischen Goethe und
Rasputin hin und her gerissen, daß ich selbst beim besten

Willen keine Zeit für Ringelreihn und Abzählspiele fand. Sooft ich aber gleich einem Gelehrten die Bücher mied, sogar als Buchstabengräber verfluchte und auf Kontakt mit dem einfachen Volk aus war, stieß ich auf die Gören unseres Mietshauses, durfte froh sein, wenn es mir nach einiger Berührung mit jenen Kannibalen gelang, heil zu meiner Lektüre zurückzufinden.

Oskar konnte die Wohnung seiner Eltern entweder durch den Laden verlassen, dann stand er auf dem Labesweg, oder er schlug die Wohnungstür hinter sich zu, befand sich im Treppenhaus, hatte links die Möglichkeit zur Straße geradeaus, die vier Treppen hoch zum Dachboden, wo der Musiker Meyn die Trompete blies, und als letzte Wahl bot sich der Hof des Mietshauses. Die Straße, das war Kopfsteinpflaster. Auf dem gestampften Sand des Hofes vermehrten sich Kaninchen und wurden Teppiche geklopft. Der Dachboden bot, außer gelegentlichen Debatten mit dem betrunkenen Herrn Meyn, Ausblick, Fernsicht und jenes hübsche aber trügerische Freiheitsgefühl, das alle Turmbesteiger suchen, das Mansardenbewohner zu Schwärmern macht.

(*Danziger Trilogie*, Luchterhand, Darmstadt 1980, pp. 79–80)

Grammar	tense	past in narrative, but present in the first paragraph to refer to the time of narration	
	indirect speech	present subjunctive used	ich **sei** . . . gewesen
	case	genitive used freely	**unseres** Mietshauses **des** Hofes
	demonstratives	use of *jener*	mit **jenen** Kannibalen **jenes** . . . Freiheitsgefühl
Sentence construction	inversion + **doch**	war ich **doch** so . . . beansprucht	
	participle phrases	**von mir behandelt**	
	subordination	Nearly 50% of clauses are subordinate.	
	sentence length	There are 32 clauses in 8 sentences. Most of the sentences have three or more clauses and some are extremely complex, eg the single sentence of the first paragraph and the last of the second.	

Vocabulary	The sheer range of vocabulary is striking.

The first paragraph has rather technical and formal terms such as Fräulein Dr Hornstetter would use: **kontaktarm, näheren Umgang pflegen**.

The second paragraph has much rather lofty diction, typically R3a, which in the mouth of this narrator and linked to the very elaborate sentence construction has a pompous ring which might not be wholly serious:

betreffen	**meiden**	**jene Kannibalen**
mag	**nach einiger**	**heil zurückfinden**
Lehrbetrieb	**Berührung**	**Lektüre**
gleich einem		
Gelehrten		

The third paragraph of third-person narrative is more neutral, although it still has those characteristic elements which are restricted to the written registers:

sich befinden	**Ausblick**	**jenes trügerische**
sich bieten	**Fernsicht**	**Freiheitsgefühl**
sich vermehren		**Schwärmer**

A last noticeable feature is the extensive use of imaginative compounds, some of which will be the author's invention:

Zigarettenlänge	**Turmbesteiger**
Buchstabengräber	**Mansardenbewohner**

Interjections, fillers and particles	The use of these is very limited: typically the few that occur (**nun, doch, aber**) are in the second paragraph where a first-person narrator is 'speaking'.
Regionalisms	Only **Gören** (N) *children*.

1.6.5 Non-literary prose: the modern city (R3b)

A very characteristic piece of modern specialist writing (*Fachsprache*) from a handbook on architecture for the interested layman. Its complexity derives from extensive use of noun constructions rather than from subordination.

Struktur und Gestalt der Städte verändern sich im 19. und 20. Jh. schnell entsprechend der Wandlung der städtischen Gesellschaft im Industriezeitalter. Die Konzentration von Wohnungen gehört seit je zu den Kennzeichen der Städte. Sie ist zur Erfüllung der städtischen Funktion notwendig. Das Gegenbild, die Gartenstadt, ignoriert die tatsächliche Situation und die Rolle der Großstadt. Sie kann deren Funktionen nur ergänzen. Das Ziel muß sein, die Großstadt aufzulockern, ohne die Konzentration preiszugeben und zugleich die Landschaft vor der Zersiedelung zu bewahren.
   Um die Wohnungsqualität innerhalb der Städte zu verbessern, muß die Struktur geändert werden. Die starre Bindung der Häuser an das Blocksystem und die ,,Kor-

ridor-Straße" mit ihrem Schema Fahrbahn–Bürgersteig–Hauswand gehört zu den Ursachen der Unwohnlichkeit und Eintönigkeit vieler Stadtviertel. Zur ermüdenden Wiederholung des gleichen Schemas kommt noch die Zunahme des lebensgefährlichen motorisierten Verkehrs einschließlich der Belastung durch Lärm und Abgase. Die Fußgänger werden auf den Bürgersteig gedrängt, die die Häuser verbindende Grundebene der Straße in parallele Bahnen zerteilt.

Die Erweiterung des privaten Raumes durch die Straße als öffentlichen Schauplatz und Spielraum des städtischen Lebens fällt der Verkehrsfunktion zum Opfer. Selbst diese kann sie oft nur mangelhaft erfüllen. Sie leidet an Erstickung und Bewegungsmangel.

(Werner Müller and Gunther Vogel, *dtv-Atlas zur Baukunst*, dtv, Munich 1981, p. 529)

Grammar	tense	present throughout
	voice	use of passive suits the impersonal tone, eg: muß die Struktur **geändert werden**
	case	wide use of genitives (more genitive than dative), eg: Rolle **der** Großstadt **des** privaten Raumes
	prepositions	use of prepositions with the genitive, eg: **innerhalb** **einschließlich**
	demonstratives	used for possessive to avoid ambiguity, eg: **deren** Funktion
Sentence construction	constructions with verbal nouns	zur **Erfüllung** der städtischen Funktion die starre **Bindung** der Häuser an das Blocksystem zur ermüdenden **Wiederholung** des gleichen Schemas
	'blocks' of nouns linked by genitives or prepositions	**entsprechend der Wandlung der städtischen Gesellschaft** **den Ursachen der Unwohnlichkeit und Eintönigkeit vieler Stadtviertel**
	phrasal verbs	die Erweiterung . . . **fällt** der Verkehrsfunktion **zum Opfer**
	extended epithets (see **1.4.2**)	die **die Häuser verbindende** Grundebene
	NO subordination	The whole passage consists entirely of main clauses with a few infinitive constructions.

The preference for strings of nouns rather than subordination is very typical of this register. This reinforces the factual, impersonal tone and gives an impression of preciseness.

Vocabulary	Highly specialized and abstract, exclusively R2 and R3:

Erfüllung	**Zersiedelung**	**Abgase**
auflockern	**Unwohnlichkeit**	**Erstickung**
preisgeben	**Belastung**	

There are many foreign words, often with specialized meanings:

Struktur	**ignorieren**	**parallel**
Konzentration	**Schema**	
Funktion	**motorisiert**	

Many compound words, often with foreign elements. These again mainly belong to specialist terminology:

Industriezeitalter	**Blocksystem**	**Bewegungs-**
Gartenstadt	**Grundebene**	**mangel**
Wohnungsqualität	**Verkehrsfunktion**	

As might be expected in this very strictly written register, interjections, fillers and particles are entirely absent, as are regionalisms.

1.6.6 *Süddeutsche Zeitung* leading article (R3a/R3b)

A representative piece of serious journalism from a leading article discussing an Italian politician's remarks (made in 1984) about the possibility of German reunification and West German reactions to it. The prevailing tone is that of presenting a balanced and well-considered argument. The register is essentially R3b, but less typical of that register than **1.6.5**, and with more elements closer to literary R3a.

Diplomatischer Krach um Realitäten

Giulio Andreotti hat mit der Art, in welcher er seinen Wunsch nach einem Fortbestehen der beiden deutschen Staaten vortrug, sicher einen Teil jener Vorwürfe gerechtfertigt, die gegen ihn erhoben werden. Deshalb hat er aber nicht, wie es ihm unterstellt wird, seine Nachbarn jenseits der Alpen bewußt vor den Kopf stoßen wollen. Der italienische Außenminister war offenbar über die Heftigkeit des Echos selbst erstaunt.

So ist denn auch das eigentliche Ereignis nicht die unverblümte Offenheit, mit der Andreotti seine Haltung beschrieben hat, sondern die geradezu eruptive Reaktion von Politikern der CDU/CSU darauf. Die schnodderige Art, mit der Regierungssprecher Peter Boenisch den italienischen Minister und gleich den ehemaligen österreichischen Bundeskanzler Bruno Kreisky herunterputzte, mochte dem Bedürfnis entsprechen, die Angelegenheit schnell zu beenden. Aber dem Bundeskanzler, der wissen ließ, ihm seien die Äußerungen seines christlich-demokratischen Parteifreundes ,,absolut unverständlich'', müßte die Denkweise Andreottis eigentlich geläufig sein. Andererseits kennt auch Andreotti die Mentalität und die

Empfindlichkeiten der Bundesdeutschen zu genau, als daß ihm bloß ein Schnitzer unterlaufen wäre.

Es muß also einen Grund dafür geben, daß sich die Diskussion über die deutsche Zukunft gerade jetzt derart zuspitzt. Diplomatisch verklausuliert war es nicht, was Andreotti formulierte, auch war das Forum eines kommunistischen Pressefestes nicht gerade der geeignete Schauplatz, und die Warnung vor dem ,,Pan-Germanismus'' ist nicht nur ungenau, sondern auch unsinnig und unangebracht. Gleichwohl bildet die Substanz des Gedankenganges, es bestünden zwei deutsche Staaten, und zwei sollten es bleiben, seit Jahren einen festen Bestandteil dessen, was nahezu alle Nachbarn im Westen wie im Osten denken, gelegentlich sogar, wenn auch etwas geschickter, formulieren.

(*Süddeutsche Zeitung*, Munich, 17 September 1984)

Grammar	Formal and correct in all respects.	
	verb forms	full range of tenses and moods used, with a few passive constructions
		past subj in *als daß* clause after *zu* + adj, eg: zu genau, als daß ihm . . . unterlaufen **wäre**
		one-word past subj, eg: **bestünden**
	indirect speech	correct variation of pres and past subj, eg: ihm **seien**... es **bestünden**...
	case	full use of gen, also with the prep *jenseits* and in the demonstrative *dessen*
	relative pronoun	*welcher* used for variation
Sentence construction	subordination	Nearly 50% of clauses are subordinate (ie nearer **1.6.4** than **1.6.5**), but sentences are not overlong or complex. The majority consist of a main clause with one subordinate, most often a relative clause.
	first element	More than half the main clauses begin with an element other than the subject. This usually links back to the preceding sentence and maintains the flow of the argument.
	'blocks' of nouns linked by gen or prep	used much more sparingly than in **1.6.5**, but not wholly absent, eg: **seinen Wunsch nach einem Fortbestehen der beiden deutschen Staaten**

Vocabulary	Mainly kept on a fairly formal level in keeping with the serious tone:

vortragen	Ereignis	derart
Vorwurf	mochte	unangebracht
rechtfertigen	Angelegenheit	gleichwohl
erheben	Äußerung	gelegentlich
unterstellen	Empfindlichkeit	
Heftigkeit	unterlaufen	

There are some set phrases characteristic of political subjects:

die unverblümte Offenheit	diplomatisch verklausuliert
dem Bedürfnis entsprechen	der geeignete Schauplatz
absolut unverständlich	ein fester Bestandteil

The occasional R1 colloquialisms and idioms serve to enliven the argument:

jdn vor den Kopf stoßen	herunterputzen
schnodderig	der Schnitzer

Considerable use of foreign words, often of a specialist nature:

Echo	Diskussion	Forum
eruptive Reaktion	formulieren	Substanz
Mentalität		

Link words	The argument is structured carefully through the use of particles and other adverbs which make the logical progression clear and serve to emphasize the writer's main points:

sicher	bloß
offenbar	also
eigentlich	derart
andererseits	gleichwohl

deshalb . . . aber	auch war . . . nicht gerade
so ist denn auch…	nicht nur. . . , sondern auch

2 Words and meanings

2.1 Problems of meaning

More than two-thirds of errors made by advanced English-speaking learners of German involve matters of vocabulary. The central problem is that different languages reflect a different perspective of the world in their vocabulary. Each language divides up things, ideas, events, etc, in terms of words from a quite different viewpoint, categorizing and drawing distinctions in an individual way. The result is not just that there are words in German which are 'untranslatable', such as *gemütlich*, but that for most of the vocabulary we do not find any one-to-one correspondences between an English word and a German word. Cases of exact equivalence, such as *Baum*/tree or *Tisch*/table are relatively rare. Learning German involves learning how to break out of one's own framework of meaning and operate in the framework peculiar to German. As we are dealing with individual words, there are no rules; each word has to be taken on its own terms and there may be contexts where more than one will serve equally for a particular English word.

The following sections aim to elucidate some of the most confusing cases where the range of meaning of a word or group of words in one of the languages does not correspond to that of the nearest equivalents in the other.

2.1.1 Problems of meaning: English–German examples

This section lists, in alphabetical order, English words which most commonly cause problems for learners of German because the English word covers a wider area of meaning than any single word in German; there are, of course, many more than can be dealt with here.

ACCEPT	etw **annehmen** etw **akzeptieren**	to take sth offered (eg gift, suggestion)
	etw **gelten lassen** etw **akzeptieren**	to take sth as valid (eg excuses, arguments)
	jdn **akzeptieren**	to accept sb (eg as a friend)
	etw **einsehen**	to recognize, realize sth
	etw **hinnehmen**	to put up with sth

⋙→

[ACCEPT]	jdn in etw **aufnehmen**	to admit sb to sth (eg to a club)
	etw **übernehmen** etw auf sich **nehmen** }	to take sth on (eg task)
ACCIDENT	**das Unglück** **der Unfall**	fairly major, disaster (eg rail, plane) less serious, not necessarily fatal (eg car, home, work)
	das Mißgeschick } **das Malheur** (R1) }	rather minor, mishap
ACCIDENTALLY	**versehentlich** } **aus Versehen** }	inadvertently
	zufällig	by chance
ACCOMPLISH-MENT	**die Vollendung**	completion
	die Durchführung	execution
	die Leistung	achievement
	die Fertigkeit	skill
ACTUALLY see **really**		
ADMIT	jdn (zu etw (dat)) **zulassen** jdn (in etw) **hin-/hereinlassen**	to admit sb to sth, let sb in
	etw **zugeben**	to confess sth
ADVISE	jdm **raten**	to advise sb (general sense)
	jdn **beraten**	to advise sb at length (esp professionally)
	jdm von etw (dat) **abraten**	to advise sb against sth
	jdm **zuraten**, etw zu tun	to advise sb in favour of doing sth
	jdn von etw (dat) **unterrichten** jdn von etw (dat) **verständigen** jdn von etw (dat) **in Kenntnis setzen** (R3b) }	to inform sb of sth
ADVERTISING/ ADVERTISE-MENT	**die Werbung**	advertising (general sense)
	die Reklame	commercial advertisement
	die Annonce **die Anzeige** } **das Inserat**	small ad
	der Werbespot	television commercial

AFRAID see **fear**

AGAIN	**wieder**	once more as before
	noch einmal	one more time
	nochmals **wiederum** }	once again, stressing repetition

AGE	**das Alter**	length, stage of life; old age
	das Zeitalter	(historical) period

AGREE	jdm **zustimmen** mit jdm **einverstanden** **sein** mit jdm **übereinstimmen** (R3) }	to share sb's opinion
	etw (dat) **zustimmen** etw **billigen** mit etw (dat) **einverstanden** **sein** }	not to object to sth
	zu etw (dat) **stimmen** mit etw (dat) **übereinstimmen** }	to tally, fit in with sth
	sich mit jdm **einigen** mit jdm **einig werden** }	to reach an agreement with sb
	etw **verabreden** etw **vereinbaren** }	to agree (on) sth (eg dates, plan)
	sich bereit erklären, etw zu tun	to be prepared to do sth
	in etw **einwilligen** (R3)	to consent to sth
	zugeben, daß...	to admit that...

ALTER see **change**

APPEARANCE	**das Erscheinen**	action of becoming visible
	der Schein	outward look (deceptive)
	der Anschein	outward look (judged to be true)
	das Aussehen	general look of sb or sth
	das Äußere(s)	outward appearance of sb (eg clothes, face)
	die Erscheinung	phenomenon, apparition

ASK	jdn **fragen**	to ask sb (a question)
	eine Frage **stellen**	to ask a question
	jdn um etw **bitten** jdn um etw **ersuchen** (R3) }	to request sth from sb
	jdn zu etw (dat) **auffordern**	to request sth from sb (forcefully)
	etw **verlangen** etw **fordern** }	to demand, require sth (person as subject)
	etw **verlangen** etw **erfordern** (R3) }	to demand, require sth (thing as subject)

	nach jdm/etw (dat)
	  fragen
	sich nach jdm/etw (dat)
	  erkundigen (R3) }
		to enquire about sb/sth

	jdn **einladen**	to invite sb
AVOID	jdm/etw (dat) aus dem Weg **gehen** jdn/etw **meiden** (R3) }	to keep clear of sb/sth
	etw **vermeiden**	to manage not to do sth
	jdm/etw (dat) **ausweichen**	to steer clear of sth (eg danger)
	etw **um'gehen**	to find a way round sth (eg obstacle)
BAD	**schlecht**	not good, of sth which can possibly be good given other conditions
	schlimm **arg** (S) }	inherently bad, of sth which cannot possibly ever be good
BANK	das **Ufer**	shore of river, lake, etc
	der **Damm**	embankment
	der **Abhang**	slope
	die **Sandbank**, **Wolkenbank** }	sandbank, cloudbank
	die **Bank**	financial establishment
BEHAVE	sich **verhalten**	to have a particular attitude
	sich **benehmen**	to behave well, observe accepted standards
	sich **betragen** (R3)	to conduct oneself

' stressed syllables
are preceded by a
stress mark

BELONG	jdm **gehören**	to be the possession of sb
	etw (dat) **angehören**	to be a member of sth (eg club)
	zu etw (dat) **gehören**	to be a part of sth, be one of sth
BLAME	jdm **Vorwürfe machen** } jdn **tadeln**	to censure sb, say that what sb did was wrong
	jdn **beschuldigen** } jdm **die Schuld geben**	to accuse sb, fix the blame on sb
BOX	der **Kasten**	solid, fair-sized box or case; crate (for bottles) (S also: cupboard)
	die **Kiste**	wooden packing-case or chest (eg for tea, cigars)
	das **Kästchen**	small wooden box, casket (eg for jewels)
	der **Karton**	cardboard box
	die **Schachtel**	flat, flimsy box, packet (eg for matches, chocolates)
	die **Dose**	small box; tin can
BREAK	**brechen** (tr or itr)	to break cleanly, of solid objects (eg arm, mast, branch)
	zerbrechen (tr or itr)	to break into fragments (eg window)
	ein Ei aufschlagen	to break an egg
	etw **unterbrechen**	to interrupt sth (eg journey)
	(zer)reißen (tr or itr)	to snap, of non-hard things (eg string)
	kaputt sein (R1)	to be broken
	kaputtgehen (itr) (R1)	to break (colloquially, of almost anything)
BRIGHT	**hell**	not dark (of light)
	leuchtend	glowing (of colours)
	strahlend	shining (eg of sun, eyes, jewel)
	heiter	cheerful (eg of weather, day, person)
	glänzend	gleaming (eg of metal, prospects)
	intelligent	clever
BRUSH	die **Bürste**	stiff brush, for cleaning (eg hair, shoes)
	der **Pinsel**	soft brush for applying sth (eg paint)
	der **Besen**	broom, for sweeping

CALL	(etw) **rufen**	to shout (sth) out
	jdn/etw **herbeirufen**	to summon sb/sth (eg doctor, taxi)
	jdn **anrufen**	to call sb on the telephone
	jdm etw **zurufen**	to call sth out to sb
	jdn etw **nennen**	to call, name sb sth
	heißen	to be called
	jdn **besuchen** bei jdm **vorbeischauen** (R1) bei jdm **vorbeikommen** (R1)	to call on sb
	jdn/etw **abholen**	to call for sb, pick sb up
CARE	**die Sorge**	worry, anxiety
	die Sorgfalt	attentiveness, carefulness
	die Pflege	looking after sb/sth
	die Vorsicht	attention, heed
CAREFUL	**sorgfältig**	painstaking, taking care in doing sth
	vorsichtig	cautious, avoiding mishaps
CARELESS	**nachlässig**	negligent (opposite of *sorgfältig*)
	unvorsichtig	not paying attention
	leichtsinnig	foolishly thoughtless
	sorglos	carefree, unworried
CASE see **box**		
CASTLE	**die Burg**	medieval fortress
	das Schloß	stately home, palace
CATHEDRAL	**der Dom**	within German-speaking countries
	die Kathedrale	outside German-speaking countries
	das Münster	in a few specific cities mainly in SW (Strasbourg, Basle, Freiburg, Ulm, Zürich and Essen)
CAUSE	**die Ursache**	sth producing an effect
	der Grund **der Anlaß**	reason, motivation

CHANGE	etw **ändern**	to change sth fairly radically, esp in sudden action and in essential features
	etw **verändern**	to alter sth less radically, esp in gradual process and in external appearance

NOTE: the reflexives *sich ändern* and *sich verändern* are used for intransitive *to change* or *to alter* in the above meanings.

	etw **wechseln**	to substitute sth for another of the same kind (eg job, topic)
	etw **tauschen**	to swap sth for one of the same value
	etw **umtauschen**	to exchange sth (eg goods in shop, money)

NOTE: *tauschen* and *wechseln* differ in their basic meanings, but this difference may not be vital in certain contexts.

	jdn/etw **verwandeln**	to transform sb/sth completely (eg by magic)
	sich **umziehen**	to get changed (clothes)
	umsteigen	to change (trains, buses, planes, etc)
CLEVER	**klug**	sensible, clear-headed
	intelligent	mentally gifted, bright
	geschickt	skilful, dexterous
	schlau	astute, ingenious
	clever (R1)	smart, sharp
	gescheit	shrewd, quick-witted
CLIMB	auf/über etw **klettern**	to clamber up/over sth, using hands
	etw **ersteigen**	to reach the top of sth (eg mountain)
	etw **besteigen**	to climb, ascend sth (not necessarily reaching the top)
	auf etw **steigen**	climb up (onto) sth, ascend sth
	steigen	to climb, ascend (itr)
CLOSE	etw **schließen** (R3) } etw **zumachen**	to shut, close sth
	geschlossen sein } **dicht sein** (R1)	to be shut (eg shop, door)
	schließen } **zugehen** (R1)	to shut, close (itr)
	zumachen (R1)	to shut (itr: of shop, factory)
	etw **sperren**	to close sth off, block access to sth (eg road, port, tunnel)

COAT see **jacket**

COLLECT	etw **sammeln**	to collect things to keep (eg stamps) or for use (eg berries, wood)
	etw **ansammeln**	to accumulate things (eg valuable objects)
	sich ansammeln	to accumulate (itr: eg crowds)
	etw **einsammeln**	to take one from each person (eg tickets)
	sich versammeln **zusammenkommen** }	to assemble in a place (of people)
	jdn/etw **abholen**	to pick sb/sth up
	Geld einnehmen } **kassieren**	to collect money
COMPLAIN	**sich** (über etw) **beschweren** (etw) **reklamieren** }	to make a complaint (about sth)
	sich (über etw) **beklagen** } (über etw) **klagen**	to express annoyance (about sth)
	meckern (R1)	to grouse
CONTENT(S)	**der Inhalt**	contents, what is physically in sth
	der Gehalt	content in terms of ideas; proportion of sth in sth
CONTINUE	etw **weiterführen** } etw **fortsetzen** (R3)	to continue sth
	fortfahren, etw zu tun (R3)	to continue to do sth
	weitermachen (R1)	to carry on (itr)
	NOTE: the most natural German equivalent of 'to continue', 'to carry on doing sth' is most often *weiter* with an appropriate verb, see **5.2.4**.	
COPY	**die Kopie**	replica, exact copy
	das Exemplar	one of a number (eg book)
COW/CATTLE	**die Kuh**	cow, ie the female animal
	das Vieh	livestock, esp, but not only, cattle
	das Rind	head of cattle (R1 also: beef)
	das Rindvieh	cattle as species (R1*: term of abuse)

CROSS	NOTE: the most usual R2 equivalent of 'to cross' is, in transitive uses, *über etw gehen*, *fahren*, etc, in intransitive uses *hinübergehen*, *hinüberfahren*, etc.	
	sich kreuzen	to pass one another (eg trains, letters)
	etw **über'queren** (R3)	to go from one side of sth to the other (eg road)
	etw **passieren**	to pass through or over sth (eg frontier)
' stressed syllables are preceded by a stress mark	etw **über'schreiten** (R3)	to step over sth (esp a line, eg railway)
	etw **durch'queren** (R3)	to go across sth of wide area (eg desert)
CRY	**weinen** **heulen** (R1) }	to weep, cry tears
	(etw) **schreien**	to shout, scream (sth), often inarticulate (eg in fear)
	(etw) **rufen**	to call (sth), usually articulate
	(etw) **brüllen**	to yell, roar (sth), esp in excitement or anger, also of animals
DAMAGE	etw **beschädigen**	to cause actual physical damage to sth
	jdm/etw (dat) **schaden**	to be bad for sb/sth
	jdn/etw **schädigen**	to be to the disadvantage of sb/sth (eg reputation, business)
DARK	**dunkel**	not bright (opposite of *hell*)
	düster (R3)	gloomy, with little light and thus unpleasant
	finster (R3)	pitch black, with no light and thus sinister
	trübe	dull, dim (eg of light), murky (eg of water)
DECIDE	etw **beschließen**	to reach a decision to do sth (general sense)
	sich zu etw (dat) **entschließen**	to reach a firm decision to do sth after due consideration
	sich (für etw) **entscheiden**	to decide (on sth) by choosing from the available alternatives
	etw **bestimmen**	to fix, determine sth (eg time, place)
	jdn zu etw (dat) **bewegen** (R3) jdn zu etw (dat) **bestimmen** }	to decide, induce sb to do sth

DEMAND see **ask**

DENY	etw **leugnen** etw **bestreiten** }	to dispute truth of sth
	etw **ableugnen**	to dispute sth forcefully
	jdn/etw **verleugnen**	to disown sb/sth (eg one's origins)
	jdm etw **versagen** (R3) jdm etw **verweigern** }	to refuse sb sth
DIE	**sterben** **abkratzen** (R1), **krepieren** (R1) }	to die (general sense)
	umkommen **ums Leben kommen** }	be killed (eg in accident)
	fallen	die in battle
	entschlafen (R3)	pass away (euphemism)
DIFFERENT	**verschieden**	not the same as each other, various
	ander	not the same as before, another
	unterschiedlich	varied
DOUBT	etw **bezweifeln**	to doubt sth which has been taken to be true or accurate
	an jdm/etw (dat) **zweifeln**	to have doubts about sb/sth
	etw **anzweifeln**	to question sth (eg sb's honesty)
ENTRY/ **ENTRANCE**	**der Eingang**	way in
	die Einfahrt	way in for vehicles
	der Zugang	(point of) access
	der Eintritt	act of entering, admission
	der Zutritt	right of entry, admittance
	der Einlaß	being allowed in
	die Einreise	entry to a country
	der Auftritt	entrance on stage
	die Aufnahme	admittance (eg to a club) as a member
	der Eintrag	entry in book (eg dictionary, ledger)
EVENT	**das Ereignis**	definite, single event
	die Begebenheit (R3)	chance occurrence, esp extraordinary
	das Vorkommnis (R3)	single occurrence, esp unpleasant
	der Vorgang	event seen as process (pl *Vorgänge* = sequence of events)
	der Vorfall	unexpected incident

	der **Zwischenfall** (R3)	incident, esp political or diplomatic
	die **Veranstaltung**	organized function
	der **Fall**	case (cf *im Falle eines Krieges*)
	das **Vorkommen**	occurrence (eg precious metals, minerals, etc)
EXAMINE	jdn/etw **untersuchen**	to subject sb/sth to careful scrutiny, investigate sb/sth
	etw **prüfen**	to test sth for genuineness or accuracy (eg jewels, accounts)
	jdn **prüfen**	to subject sb (eg candidate) to an examination
	etw **kontrollieren**	to check, scrutinize sth (eg passport)
EXPERIENCE	die **Erfahrung**	knowledge, skills acquired over time
	das **Erlebnis**	event, sensation which one has experienced
FALL	**fallen**	to fall (general sense)
	stürzen	to fall violently, usually causing injury or damage (eg from height, off bicycle)
FAT	**dick**	corpulent, large, hefty (of people)
	fett	containing fat (R1 also = fat – of people in pejorative sense)
	fettig	greasy, covered in fat
FEAR/ FRIGHTEN	**sich** (um jdn/etw) **ängstigen**	to be worried (about sb/sth)
	jdn **beängstigen**	to worry sb, make sb anxious
	Angst haben	to be rather afraid, uneasy (fairly weak)
	etw **befürchten**	to be convinced that sth unpleasant will happen
	jdn/etw **fürchten**	to be in awe, dread of sb/sth
	sich vor jdm/etw (dat) **fürchten**	to be frightened of sb/sth (fairly strong)
	es tut mir leid(, daß . . .)	I am sorry, I regret (that . . .)
	jdm **angst machen** (see **5.4.1**) jdn **in Angst versetzen**	to scare, frighten sb
	jdn **erschrecken** NOTE: *weak* verb, see **3.3.4**	to startle sb, frighten sb suddenly
	erschrecken (R3) NOTE: *strong* verb, see **3.3.4**	to be physically frightened (suddenly)

FEEL	etw **fühlen**	to perceive sth through the senses
	etw **empfinden**	to be sensitive to sth (eg cold); feel emotions (eg joy, sorrow, respect)
	etw **spüren**	to be aware of sth, notice, sense sth
	(nach etw (dat)) **tasten**	to grope, feel (for sth) searchingly
	etw **betasten**	to feel sth to test quality
	meinen(, daß . . .)	to feel, be of the opinion (that . . .)
	sich + adj **fühlen**	(of people) to feel + adj, eg well, sick, tired
	sich + adj **anfühlen**	(of things) to feel + adj, eg hard, hot, damp
FIGHT	(gegen jdn/etw) **kämpfen**	to fight (sb/sth), esp in prolonged struggle
	etw **bekämpfen**	to combat sth (eg disease, fascism)
	fechten	to fence
	sich (mit jdm) **streiten**	to argue, quarrel (with sb), possibly, but not necessarily, physically
	sich schlagen **sich prügeln** **sich hauen** (R1)	to have a fight
	boxen	to box
FINALLY	**endlich**	after a long time (often impatient)
	endgültig	for ever, definitive(ly)
	zum Schluß **schließlich**	eventually, in the end, after all
FIRE	**das Feuer**	fire as element
	der Brand	a fire, causing damage (eg house, forest)
(AT) FIRST	**zuerst**	before the rest
	zunächst **erst mal** (R1)	initially, for the moment
	erstmals **zum erstenmal**	for the first time
	erst	*first,* followed by *dann* in series
	erstens	*first(ly)* in list, followed by *zweitens*, *drittens*, etc
FLOW	**fließen**	neutral equivalent of *to flow*
	strömen	to pour out, flow in large masses, stream

FOLLOW	(jdm/etw (dat)) **folgen** (R3)	to follow (sb/sth)
	NOTE: in this neutral sense R1 and R2 most often use an appropriate verb of motion prefixed by *nach-* or *hinterher-*, eg *jdm nachlaufen*.	
	auf jdn/etw **folgen** jdm/etw (dat) **folgen** }	to succeed sb/sth in chronological sequence
	aus etw (dat) **folgen**	to follow from sth (logically)
	etw **befolgen**	to act in accordance with sth (eg orders)
	jdn **verfolgen**	to pursue sb (eg thief); persecute sb
	etw **verfolgen**	to follow sth keenly (eg aims, TV series)
	etw **besuchen**	to attend sth (eg course)
	jdn/etw **verstehen**	to understand sb/sth (eg Do you follow me?)
FOOD	**das Essen**	food for a meal
	die Lebensmittel (pl) **die Nahrungsmittel** (pl) }	foodstuffs, comestibles
	die Speise	dish (usually in compound, eg *Süßspeise*; in R3 also used for Engl *nourishment*)
	die Nahrung	nourishment, sustenance
	die Kost	fare, type of food
	das Futter	food for animals (in R1 also used for Engl *grub*)
FORCE	jdn (zu etw (dat)) **zwingen**	to force, compel sb (to sth)
	etw (von jdm) **erzwingen**	to force sth (from sb)
	jdn/etw **bezwingen**	to overcome sb/sth (eg enemy, fear)
	jdm etw **aufzwingen**	to force sth on sb
FREEZE	**es friert**	there is a frost, it is freezing
	ich friere **mich friert** (R3) }	I am cold
	frieren **gefrieren** }	to turn to ice, be covered with ice
	zufrieren	to freeze over (eg of lake)
	erfrieren	to freeze to death
	einfrieren	to freeze up (eg of pipes)
	etw **einfrieren**	to freeze sth (eg food, post in institution)

FRUIT	**die Frucht**	fruit (general sense)
	das Obst (no pl, see **3.1.6c**)	edible fruit (eg apples, pears)
GARAGE	**die Garage**	place to store cars, etc
	die Werkstatt	repair shop for cars, etc
	die Tankstelle	petrol station
GATHER see **collect**		
GRASP	jdn/etw **ergreifen**	to grasp, take hold of sb/sth in sudden movement (also: opportunity, power, etc)
	jdn/etw **schnappen** (R1)	= *ergreifen* (in literal senses only)
	nach etw (dat) **greifen** nach etw (dat) **graps(ch)en** (N + C) nach etw (dat) **langen** (S)	to grasp, snatch at sth, reach quickly for sth
	jdn **packen**	to grab sb violently and keep tight hold
	jdn/etw **fassen**	to seize sb/sth firmly and keep hold
	sich jds/etw (gen) **bemächtigen** (R3)	to take control of sb/sth (eg radio station)
	etw **beschlagnahmen** (R3)	to confiscate sth (eg contraband)
	etw **begreifen** etw **erfassen**	to comprehend sth
GREET	(jdn) **grüßen**	to say hello (to sb); give one's regards to sb
	jdn **begrüßen** jdn **willkommen heißen** (R3)	to welcome sb
GRIN	**grinsen** **feixen** (R1)	to grin, smirk, esp scornfully or unpleasantly
	schmunzeln **lächeln**	to grin in a friendly or pleasant way
GROW (UP)	**wachsen**	to grow (general sense)
	größer werden (R1)	to grow (of children)
	aufwachsen	to grow up, spend one's childhood
	heranwachsen (R3)	to grow up, stressing development
	erwachsen werden	to become adult

	zunehmen	to increase in size or quantity
	adj + **werden**	to grow, get, become + adj (eg large, red)
	etw **ziehen**	to grow sth (plants)
	etw **anbauen**	to grow sth (plants) commercially
	etw **züchten**	to grow sth (plants), ie cultivate new types
GUESS	(etw) **raten**	to have a guess (at sth)
	etw **erraten**	to guess sth correctly
	etw **schätzen**	to estimate sth (eg weight)
	etw **vermuten**	to suppose sth
HAPPEN/ OCCUR	(jdm) **geschehen** (jdm) **passieren** (R1/R2) }	to happen (to sb) (general sense)
	sich ereignen **sich zutragen** (R3) }	to happen (of unusual or remarkable event)
	jdm **zustoßen** (R3) jdm **widerfahren** (R3) }	to befall sb
	vorfallen (R2/R3)	to happen (rather unexpectedly)
	vorkommen	to occur (ie be found); take place (of sth unpleasant)
	erfolgen	to take place (as a result)

HARM see **damage**

HILL see **mountain**

HIRE see **rent**

HOLIDAY(S)	**der Urlaub**	leave (from work), vacation
	die Ferien (pl)	institutional break (eg from school)
	der Feiertag	public, bank holiday

NOTE: in many contexts the distinction between *Urlaub* and *Ferien* is unimportant, and they are often used interchangeably, especially in R1.

IDEA	**die Idee**	notion, thought; philosophical idea
	der Einfall	idea, plan which occurs to one suddenly
	die Vorstellung	image in the mind, idea one has of sth
	der Begriff	concept, generic idea
	die Absicht	intention, plan of action
	die Meinung	opinion
	die Ahnung	inkling, suspicion

IMAGINE	**sich** (dat) etw **vorstellen**	to make oneself a mental picture of sth, possibly correct, possibly not
	sich (dat) etw **einbilden**	merely to imagine sth which is quite illusory
IMPROVE	jdn/etw **bessern**	to make sb/sth rather better
	sich bessern	to become rather better

NOTE: *(sich) bessern* is used especially with regard to health, morals, social conditions, situation in life, etc.

	sich verbessern	to better oneself (in career); do better (in sport); correct oneself
	etw **verbessern**	to correct sth, bring sth nearer to ideal, improve on sth (eg quality of product)

INCIDENT see **event**

INHABITANT(S)	**der Bewohner**	inhabitant, occupier, sb who happens to live in a particular place, road, house
	der Einwohner	resident, permanent inhabitant (eg of a city) with some legal or official status
	der Einheimische(r)	native, sb who belongs to a place
	der Eingeborene(r)	primitive, aboriginal native
	die Bevölkerung	inhabitants of a city, etc, seen as a collective whole
JACKET	**die Jacke** / **der Rock** (S)	jacket (general sense)
	das Jackett / **der** (AU **das**) **Sakko**	jacket of suit
	der Mantel	(over-)coat
JOB	**die Arbeit**	work in general (esp manual), piece of work
	die Aufgabe	specific task set sb
	der Auftrag	order, commission, specific piece of work relating to one's trade or profession
	die Stelle	paid job, position of employment
	der Job (R1)	casual or part-time job
	die Stellung	situation in general
	der Posten	specific post, esp in administration or commerce (eg *stellvertretender Direktor*)
	der Beruf	employment of a professional nature, (skilled) trade

KEEP	jdn/etw **behalten**	not to give sth away, not to allow sb to go
	etw **beibehalten**	retain sth (rather emphatic)
	etw **erhalten** etw **bewahren** (R3) }	to preserve, maintain sth
	etw **aufheben** etw **aufbewahren** (R3) }	to look after sth, put sth aside
	etw + adj **halten**	to keep sth + adj (eg clean, tidy)
	etw **halten**	to keep sth (pets)
	sich halten	to stay fresh (of food)
	jdn vor etw (dat) **bewahren**	to keep, protect sb from sth
	etw **unterhalten**	to keep sth going, maintain sth (eg building)
	jdn **unterhalten** jdn **versorgen** }	to provide for sb (eg family)
KNOW	jdn/etw **kennen**	to be familiar with sb/sth
	(etw) **wissen**	to have knowledge (of sth)
	eine Sprache **können**	to be able to speak a language
	bekannt sein	to be known
KNOWLEDGE	**das Wissen**	knowledge in general, total knowledge which a person possesses
	die Kenntnis	specific (piece of) knowledge
	die Kenntnisse (pl)	specialized knowledge in a certain field
	die Erkenntnis	knowledge of the nature of things gained through perception or experience
LEARN	(etw) **lernen**	to learn (sth) by effort, through study
	etw **erlernen**	to learn sth completely (eg language, skill)
	etw **erfahren**	to learn sth by chance, find sth out

$\ggg\!\!\rightarrow$

LEAVE	etw **verlassen**	to go away from sb/sth
	(weg)gehen \} **losgehen** (R1)	to depart
	abfahren \} **losfahren** (R1)	to depart (in vehicle, by train, etc)
	etw **lassen**	to allow sth to remain (in a particular place or in a certain condition)
	etw **liegenlassen** \} etw **vergessen**	to leave sth behind (esp in sense of *forget*)
	jdn/etw **zurücklassen** \} jdn/etw **dalassen** (R1)	not to take sb/sth with one, leave sb/sth behind
	jdn/etw **hinterlassen**	to leave sth behind (after death; for sb, as sign that one has been there)
	jdm etw **überlassen**	to leave sth in sb's care, entrust sth to sb

(AT) LAST see **finally**

LIFT	jdn/etw **heben**	to move sb/sth higher
	etw **hochheben** \} etw **erheben** (R3)	to raise sth up high (eg hand, glass)
	jdn/etw **aufheben**	to pick sb/sth up
	etw **erhöhen**	to make sth higher (eg wall, prices)

LIKE	jdn/etw **lieben**	to love sb/sth
	jdn **liebhaben**	to be fond of sb
	jdn/etw **gernhaben**	to like sb/sth (esp an established affection)
	etw **gefällt** jdm (see **4.1.1**)	sb likes sth (esp on the basis of a first impression)
	jdn/etw **mögen** (see **4.6**)	to like sb/sth (esp people or food)

NOTE: referring to people and food, *gernhaben* and *mögen* are very similar in meaning; *mögen* is rather more frequently used with a negative. With verbs, eg 'to like doing sth', German most often uses *gern* with an appropriate verb, see **5.2.4**, eg *ich reite gern* 'I like horse-riding'.

LITTLE see **small**

| **LIVE** | **leben** | to be alive, have a certain lifestyle |
| | **wohnen** | to dwell |

LOCK	**abschließen** (tr or itr) **absperren** (tr or itr) (SE) }	to lock (eg house, car, door)
	etw **verschließen**	to lock sth (small, eg case, box)
	jdn **einsperren** jdn/etw **einschließen** } etw **wegschließen**	to lock sb up, lock sth away
LOVE see **like**		
MAN	**der Mensch**	man as species, as opposed to animals
	der Mann	male human, as opposed to woman
MARRY	(jdn) **heiraten** **sich** (mit jdm) } **vermählen** (R3)	to get married (to sb)
	(mit jdm) **verheiratet sein**	to be married (to sb)
	jdn **trauen**	to marry sb (ie perform the ceremony)
MEAN	etw **bedeuten**	to signify sth
	etw **heißen**	to have a certain meaning (eg of foreign word)
	etw **besagen**	to make sth clear, express sth
	jdn/etw **meinen**	to have sb/sth in mind, intend sb/sth (esp in questions, eg 'Who/What do you mean?')
	etw **vorhaben**	to mean to do sth
MEET	jdm **begegnen** (R3)	to meet sb (by chance)
	jdn **treffen**	to meet sb (by chance or arrangement)
	sich (mit jdm) **treffen**	to meet (sb) by arrangement
	auf jdn/etw **treffen**	to come across sb/sth
	(mit jdm) **zusammentreffen**	to have a meeting (with sb)
	jdn **kennenlernen**	to meet sb for the first time
	jdn **abholen**	to pick sb up
MEMORY	**das Gedächtnis**	faculty of remembering
	die Erinnerung	remembrance, recollection
	der Speicher	memory of computer or calculator

MISS	jdn/etw **vermissen**	to notice, regret the absence of sb/sth
	etw **verfehlen**	not to get the right sth (eg path, purpose)
	etw **verpassen**	to come too late for sth (eg train), let sth slip (eg opportunity)
	etw **versäumen**	not to do sth one ought to have done (eg miss an opportunity)

NOTE: the German equivalent of English 'miss' in intransitive senses is most often *daneben* with an appropriate verb, eg *er hat daneben geschossen*. *Versäumen* and *verpassen* are close in meaning and interchangeable in many contexts, although in general *versäumen* is more reproachful.

MISTAKE	**der Fehler**	error, fault, defect
	der Irrtum	mistaken belief or judgement
MOUNTAIN	**der Berg**	mountain, hill
	der Hang	slope, incline
	der Hügel (esp N)	rather small hill, often solitary
	das Gebirge	mountains, hills
NARROW	schmal	of small width or breadth (opposite of *breit*)
	eng	constricted, difficult to get through (opposite of *weit*)
NECK	**der Hals**	whole neck or throat, also of bottles
	der Nacken **das Genick** (R3) }	nape, back of neck
NIGHT	**die Nacht**	period between bedtime and dawn
	der Abend	period between sunset and bedtime
NOISE see **sound**		
NOTICE	jdn/etw **bemerken**	to become aware of sth
	etw **merken**	to perceive, realize sth abstract (eg intention, deceit)
	etw **spüren**	to sense, feel sth (eg smell, pain, cold)
NUMBER	**die Anzahl**	rather vague, indefinite number
	die Zahl	quite specific number
	die Nummer	numbers in series applied to sth (eg house, car, telephone)
	die Ziffer	actual figure itself (eg 4, 7)
OCCUR see **happen/occur**		

OCCURRENCE see **event**

ODD	**merkwürdig** **seltsam** **sonderbar** **wunderlich**	odd, out of the ordinary
	eigenartig	peculiar, with odd individual characteristics
	komisch	funny, peculiar
	fremd	unfamiliar, strange
	unheimlich	uncanny, weird
	ungerade (Zahl)	odd (number)
OFFER	jdm etw **anbieten**	to hand sth to sb for acceptance
	(jdm) etw **bieten**	to afford sth, make sth available (to sb) (usually sth abstract, eg opportunity)
OFFICER	**der Offizier**	military officer
	der Beamte(r)	civilian official (incl eg policeman), civil servant (officer of the State)
ONLY	**nur** **bloß** (R1/R2)	limiting (ie that number and no more, at that time and only then, see **2.6**)
	erst	indicating more to follow, that there is time left, or that sth is not happening before a certain time (see **2.6**)
OPEN	etw **aufmachen** etw **öffnen** (R3)	to open sth (general sense)
	etw **aufschließen**	to unlock sth
	etw **eröffnen**	to perform the opening of sth (eg school, exhibition, proceedings)
	aufgehen **sich öffnen** (R3)	to open (itr)
ORDER	jdm **befehlen** jdm **gebieten** (R3)	to command sb (eg to do sth)
	etw **befehlen** etw **gebieten** (R3)	to order sth (eg silence)
	etw **anordnen**	to decree sth (esp of official); arrange sth according to a system
	etw **ordnen**	to sort sth into order, organize sth
	etw **bestellen**	to make an order to be provided with sth
ORGAN	**das Organ**	part of body, etc
	die Orgel	musical instrument

PACKET	**das Paket**	large package, packet (eg for washing powder); large postal parcel
	die Packung } **das Päckchen** }	small package or packet (eg for tea, cigarettes); *Päckchen* also small postal parcel
PAINT	etw **(an)streichen**	to put paint on sth (eg house, fence)
	(jdn/etw) **malen**	to paint a picture (of sb/sth)

PARCEL see **packet**

PATH see **street**

PAY	(etw für etw) **zahlen**	to pay (sth – always a sum of money – for sth; in R1 also used for *bezahlen*)
	bei jdm **zahlen**	to pay sb (ie waiter, bus conductor)
	etw **bezahlen**	to pay for sth
	jdn **bezahlen**	to pay sb
PEOPLE	**die Menschen** (pl)	people as individuals
	die Leute (pl)	people as a mass (in R1 also used for *Menschen*)
	das Volk	people as a nation or community; the 'common' people

NOTE: as an indefinite (= *they*), *man* is used in German where English will often have *people*, eg: *man sagt = people say*.

PERSUADE	jdn von etw (dat) **überzeugen**	to convince sb of sth
	jdn **überreden**, etw zu tun	to talk sb into doing sth
	jdn (dazu) **bewegen**, etw zu tun (R3)	to induce sb to do sth
	jdm etw **einreden**	to talk sb into believing sth
PLACE	**der Ort**	place in general, not precise
	die Stelle	precise spot, usually with a certain relevance or in relation to surroundings
	die Ortschaft	village, settlement
	der Platz	place to do sth specific (eg to sit down, to play sth, etc); square (in town); room, space (of sufficient size to do sth)

POUR	etw **gießen**	to pour sth (only liquids)
	etw **streuen**	to pour, strew sth (having grains, eg sand)
	etw **schütten**	to pour sth in large quantities
	(jdm etw) **einschenken**	to pour (sb sth, ie a drink)
	strömen **sich ergießen** (R3) $\Big\}$	to pour (out) (itr – also of people)
	gießen (itr)	to pour (of rain)
POWER	**die Macht**	power, ability to control (esp latent)
	die Gewalt	power exercised, force, violence, might
	die Kraft	physical strength
	die Stärke	measurable strength, size, intensity
PRESENT	**aktuell**	topical, current, relating to the present
	anwesend	in attendance
	vorhanden	existing in a place, available
	augenblicklich **gegenwärtig** **derzeitig** (R3 – adj only) $\Big\}$	of/at the present moment
PREVENT	jdn an etw **hindern**	to stop, impede sb in sth
	etw **verhindern**	to make sth impossible
	jdn/etw **behindern**	to obstruct, hinder sb/sth
PUSH	(jdn/etw) **schieben**	to move (sb/sth) by pushing (esp along a surface)
	(jdn/etw) **stoßen** **schubsen** (R1) $\Big\}$	to give a short, violent shove (to sb/sth)
	(jdn/etw) **drücken**	to apply pressure (to sb/sth, eg door, button)
	drängen **drängeln** (R1) $\Big\}$	to push, press forward (of people)

$\ggg\!\!\rightarrow$

PUT	jdn/etw **stellen**	to put sb/sth so that it then stands (ie *steht*; eg chair in corner, bottle, plate on table)
	jdn/etw **setzen**	to put sb/sth so that it then sits (ie *sitzt*; eg child on chair, pot on stove)
	jdn/etw **legen**	to put sb/sth so that it then lies (ie *liegt*; eg book on table, person on couch)
	jdn/etw **stecken**	to put sb/sth so that it is then hidden from view (ie *steckt*; eg hand in pocket, letter in mailbox)
	etw **hängen**	to put sth so that it then hangs (ie *hängt*; eg picture on wall)
	etw in etw **(hinein)geben**	to add sth to sth (eg salt to stew)
	NOTE: in R1, *tun* commonly replaces these more specific words.	

QUIET	**leise**	not loud
	ruhig	calm (of people or things), undisturbed
	still	silent, not talkative

READY	**bereit**	prepared, willing
	fertig	finished, completed

REALIZE	etw **erkennen** etw **begreifen** etw **einsehen**	to appreciate, comprehend sth
	etw **wird** jdm **klar** etw **geht** jdm **auf**	sth becomes apparent to sb
	etw **(be)merken**	to notice sth; see also **notice**
	etw **feststellen**	to discover sth, find sth out
	etw **verwirklichen** etw **realisieren** (R3)	to make sth real (eg plans, aims)

REALLY/ ACTUALLY	**wirklich** **tatsächlich** **in der Tat** **wahrhaftig** (R2/R3)	in actual fact, in reality (as opposed to imagination or illusion)
	eigentlich **an (und für) sich**	originally, strictly speaking, at bottom, as a matter of fact
	übrigens	by the way

REFUSE	**sich weigern** (, etw zu tun)	to refuse (to do sth – of people)
	etw **nicht (tun) wollen**	to refuse (to do sth – of things)

	(jdm) etw **verweigern** ⎫ (jdm) etw **versagen** ⎬	to refuse, not to grant (sb) sth
	etw **ablehnen**	to decline sth, turn sth down
RENT	etw **mieten**	to rent, hire sth (from sb)
	etw **vermieten**	to rent, hire sth (to sb)

RAISE see **lift**

RISE	**aufstehen** ⎫ **sich erheben** (R3) ⎬	to get up, rise
	steigen	to rise upwards, ascend (itr)

ROAD see **street**

ROOM	**das Zimmer**	room in private house
	die Stube (S)	living–room
	die Kammer	box-room (in S also used for *Schlafzimmer*)
	der Saal	very large room, hall (eg for concerts)
	der Raum	large space in most senses (eg for sth to fit into); room (in public building)
ROPE	**das Seil**	rope
	der Strick	thin rope, esp for tying things (also hangman's rope)
	das Tau	thick rope, cable (esp on ships)
SAME	**derselbe**	the very same one
	der gleiche	another identical one
	NOTE: in R1 *derselbe* and *der gleiche* are used interchangeably.	
SATISFY	jdn/etw **befriedigen**	to satisfy, gratify sb/sth, ie (sb in his) desires, claims, curiosity, etc
	jdn **zufriedenstellen**	to make sb contented (eg customer)
	(mit etw (dat)) **zufriedensein** ⎫ sich (mit etw (dat)) ⎬ **zufriedengeben**	to be satisfied (with sth)
	satt sein ⎫ **gesättigt sein** ⎬	to have had enough to eat
	etw **erfüllen**	to fulfil sth (eg conditions, equation)
	etw (dat) **genügen**	to comply with sth (eg requirements)
	jdn (von etw (dat)) **überzeugen**	to convince sb (of sth)

SAVE	jdn (vor etw (dat)) **retten**	to save sb (from sth, eg danger)
	etw **sparen**	not to use sth (eg money, time)
	etw **schonen**	to go easy on sth (eg eyes, clothes)
	etw **ersparen**	to save (money)
	jdm etw **ersparen**	to save sb sth (esp unpleasant details)
	sich etw (dat) **ersparen**	to avoid sth (eg trouble)
	etw **aufsparen**	to put sth to one side for later
SECRET	**geheim**	deliberately kept from public view
	heimlich	(kept) hidden, invisible, clandestine
SEIZE see **grasp**		
SHINE	**leuchten**	give out or reflect light (general term) (esp of lamps, etc)
	glänzen	reflect light, gleam, sparkle (esp of things which do not give out their own light)
	scheinen	give out light (of sun, moon, lamps)
SHUT see **close**		
SHY	**scheu**	timorous, esp used of animals or expressions of emotion (smile, glance, etc)
	schüchtern	of a reserved, introverted nature (of people)
SIMPLE	**einfach** **leicht**	uncomplicated, easy
	einfältig **simpel**	simple-minded
	schlicht	plain, straightforward (positive sense)
SKIN	**die Haut**	skin of human or animal (no fur)
	das Fell	animal skin with fur
	die Schale	skin, peel, rind (eg fruit, vegetable)
SMALL	**klein**	small in size
	gering	slight, low, small in value or importance
SMELL	**der Geruch** **der Geschmack** (SW)	smell (general sense)
	der Duft	pleasant smell, fragrance
	der Gestank	unpleasant smell, stench

SOUND	**das Geräusch**	any indistinct sound or noise (general sense)
	der Lärm	loud, unpleasant noise
	der Krach	crashing noise (in R1 also used for *Lärm*)
	der Klang	resonant, musical sound
	der Ton	single musical note; tone (of voice)
	der Laut	sound made by humans or animals (eg speech sound)
	der Schall	sound as a physical phenomenon (eg *Schallgeschwindigkeit*); clear and distinct sound (eg bell)

SPACE see **room** and **place**

SPEND	**Geld ausgeben**	to spend money
	etw **verbrauchen**	to use sth up (eg strength, energy)
	etw **verbringen** etw **zubringen** }	to pass sth (eg time)
SPREAD	etw **ausbreiten**	to spread sth (out), extend sth evenly (eg wings, map on floor)
	etw **verbreiten**	to disseminate sth, ie spread sth patchily over wide area (eg disease, panic)
	etw **verteilen**	to distribute sth (eg forces, payments, cushions round room)

NOTE: the reflexives *sich ausbreiten*, *sich verbreiten* and *sich verteilen* are used for intransitive *spread* in the above meanings.

	sich erstrecken	to extend, stretch over an area (without movement, eg forest to horizon)
	sich ausdehnen	to move, stretch out over a wide area (eg war, fog); also = *sich erstrecken*
	etw (auf etw) **streichen** etw (auf etw) **schmieren** }	to spread sth (on sth, eg butter on bread)
	um sich greifen	spread out from centre (esp of pernicious things, eg disease, fire, trouble)
STEP	**der Schritt**	pace (of person); stride
	der (Fuß)tritt	sound of human step
	die Stufe	individual step or stair
	die Treppe **die Stiege** (AU) }	stairs, staircase, flight of steps

STOP	jdn/etw **anhalten**	to stop sb/sth (person or vehicle in motion)
	halten	to come to a halt (esp of scheduled stop for vehicles; also of people)
	anhalten	to come to a halt (esp of temporary, unplanned stop of vehicles or people)
	stehenbleiben	to come to a halt (esp people); break down (eg machine, vehicle)
	jdn/etw **aufhalten**	to prevent sb/sth from continuing
	etw **abstellen**	to switch sth off (eg motor, machine)
	etw **einstellen**	to suspend sth (eg work, payment, production)
	jdn von etw (dat) **abhalten**	to stop sb from (doing) sth
	(mit etw (dat)) **aufhören**	to cease (sth, eg an activity)

NOTE: *stoppen* may be used instead of *halten, anhalten, aufhalten, abstellen* or *einstellen*, especially in R1.

STRANGE see **odd**

STREET	die **Straße**	surfaced street or road
	die **Gasse**	lane, alley (AU, CH also: street in town)
	der **Weg**	unsurfaced, but well-defined road or path
	der **Pfad**	ill-defined, merely trodden path

STRENGTH see **power**

STRING	die **Schnur** (S) der **Bindfaden** (N + C) die **Kordel** (C, esp Rheinland) der **Spagat** (AU)	string
	die **Saite**	string of instrument

SUSPICIOUS	**verdächtig** **suspekt**	arousing suspicion
	mißtrauisch **stutzig** **argwöhnisch** (R3)	inclined to have suspicions, distrustful

TAKE	jdn/etw **nehmen**	to remove, take hold of, receive sb/sth
	jdn/etw wohin **bringen**	to convey, accompany sb/sth to a place (eg cases upstairs, sb to station)
	etw **brauchen**	to take sth (of time, eg to take two hours to do sth)

TALL	groß ⎱ lang (R1) ⎰	tall (of people)
	hoch	tall (of things, eg tree, tower)

THEN	dann	then (for sequences of events or referring to present or future)
	damals	then (ie at that time in the past)
	denn (see 2.6)	then (in questions, ie 'What are you doing, then?')

THICK	dick	measuring a long way through (eg book, layer, wall); also of soup
	dicht	packed together, dense (eg trees, hair, traffic); also = not leaky

THING	das Ding	in sing: concrete object in pl: concrete objects; matters of a relatively serious nature
	die Sache	in sing: matter, affair, business in pl: personal belongings; matters, affairs of a rather nebulous, less serious kind

NOTE: the German equivalent of *thing(s)* is often an adjective used as a noun, eg *das Wichtige*, see **3.4.4**.

THINK	(etw) denken	to form (sth) in the mind, have (sth) in the mind as an idea
	(etw) glauben	to believe (sth)
	(etw) meinen	to hold (sth) as an opinion

NOTE: *glauben* and *meinen* are close in meaning and often interchangeable.

sich (dat) etw denken ⎱ sich (dat) etw vorstellen ⎰	to imagine sth
viel (etc) von jdm/etw (dat) halten	to think a lot (etc) of sb/sth
jdn/etw für jdn/etw halten ⎱ jdn/etw als jdn/etw betrachten ⎰	to take sb/sth for sb/sth; think that sb/sth is sb/sth
sich (dat) etw überlegen ⎱ über etw nachdenken ⎰	to think about sth

THREATEN	(jdm mit etw (dat)) **drohen**	to warn, threaten (sb with sth) in general way, not necessarily involving force
	jdn/etw (mit etw (dat)) **bedrohen**	to threaten sb/sth (with sth), involving direct, physical force; endanger sb/sth
	(jdm) etw **androhen**	to threaten (sb with) sth abstract (eg punishment, revenge)
TIME	**die Zeit**	time as duration, fourth dimension
	das Mal	occasion
TOUCH	jdn/etw **berühren**	to come into (slight) contact with sb/sth
	jdn/etw **anfassen** jdn/etw **angreifen** (S) an etw **rühren** (R3) }	to touch (and get hold of) sb/sth with the hand
	jdn/etw nicht **anrühren**	not to touch sb/sth (eg me, food, money)

NOTE: *anrühren* is normally only used with a negative.

	jdn **rühren** jdn **bewegen** (R3) }	to move sb emotionally
TURN	etw **drehen**	to spin, revolve sth (eg knob, key, wheel)

NOTE: *sich drehen* is used for intransitive *turn* in this sense.

	etw **umdrehen**	to turn sth round, turn sth over, eg revolve sth through 180° on its own axis
	sich umdrehen	to turn round, turn over (esp of people)
	(etw) **umkippen**	to turn (sth) upside down (eg car, plate)
	(etw) **wenden**	to turn (sth) onto the other side or to face in another direction (eg steak, page, car, glance, head)
	etw wohin **kehren**	to turn sth to face in a certain direction (eg sail to the wind)
	etw (von etw (dat)) **abwenden**	to turn sth away, aside (from sth)
	umkehren	to turn round and go back
	wohin **(ein)biegen**	to turn off straight course in new direction
	abbiegen	to turn off (one road into another)
UNDER-STANDING	**die Vernunft**	good sense, reasonableness
	der Verstand	ability to understand, wit(s), intellect, reason

	die Verständnis	act of understanding, sympathy
	die Verständigung	mutual understanding, agreement
	das Einverständnis	consent
	die Einsicht	insight, realization, understanding of sth specific
USE	etw **benutzen, benützen** (S) (see **2.2.4**) **sich** etw (gen) **bedienen** (R3)	to make use of sth for a particular purpose
	etw **gebrauchen**	to find a use for sth in accordance with its intended purpose
	etw **verwenden**	to utilize sth, often for a purpose for which it was not intended

NOTE: *benutzen, gebrauchen, verwenden* are very close in meaning and in R1 and R2 are often used interchangeably.

	etw **verwerten** (R3)	to utilize sth in a new way (esp left-overs, ideas)
	etw **verbrauchen**	to use sth up, consume sth
	etw (auf etw) **anwenden**	to apply sth (to sth)
	etw **(aus)nutzen, (aus)nützen** (S) (see **2.2.4**)	to make full use of sth, exploit sth
VIEW	**der Blick**	view in general, into, onto sth

NOTE: *Blick* is *not* used with a following genitive phrase.

	die Ansicht	view **of** sth (also = *Meinung*)
	die Aussicht	(panoramic) view **from** a place, prospect
	der Ausblick	outlook from a place, perhaps restricted
	die Sicht	range of vision (eg *in Sicht kommen*)
WAKE (UP)	jdn **(auf)wecken** jdn **erwecken** (R3)	to wake sb (up)
	wach werden **aufwachen** **erwachen** (R3)	to wake up, awake
	etw **erwecken** (R3)	to awaken, arouse sth (eg emotions)
	wachen	to stay awake, be awake, keep watch
WALL	**die Wand**	wall of building, inside or outside
	die Mauer	outside wall of brick, stone, etc
	der Wall (R3)	rampart, fortification

WASH (UP)	jdn/etw **waschen**	to wash sb/sth (general sense)
	sich waschen	to wash (of people)
	(etw) **spülen** (etw) **abwaschen** }	to wash sth (up) (ie dishes)
	etw wohin **spülen**	to wash sth up in a place (of waves, river)

WELCOME see **greet**

2.1.2   Problems of meaning: German–English examples

In this section are common examples of German words which are often confusing because of their wide range of meaning. They are given in alphabetical order, together with their most usual English equivalents.

NOTE: In some instances compounds can be used if the simple word might be ambiguous. If this is so, the appropriate compound is given in italics. However, all registers, and especially R1, normally prefer the simple word as long as there is no chance of ambiguity.

der Absatz		heel (ie of shoe: *Schuhabsatz*) paragraph landing (ie on stairs: *Treppenabsatz*) (R3b) sales (ie of goods or services)
etw **annehmen**		to accept sth to presume, assume sth
anziehen	*etw anziehen* *sich anziehen* *jdn/etw anziehen*	to put sth on (clothes) to get dressed to attract sb/sth
etw **bemerken**		to notice sth to remark sth
das Blatt		leaf sheet (of paper) hand (of cards)
der Boden		ground floor (*Fußboden*) bottom (eg of cup, sea) (N + C, AU) loft (*Dachboden*)
die Decke		ceiling blanket (*Wolldecke*) quilt, duvet (*Steppdecke*) covering (eg surface of road: *Straßendecke*)

dicht		dense (eg trees, fog)
		thick (eg hair, feathers)
		heavy (eg traffic)
		close (to sth = *an etw*)
		(water-, air-) tight (*wasserdicht, luftdicht*)
		(R1) shut (eg of shop)
dick		fat (of people)
		thick (eg tree-trunk, wall, soup)
		(R1) big (eg car, business, wallet)
einfallen	*einfallen* (itr)	to join in (eg singing)
		to cave in
		(R3a) to fall (eg night)
	in etw einfallen	to invade sth (eg country)
	jdm einfallen	to occur to sb
etw **erfahren**		to learn sth, find out about sth
		to experience sth
etw **erklären**		to explain sth
		to declare sth
erst		first (if followed by *dann*, see **2.1.1**)
		only (see **2.1.1**)
		modal particle (see **2.6**)
das Fach		compartment (eg in bag)
		pigeon-hole
		subject (eg at school: *Schulfach, Studienfach*)
der Fall		fall
		case, instance
die Farbe		colour
		paint
der Fehler		mistake
		fault, defect
fertig		finished
		ready
		(R1) whacked, tired out
fremd		strange
		foreign
		someone else's
der Gang		corridor, passage
		gait, way of walking
		course (eg of events, of meal)
		gear (in car)
		operation (eg of machine)

die Geschichte		story history (R1) matter, affair, business
gleich		same equal(ly) immediately, at once
der Grund		reason bottom (eg of sea) ground
der Hahn		cock, rooster tap (eg for water, gas: *Wasserhahn, Gashahn*)
der Hals		neck throat
hell		bright (of light) light, pale (of colours)
der Himmel		sky (*am Himmel* = in the sky) heaven (*im Himmel* = in heaven)
die Kapelle		chapel band
die Karte		card (*Spielkarte*) ticket (*Fahrkarte, Eintrittskarte*, etc) map (*Landkarte*) menu (*Speisekarte*)
das Kissen		cushion pillow
kosten	*kosten* *(etw) kosten*	to cost to taste (sth)
das Kreuz		cross small of the back
das Land		country (as opposed to town) land (as opposed to water) province, state (*Bundesland*)
die Landschaft		countryside landscape scenery
der, die, das letzte		the last, the latest
meinen	*meinen(, daß...)* *jdn/etw meinen*	to think, be of the opinion (that . . .) to mean sb/sth

der, die, das nächste		the next the nearest the shortest, quickest (eg way)
packen	*jdn packen* (R1) *etw packen*	to grab, grip sb to pack sth (eg suitcase) (R1) to manage (to do) sth
die Politik		politics policy
der Preis		price prize
der Rat		advice council (eg of town: *Stadtrat*) councillor, official
raten	*jdm raten* *(etw) raten*	to advise sb to guess (sth)
reichen	*reichen* (itr) *jdm etw reichen*	to extend, stretch to be enough to pass sb sth
der Schein		appearance certificate banknote (*Geldschein*) light, glow (eg of sun: *Sonnenschein*, etc) ticket (larger ones, plane ticket)
scheinen		to seem, appear to shine (see **2.1.1**)
das Schloß		castle, mansion lock
sicher		safe sure, certain secure
die Spannung		tension suspense voltage
die Stimme		voice vote
der Stock		stick storey, floor (in building = *das Stockwerk*)
der Stoff		material, fabric substance subject, topic (eg of discussion)

tragen	*jdn/etw tragen*	to carry sb/sth
	etw tragen	to wear sth (clothes)
		to bear sth (eg name, costs)
treffen	*jdn treffen*	to meet sb (see **2.1.1**)
	jdn/etw treffen	to hit sb/sth
umziehen	*'umziehen*	to move (house)
	sich 'umziehen	to get changed (clothes)
unterhalten	*jdn/etw unter'halten*	to maintain, support sb/sth
	jdn unter'halten	to entertain sb
	sich unter'halten	to have a talk, to enjoy oneself
der Versuch		try, attempt
		experiment, test
vorstellen	*sich (dat) etw vorstellen*	to imagine sth
	jdn (jdm) vorstellen	to introduce sb (to sb)
wählen	*(jdn) wählen*	to vote (for sb)
	jdn wählen	to elect sb
	jdn/etw wählen	to choose sb/sth
	wählen	to dial (on telephone)
weit		wide, broad
		long (eg way, journey)
		far (as adverb)
die Wirtschaft		economy
		pub (*Gastwirtschaft*)
		(R1) trouble, bother
zeigen	*jdm etw zeigen*	to show sb sth
	auf jdn/etw zeigen	to point to sb/sth
der Zug		train
		draught (*Luftzug*)
		procession (*Straßenzug*)
		feature, trait (*Charakterzug*)

' stressed syllables
are preceded by a
stress mark

2.2 Easily confused words

2.2.1 Easily confused words: similar form – different meaning

Some German words look so much alike that they can be confusing even for the advanced learner. A selection of such words is given in this section, grouped into pairs or sets. A number of these words are similar because they are built up from the same root, often using the prefixes and suffixes explained in **2.3**. This means that the relevant words cannot always be given in alphabetical order, so that it is important to look at each group of words as a whole.

die Achsel shoulder	**die Achse** axle
der Akt act; nude (painting); (AU also = file)	**die Akte** file
der Antrag application etw **beantragen** to apply for sth	**der Auftrag** order jdn (mit etw) **beauftragen** to instruct sb to do sth (= jdm etw **auftragen** (R3))
die Aufführung performance	**die Ausführung** carrying out (task, etc)
die Aufgabe task	**die Ausgabe** issue; edition
aufrüsten to arm (ie get weapons)	jdn/etw **ausrüsten** to equip sb/sth
etw **ausarbeiten** to work sth out	etw **herausarbeiten** to make sth clear
jdm etw **ausrichten** to tell sb sth etw **verrichten** to perform sth (eg task)	etw **einrichten** to furnish sth
der Ball ball	**der Ballen** bale
der Band (cf. **2.2.2**) volume **das Band** ribbon **die Bande** gang **der Verband** bandage; association	**der Bund** (cf. **2.2.2**) confederation **das Bund** bundle, bunch **das Bündnis** alliance **die Verbundenheit** obligingness

R1* = vulgar
R1 = informal
    colloquial
R2 = neutral
R3 = formal
R3a = literary
R3b = non-literary
(see 1.1.5)

N = North
C = Central
S = South
SW = South West
SE = South East
AU = Austria
CH = Switzerland
(see 1.2.3)

⟫→

die Verbindung connection	**die Verbindlichkeit** obligingness
bedingungslos unconditional	**unbedingt** absolute
der Beruf profession	**die Berufung** calling; vocation; (legal) appeal
etw **beurteilen** to judge sth	jdn **verurteilen** to condemn sb
etw **bezeichnen** to indicate, mean sth	etw **verzeichnen** to record, note sth

das Bild picture, image	**die Bildung** education; formation
die Ausbildung training	
jdn **ausbilden** to train sb	etw **herausbilden** to develop sth

jdn um etw **bitten** (bat – gebeten) to ask sb for sth jdm etw **bieten** (bot – geboten) to offer sb sth	**beten** (betete – gebetet) to pray **betteln** (bettelte – gebettelt) to beg

blinken (R1) to indicate (in car)	**blinzeln** to blink
jdn **blenden** to blind sb	

böse wicked; cross, vexed	**boshaft** spiteful
böswillig malicious	

der Brauch custom **gebraucht** used; second-hand	**der Gebrauch** use **gebräuchlich** customary

etw **brauchen** to need sth	etw **gebrauchen** to use sth
etw **verbrauchen** to consume sth	

der Busch bush	**die Böschung** slope
das Café café	**der 'Kaffee** (AU **der Kaf'fee**) coffee
der Dank thanks	**der Gedanke** thought

' stressed syllables
are preceded by a
stress mark

dauern	etw/jdn **bedauern**
to last; to pity (R3)	to regret sth; to feel pity for sb
bedauerlich	**bedauernswert**
regrettable	pitiful (R3)

die Decke	**der Deckel**
ceiling; blanket	cover; lid
die Deckung	**das Gedeck**
cover (to hide in)	place (laid at table)

denken
to think

etw **bedenken**
to consider sth

jds/etw (gen) **gedenken** (R3)
to remember sb/sth

durch etw **dringen**
to penetrate sth

auf etw **dringen**
to insist on sth

jdn **drängen**
to push sb (in crowd)

auf etw **drängen**
to press for sth

jdn **bedrängen**
to put pressure on sb

etw **drücken**
to press sth

etw **drucken**
to print sth

etw **ausdrücken**
to express sth

etw **eindrücken**
to push sth in

jdn **beeindrucken**
to impress sb

der Ausdruck
expression

der Eindruck
impression

die Ehre
honour

die Ehrfurcht
reverence

der Ehrgeiz
ambition

ehrbar (R3)
respectable

ehrenhaft
honourable

ehrenvoll
distinguished

ehrlich
honest

ehrwürdig
venerable

die Eigenschaft	**die Eigenart**
quality; feature	individuality
das Eigentum	**die Eigentümlichkeit**
property	peculiarity

einfach
simple

einfältig
simple (-minded)

einheitlich
uniform

einig
agreed

einsam
lonely

einzig
only (as adjective)

einzeln
single; individual

vereinzelt
occasional

---

jdm **einfallen**
to occur to sb

auf etw **hereinfallen** (R1)
to be taken in by sth

---

empfänglich
receptive; susceptible

empfindlich
sensitive

---

endlos
endless

endlich
at last; finally

unendlich
infinite

---

der Entschluß
decision

die Entschlossenheit
determination

---

erst
first; only

erstens
first(ly)

zuerst
at first

erstmals
for the first time

---

die Etikette
etiquette (AU, CH also label)

das Etikett
label

---

der Fahrer
driver

der Führer
leader; guide

---

etw **fordern**
to demand sth

jdn/etw **fördern**
to support sb/sth

etw **erfordern** (R3)
to necessitate sth

jdn/etw **befördern**
to promote sb; to transport sth

die Forderung
demand; claim

die Förderung
support; promotion

---

geistig
intellectual; mental

geistlich
spiritual

geistreich
witty

---

die Gelegenheit
opportunity

die Angelegenheit
matter; affair

---

die Gemeinheit
meanness

die Gemeinschaft
community

die Gemeinsamkeit
common ground

---

etw **gewohnt sein**
to be used to sth

sich an etw **gewöhnen**
to get used to sth

der Gläubige(r) believer	**der Gläubiger** creditor

gleich same; immediately **zugleich** at the same time **gleichgültig** indifferent	**gleichfalls** likewise **gleichmäßig** even; regular **gleichviel** (R3) none the less

das Grab grave **graben** to dig	**der Graben** ditch jdn **begraben** to bury sb

grausam cruel	**grauenhaft** atrocious

gründlich thorough	**grundsätzlich** fundamental

der Hahn cock, rooster; tap, faucet	**die Henne** hen

das Huhn
 chicken

der Handel trade	**die Handlung** action

das Herd stove	**die Herde** herd

die Höhe height	**die Anhöhe** hill

der Inder Indian	**der Indianer** (Red Indian) Native American

der Kegel skittle; cone	**die Kugel** ball; sphere

kostbar precious **die Kost** (R3) food, fare	**köstlich** exquisite **die Kosten** (pl) cost(s)

jdm **kündigen** to give notice to sb, fire sb	etw **verkünden** (R3) to announce sth

sich erkundigen
 to inquire

künstlich artificial	**künstlerisch** artistic

lebendig alive; living	**lebhaft** lively; vivid

etw **legen** (legte – gelegt)   **liegen** (lag – gelegen)
  to put, lay sth   to lie, be lying (down)
              lügen (log – gelogen)
                to tell lies

---

das Leid   **das Leiden**
  sorrow, grief   suffering; illness
              die Leidenschaft
                passion; enthusiasm

---

die Lerche   **die Lärche**
  lark   larch

---

das Mahl (R3a)   **die Mahlzeit**
  repast   meal
              der Gemahl (R3a)
                husband

---

etw **mieten**   etw **vermieten**
  to rent, hire sth (from sb)   to rent, hire sth (to sb)

---

der Muskel   **die Muschel**
  muscle   (sea-)shell

---

namentlich   **nämlich**
  by name; in particular   namely; because
              namhaft
                renowned

---

offiziell   **offiziös** (R3b)
  official   semi-official

---

ein paar   **ein Paar**
  a few   a pair

---

der Pfeil   **der Pfeiler**
  arrow   pillar

---

der Photograph   **die Photographie** (R3)
  photographer   photograph; photography

---

die Post   **der Posten**
  post (ie mail), post office   post (ie job)
              der Pfosten
                post (ie upright)

---

der Rahmen   **der Rahm** (S)
  frame   cream

---

rascheln   **rasseln**
  to rustle   to rattle
rauschen   **rasen**
  to roar (of water)   to race; to rave

---

rauh   **roh**
  rough   raw

---

das Recht right; law	**die Gerechtigkeit** justice
die Rechtfertigung justification	**die Berechtigung** entitlement
reisen to travel	etw **reißen** to tear sth
römisch Roman	**romanisch** Romanesque
die Sammlung collection	**die Versammlung** assembly
schadhaft faulty	**schädlich** harmful
der Schal shawl	**die Schale** bowl; peel
jdn/etw **schicken** to send sb/sth	**geschickt** shrewd
der Schlager hit (record)	**der Schläger** tennis racket
schlecht bad	**schlicht** simple
die Seite side; page	**die Saite** string (of instrument)
sonderbar peculiar	**sonderlich** particular(ly)
springen to jump	etw **sprengen** to blow sth up; to break sth apart
das Stadium stage (in development)	**das Stadion** stadium
jdn/etw **stützen** to support sb/sth	etw **stutzen** to trim sth
stutzen (itr) to hesitate	
stürzen (itr) to fall heavily; to rush	jdn/etw **stürzen** to fling sb/sth
das Tablett tray	**die Tablette** tablet
etw **tauschen** to change sth	jdn **täuschen** to deceive sb

jdm/etw (dat) **trauen** to trust sb/sth	jdm (*or* auf jdn) **vertrauen** to have confidence in sb

jdm etw **anvertrauen**
to confide, entrust sth to sb

der Tropfen drop	**der Tropf** (R1) dope, stupid person
übrigens incidentally	**im übrigen** otherwise
ungewöhnlich unusual	**außergewöhnlich** out of the ordinary
unglaublich unbelievable	**unglaubwürdig** implausible; unreliable (of person)
das Verhalten behaviour	**das Verhältnis** relationship
jdn/etw **verschonen** (R3) to spare sb/sth	etw **verschönern** to improve sth
der Versuch attempt	**die Versuchung** temptation
vorher previously; beforehand	**vorhin** just now
der Wagen cart, carriage, car	**der Waggon** goods truck (railway)

etw **wahren** (R3)
to preserve sth
jdn/etw vor jdm/etw (dat)
  bewahren
  to protect sb/sth from sb/sth
etw **gewahren** (R3)
to notice sth
etw **aufbewahren**
to keep, store sth
	währen (R3)
	to last
	
	  sich bewähren
	  to prove one's worth
	jdm etw **gewähren** (R3)
	to grant sb sth
	sich wehren
	to defend oneself

wieder again	**wider** (R3) against
wunderbar wonderful	**wunderlich** strange; odd

verwunderlich
astonishing

sich wundern to be amazed, astonished jdn/etw **bewundern** to admire sb/sth	jdn **verwundern** to astonish sb jdn **verwunden** to wound sb

2.2.2   Easily confused words: different gender – different meaning

der **Band** volume	*die* **Band** [bɛnd] band
das **Band** { ribbon (pl ¨**er**) / bond (R3a, pl **-e**)	
der **Bulle** bull (R1 also = cop)	*die* **Bulle** (papal) bull
der **Bund** confederation	*das* **Bund** bundle (eg twigs), bunch (eg radishes)
der **Erbe** heir	*das* **Erbe** inheritance
der **Flur** (N + C) hall (in house)	*die* **Flur** (R3a) meadow
der **Gang** corridor; gait (see **2.1.2**)	*die* **Gang** [gɛŋ] (R1) gang (eg robbers)
der **Gefallen** favour	*das* **Gefallen** (R3) pleasure
der **Gehalt** content (see **2.1.1**) (AU also = salary)	*das* **Gehalt** salary
der **Golf** gulf (on coast)	*das* **Golf** golf
das **Harz** resin	*der* **Harz** Harz mountains
der **Heide** heathen	*die* **Heide** heath
der **Hut** hat	*die* **Hut** guard (in a few R3 phrases only, eg *auf der Hut sein*)
der **Junge** (N + C) boy	*das* **Junge** young (of animals)
der **Kiefer** jaw	*die* **Kiefer** (N + C) pine
der **Kunde** customer	*die* **Kunde** (R3) news
der **Laster** (R1) lorry; truck	*das* **Laster** vice
der **Leiter** leader	*die* **Leiter** ladder
der **Mangel** lack; fault	*die* **Mangel** mangle
die **Mark** Mark (currency)	*das* **Mark** (bone-)marrow
die **Marsch** (N) fen	*der* **Marsch** march
das **Maß** measure	*die* **Maß** (SE) litre (of beer)
der **Mensch** human being	*das* **Mensch** (R1) woman (pejorative)
der **Messer** surveyor	*das* **Messer** knife

der **Moment**	moment	*das* **Moment** (R3b)	factor; element
der **Otter**	otter (also: *Fischotter*)	*die* **Otter**	adder (also: *Kreuzotter*)
der **Pack**	pile; pack	*das* **Pack**	rabble
das **Pony**	pony	*der* **Pony**	fringe (hair)
der **Schild**	shield	*das* **Schild**	sign; (number-) plate
der **See**	lake	*die* **See**	sea
der **Single**	single (unmarried) person	*die* **Single**	single (record)
		das **Single**	singles (tennis)
die **Steuer**	tax	*das* **Steuer**	steering wheel; tiller
der **Stift**	pen; pencil; peg	*das* **Stift**	foundation; institution (esp religious)
der **Tau**	dew	*das* **Tau**	rope; cable (esp on ship)
der **Tor** (R3)	fool	*das* **Tor**	gate
der **Verdienst**	earnings	*das* **Verdienst**	merit
das **Wehr**	weir	*die* **Wehr**	defence (mostly in compounds, eg *Feuerwehr*, and phrases, eg *sich zur Wehr setzen*)

2.2.3   Easily confused words: different plural – different meaning

Many words have more than one meaning (see **2.1.2**). With some words, each meaning has a different plural form.

das Aas	carcass (R1*) sod	**Aase**	carcasses
		Äser (R1*)	sods
der Abdruck	offprint impression	**Abdrucke**	offprints
		Abdrücke	impressions
das Band (see 2.2.2)	ribbon (R3a) bond	**Bänder**	ribbons
		Bande (R3a)	bonds
die Bank	bench bank	**Bänke**	benches
		Banken	banks
der Block	block (various meanings)	**Blöcke**	blocks (ie large pieces)
		Blocks	blocks (ie of flats, notes)

| **das Ding** | thing | **Dinge** things |
| | (R1) girl | **Dinger** (R1) things; girls |

| **das Gesicht** | face | **Gesichter** faces |
| | (R3a) vision | **Gesichte** (R3a) visions |

| **das Land** | country | **Länder** countries |
| | (R3) region | **Lande** (R3) regions |

| **der Mann** | man | **Männer** men |
| | (R3) vassal | **Mannen** (R3) vassals |

| **die Mutter** | mother | **Mütter** mothers |
| | nut (for screw) | **Muttern** nuts |

| **der Ort** | place | **Orte** places |
| | (coal-)face | **Örter** (coal-)faces |

| **der Rat** | council, official | **Räte** councils, officials |
| | advice | **Ratschläge** pieces of advice |

| **der Strauß** | bunch (of flowers) | **Sträuße** bunches |
| | ostrich | **Strauße** ostriches |

| **das Wort** | word | **Wörter** words (in isolation) |
| | | **Worte** words (connected, eg in phrase) |

NOTE: In R1 the distinction between *Wörter* and *Worte* is largely ignored and only *Worte* is used.

2.2.4 Easily confused words: different form – same meaning

Few of these sets of doublets are totally interchangeable. Often there are regional or register variations involved, and sometimes the forms may replace one another freely in one meaning but not in another. In all cases the most frequent variant is given on the left.

| **die Backe (-n)** | der Backen (-) (S) | *cheek* |

| **der Bube (-n,-n)** | der Bub (-en,-en) (S) | *boy; jack (cards)* |

| **der Bursche (-n,-n)** | der Bursch (-en,-en) (R1) | *lad* |

| **die Ecke (-n)** | das Eck (-e; AU -en) (S) | *corner* |

NOTE: *das Eck* is in general use in some compounds, eg *das Dreieck*.

| **der Felsen (-)** | der Fels (-en) | *rock* |

NOTE: in general R2 use, *Fels* may be used to mean 'rock as a substance', whereas *Felsen* rather refers to an 'individual rock'.

| **der Fleck (-e)** | der Flecken (-) | *stain, spot* |

NOTE: in practice, *Fleck* is the usual form in the singular, whilst *Flecken* is the usual form in the plural. In R3a *Flecken* can also mean 'small town'.

| **der Frieden** | der Friede (R3) | *peace* |

| **der Funke (-ns,-n)** | der Funken (-) | *spark* |

der Hirte (-n,-n)   der Hirt (-en,-en)   *shepherd*
NOTE: both are common, but some German speakers think *Hirte* is R3, whilst others are convinced that *Hirt* is R3.

der Karren (-) (S)   die Karre (-n) (N + C)   *cart (R1 also = old crock)*

der Korken (-)   der Kork (-e) (N)   *cork*
NOTE: to refer to the material *cork*, only *Kork* is used.

der Nutzen   der Nutz (R3a)   *use*
NOTE: *Nutz* is found nowadays only in set phrases, eg *zu Nutz und Frommen* ('to the greater good of').

nutzen   nützen   *to be of use*
NOTE: both are equally common, but in compounds (eg *benutzen*), *-nutzen* is more frequent, *-nützen* is mainly S.

der Ochse (-n,-n)   der Ochs (-en,-en) (S)   *ox*

der Pack (¨e)   der Packen (–)   *pile, stack*

die Ritze (-n)   der Ritz (-e) (S)   *crack*

das Rohr (-e)   die Röhre (-n)   *pipe, tube*
NOTE: *Rohr* and *Röhre* are interchangeable in the most general sense, but for specific types of 'pipe' or 'tube', usage has become fixed, eg:
    -rohr: *Gas-, Wasser-, Seh-, Fern-, Blas-, Kanonen-*
    -röhre: *Back-* (= oven), *Fernseh-, Röntgen-, Glas-, Luft-, Harn-* and all other 'anatomical' pipes, tubes and channels.

die Ruine (-n)   der Ruin   *ruin*
NOTE: *Ruine* is used to refer to a building, *Ruin* for economic ruin.

der Samen (-)   der Same (-ns,-n) (R3a)   *seed*

der Schreck   der Schrecken (S)   *scare, fright*
NOTE: only *Schrecken* is used to mean 'terror'.

schwätzen (R1)   schwatzen (S)   *chatter*

die Socke   der Socken (S)   *sock*

der Spalt (-e)   die Spalte (-n)   *gap, opening*
NOTE: only *Spalt* is used in the phrase *einen Spalt offen* (= ajar): *Spalte* also = 'column' (in newspaper).

das (CH der) Taxi   die Taxe (R1)   *taxi*

die Truppe (-n)   der Trupp (-s)   *troupe*
NOTE: *Truppe* usually refers to a large company of soldiers, players, etc: *Trupp* is usually smaller, eg a squad of soldiers or group of people.

die Tür (-en)   die Türe (-n) (CH, AU)   *door*

der Typ (-en)   die Type (-n)   *type, character (R1 also bloke, guy)*
NOTE: *Type* mainly *(printers') type* or *(odd) character*.

der Zeh (-en)   die Zehe (-n) (R3 or N)   *toe*

2.3   Word formation

An understanding of German word formation will help to widen your vocabulary because the meaning of a German word can often be deduced from the sum of its parts. This is more true of German than of English. For example, the relationship of *Frage* to *fragen* or *Dankbarkeit* to *Dank* is quite transparent, unlike that of *question* to *ask* or *gratitude* to *thanks*.

This section gives some of the more common and productive elements used to form words in modern German. It must be emphasized, though, that these processes for deriving new words are not wholly regular or predictable. For instance, *Abmachung* and *Verwirklichung* (from *abmachen* and *verwirklichen*) exist, but *Gebung* and *Nehmung* do not. Complex words, once formed, can also develop meanings of their own. *Länge*, for example, is still obviously related to *lang*, both by form and meaning, but *Sänfte*, meaning 'sedan-chair', has lost all ties of meaning to *sanft*.

```
R1* = vulgar
R1 = informal
        colloquial
R2 = neutral
R3 = formal
R3a = literary
R3b = non-literary
(see 1.1.5)
```

2.3.1   Forming nouns

(a) By adding suffixes

–chen, **–lein** (esp R3a)	forms diminutives (from nouns), eg: die Stadt → **das Städtchen** *little town* das Auge → **das Äuglein** (poetic R3a) *little eye* NOTE: Umlaut usually added.
–e	(i) denotes an action or instrument (from verbs), eg: pflegen → **die Pflege** *care* bremsen → **die Bremse** *brake* (ii) denotes a quality (from adjectives), eg: groß → **die Größe** *size* stark → **die Stärke** *strength* NOTE: Umlaut added.
–er	(i) denotes the person who does sth or an instrument (from verbs), eg: lehren → **der Lehrer** *teacher* bohren → **der Bohrer** *drill* (ii) denotes the inhabitant (from town-names), eg: Wien → **der Wiener** *Viennese* Zürich → **der Zürcher** *person from Zurich*
–erei (esp R1), **Ge...e**	denotes repeated, irritating action (from verbs), eg: fragen → **die Fragerei, das Gefrage** *lots of annoying questions*
–heit, –(ig)keit	denotes a quality (from adjectives), eg: bitter → **die Bitterkeit** *bitterness* heftig → **die Heftigkeit** *violence* geschwind → **die Geschwindigkeit** *speed*

⟫⟫⟶

-in	forms the feminine (from nouns), eg: der Arzt → **die Ärztin** *lady doctor* NOTE: Umlaut usually added.
-ler	denotes a practitioner (from nouns), eg: die Kunst → **der Künstler** *artist* NOTE: the suffix *-ler* sometimes has a pejorative sense, eg **der Kreigsgewinnler** *war profiteer*

-ling	(i) the object of the action (from verbs), eg:
	       prüfen → **der Prüfling** *examinee*
	       strafen → **der Sträfling** *prisoner*
	(ii) person of that quality, often derogatory (from adjectives), eg:
	       feige → **der Feigling** *coward*
	       fremd → **der Fremdling** *stranger*

-mittel, -stoff,
-zeug
	things used for sth (from verbs), eg:
	    waschen → **das Waschmittel** *detergent*
	    heilen → **das Heilmittel** *cure*
	    brennen → **der Brennstoff** *fuel*
	    kleben → **der Klebstoff** *glue*
	    rasieren → **das Rasierzeug** *shaving tackle*
	    fahren → **das Fahrzeug** *vehicle*

-schaft, -tum	collective or quality (from nouns), eg:
	    der Student → **die Studentenschaft** *student body*
	    der Beamte → **das Beamtentum** *civil servants*
	    der Freund → **die Freundschaft** *friendship*

-ung	action or process (from verbs), eg:
	    verwarnen → **die Verwarnung** *warning*
	    bilden → **die Bildung** *formation*

-wesen	collective organization of sth (from nouns), eg: die Erziehung → **das Erziehungswesen** *education system*

(b) By adding prefixes

Erz- (R1),
Riesen- (R1)
	augmentative, intensive, eg:
	    der Reaktionär → **der Erzreaktionär** *dyed-in-the-wool reactionary*
	    der Erfolg → **der Riesenerfolg** *enormous success*
	NOTE: R1 is very rich in other augmentative and intensive prefixes,
	eg: *Superhit, Spitzengehalt, Bombengeschäft, Heidenlärm, Höllendurst,*
	Mordsapparat, Scheißapparat, Topmanager, etc.

Fehl-, Miß-	opposite, negative, eg:
	    die Einschätzung → **das Fehleinschätzung** (R3b) *false estimation*
	    der Erfolg → **der Mißerfolg** *failure*

Grund- (R3b)	basic, essential, eg: die Tendenz → **die Grundtendenz** *basic tendency*

Haupt-	main, eg: der Bahnhof → **der Hauptbahnhof** *main station*
Nicht-	*non-*, eg: der Raucher → **der Nichtraucher** *non-smoker*
Un-	opposite, abnormal, eg: die Ruhe → **die Unruhe** *unrest* das Wetter → **das Unwetter** *bad weather*
Ur-	original, eg: die Sprache → **die Ursprache** *original language*

2.3.2   Forming adjectives

(a) By adding suffixes

-bar	*-able* (from verbs), eg: brauchen → **brauchbar** *usable*
-(e)n, -ern	made of sth (from nouns), eg: das Gold → **golden** *golden* das Holz → **hölzern** *wooden*
-haft	like sth (from nouns), eg: der Held → **heldenhaft** *heroic*
-ig	(i) having sth (from nouns), eg: das Haar → **haarig** *hairy* (ii) like sth (from nouns), eg: der Riese → **riesig** *giant* (iii) duration (from time expressions), eg: zwei Stunden → **zweistündig** *lasting two hours*
-isch	(i) having that quality (from nouns), eg: das Kind → **kindisch** *childish* (ii) origin (from geographical names), eg: England → **englisch** *English* (iii) relating to sth (from foreign nouns), eg: die Biologie → **biologisch** *biological*

⟫→

-lich	(i)	relating to a person or a thing, eg:
		der Arzt → **ärztlich** *medical*
		der Preis → **preislich** *in respect of price*
	(ii)	having that quality (from nouns), eg:
		der Fürst → **fürstlich** *princely*
	(iii)	frequency (from time expressions), eg:
		zwei Stunden → **zweistündlich** *every two hours*
	(iv)	*-able* (from verbs), eg:
		begreifen → **begreiflich** *understandable*
	(v)	*rather* (from adjectives), eg:
		rot → **rötlich** *reddish*
-(s)los		lacking in sth (from nouns), eg:
		die Hoffnung → **hoffnungslos** *hopeless*
-mäßig (R3b)	(i)	according to sth, eg:
		der Instinkt → **instinktmäßig** *instinctive*
	(ii)	with regard to sth, eg:
		der Verkehr → **verkehrsmäßig** *relating to traffic*
	(iii)	like sth, eg:
		der Fürst → **fürstenmäßig** *like a prince*

Especially in R3, a large number of suffixes which were originally separate words are now in common use, eg:

having sth:
- **-(s)voll**   rücksichtsvoll
- **-stark**   charakterstark
- **-reich**   erlebnisreich
- **-haltig**   koffeinhaltig

lacking sth:
- **-arm**   nikotinarm
- **-leer**   gedankenleer
- **-frei**   alkoholfrei

protected from sth:
- **-fest**   hitzefest
- **-echt**   kußecht
- **-sicher**   kugelsicher
- **-dicht**   schalldicht

similar to sth:
- **-förmig**   plattenförmig
- **-gleich**   maskengleich
- **-artig**   kugelartig

capable of sth:
- **-fähig**   strapazierfähig

worth(y of) sth:
- **-wert**   lesenswert
- **-würdig**   nachahmenswürdig

needing sth:
- **-bedürftig**   korrekturbedürftig

(b) By adding prefixes

un-

opposite, eg:
wahrscheinlich → **unwahrscheinlich** *improbable*

ur-

original, eg:
deutsch → **urdeutsch** *typically German*

Many more intensifying adjective prefixes are found, esp in R1, eg *erzkonservativ, extralang, hochintelligent, saudumm, superklug, tiefernst, todunglücklich, vollautomatisch.*

2.3.3 Forming verbs – inseparable prefixes

The prefixes *be-, emp-, ent-, er-, ge-, ver-* and *zer-* are always inseparable. The following meanings are common:

be-

(a) **be-** + verbs: makes transitive verbs from intransitives or converts a prepositional object into a direct object (see **4.1**).

Sie **kämpfen** gegen das Unrecht.	Sie **bekämpfen** das Unrecht.
Er hat auf meinen Brief **geantwortet.**	Er hat meinen Brief **beantwortet.**
Er **raubte** mir das Geld.	Er **beraubte** mich des Geldes. (R3)
In dieses Beet **pflanzen** wir Rosen.	Dieses Beet **bepflanzen** wir mit Rosen.
Wir **liefern** die Waren an unsere Kunden im Ausland.	Wir **beliefern** unsere Kunden im Ausland mit Waren.

(b) **be-** + nouns: to provide with sth. Sometimes the suffix *-ig-* is added.

etw be**wässer**n	*to irrigate sth*, ie to provide with **water**
etw be**klecks**en (R1)	*to splatter sth*, ie to provide with **spots**
etw be**licht**en	*to expose sth* (eg film), ie to provide with **light**
jdn be**nachricht**igen	*to notify sb*, ie to provide with **news**

(c) **be-** + adjective: to give sb/sth a quality. Again, sometimes the suffix *-ig-* is added.

etw be**feucht**en	*to moisten sth*, ie to make sth **moist**
jdn be**frei**en	*to liberate sb*, ie to make sb **free**
etw be**grad**igen	*to straighten sth*, ie to make sth **straight**
jdn be**unruhig**en	*to disturb sb*, ie to make sb **uneasy**

⟫→

ent-
(a) **ent-** + verbs: gives the idea of 'going away' or 'escaping from sb/sth' (as a dative object).

jdm ent**gleit**en	to **slip** away from sb (eg vase from hands)
jdm/etw (dat) ent**lauf**en	to **run** away, escape from sb/sth
jdm etw ent**reiß**en (R3a)	to **snatch** sth from sb
etw (dat) ent**steig**en (R3)	to get [**climb**] out of sth (eg car, train)

(b) **ent-** + nouns, adjective or verbs: to take sth away (cf the English prefixes *de-*, *dis-*).

etw ent**gift**en	to decontaminate sth, ie to take **poison** away
jdn ent**mut**igen	to discourage sb, ie to take **courage** away
etw ent**schärf**en	to defuse sth (eg tense situation), ie to make not **sharp**
jdn/etw ent**spann**en	to relax sb, slacken sth, ie to make not **tense**

er-
(a) **er-** + verbs and nouns: the basic idea is often of 'achieving' or 'finishing'. English frequently lacks a separate verb for this.

etw er**arbeit**en	to acquire sth by working for it, ie to gain by **work**
etw er**bitt**en	to ask for sth, ie to gain by **asking**
etw er**kämpf**en	to win sth, ie to gain through **struggle**
jdn er**schieß**en	to shoot sb dead, ie to finish by **shooting**

(b) **er-** + adjective: to become sth, or give sth a quality.

er**blind**en	to lose one's sight, ie to become **blind**
jdn er**munter**n	to invigorate sb, ie to make **cheerful**
er**röt**en	to blush, ie to become **red**
etw er**wärm**en	to heat sth, ie to make **warm**

ver-
This is the most frequent of these prefixes. Although it has a wide range of meanings, it very often carries the idea of 'a change of state' or of 'the end of a process'.

(a) **ver-** + verbs: with the notion of 'finishing' or 'going away'.

ver**blüh**en	to fade (of flowers), ie to finish **blooming**
etw ver**brauch**en	to use sth up, consume sth, ie to finish **using**
jdn/etw ver**dräng**en	to oust, replace sb/sth, ie to **press** away
ver**kling**en	to fade away (of sounds), ie to finish **sounding**

(b) **ver-** + verbs: with the idea of 'wrongly' or 'to excess'.

etw ver**bieg**en	to **bend** out of shape
etw ver**lern**en	to forget (how to do) sth, ie to un-**learn**
etw ver**salz**en	to oversalt sth, ie to put too much **salt** on
sich ver**wähl**en	to misdial, ie to **dial** wrongly

(c)   **ver-** + nouns and adjectives: to become sth, or give sth a quality.

ver**arm**en	*to become **poor***
ver**einsam**en	*to become **isolated***
etw ver**länger**n	*to lengthen sth, ie to make **longer***
jdn ver**sklav**en	*to enslave sb, ie to make into a **slave***

(d)   **ver-** + nouns: to provide with sth.

etw ver**glas**en	*to glaze sth, ie to provide with **glass***
etw ver**gold**en	*to gild sth, ie to provide with **gold***
jdn ver**wund**en	*to wound sb, ie to provide with **wounds***
jdn ver**zauber**n	*to enchant sb, ie to provide with **magic***

zer–

zer- + verbs: always has the idea of 'into pieces'.

etw zer**beißen**	*to crunch sth, ie to **bite** into pieces*
zer**fallen**	*to disintegrate, ie to **fall** into pieces*
etw zer**streuen**	*to scatter, disperse sth, ie to **cast** pieces **about***

2.3.4   Forming verbs – separable prefixes

Some common, less transparent uses of separable prefixes:

ab–

Finishing, completing or achieving sth, eg:

etw **abdrehen**	*to switch sth off*
etw **abkühlen**	*to cool sth down* (also itr)
Schuhe **ablaufen**	*to wear shoes out*
jdm etw **ablisten**	*to trick sb out of sth*

an–

Beginning sth, doing sth partially, eg:

anbrennen	*to catch fire, get scorched*
etw **andrehen**	*to turn sth on*
anfaulen	*to begin to go rotten*
etw **anfressen**	*to nibble at sth*

auf–

Renovation, completion, sudden starts, eg:

etw **aufessen**	*to eat sth up*
auflachen	*to burst out laughing*
aufleuchten	*to light up*
etw **aufpolieren**	*to polish sth up*

aus–

Completion, eg:

etw **ausbrennen**	*to burn sth out* (also itr)
ausdorren	*to dry up*
ausreifen	*to ripen, mature*

ein-	Become accustomed to sth, eg:

sich einarbeiten	*to get used to the work*
etw **einfahren**	*to run sth in* (eg car)
sich einleben	*to get settled in a place*

vor-	Demonstrating, performing, etc, eg:

vorbeten	*to lead the prayers*
etw **vorführen**, **vormachen**	*to demonstrate sth*
etw **vorlesen**	*to read sth out*
vortanzen	*to demonstrate a dance* (also tr)

zusammen-	Often corresponds to English *up* rather than *together*, eg:

etw **zusammenfalten**	*to fold sth up*
jdn **zusammenhauen** (R1)	*to beat sb up*
die Augen zusammenkneifen	*to screw up one's eyes*
sich zusammenrollen	*to curl up*

2.3.5 Forming verbs – variable prefixes

The following prefixes are rather confusing, as they can form both separable and inseparable verbs. In all cases, the prefix is stressed in pronunciation if the verb is separable, unstressed if it is inseparable.

durch-	This prefix always has the idea of 'through', whether separable or inseparable.

Only inseparable (very few verbs), eg: **durch'leben**, **durch'löchern**, **durch'denken**.
NOTE: **'durchdenken** is also found with identical meaning, but is less common.

Only separable (many verbs), eg: **'durchblicken**, **'durchfallen**, **'durchführen**, **'durchhalten**, **'durchkommen**, **'durchkriechen**, **'durchrosten**, **'durchsehen**.

Separable or inseparable (many verbs).
If separable, the meaning is always 'right the way through', whilst the inseparable verbs emphasize 'penetration into sth', without there necessarily being any idea of coming out the other side. But the distinction is often very fine, especially with verbs of motion, eg:

Er *ritt* durch den Wald *durch*	*He crossed the forest on horseback*
Er *durchritt* den Wald	*He rode through the forest*
Er *schnitt* das Brot *durch*	*He cut the loaf in two*
Der Fluß *durchschneidet* die Ebene	*The river cuts through the plain*

> ' stressed syllables are preceded by a stress mark

Similarly: **durchbrechen**, **durchdringen**, **durchfahren**, **durchlaufen**, **durchreisen**, **durchschauen**, **durchsetzen**, **durchstoßen**, **durchwachen**, **durchziehen**.

hinter-	*Only inseparable* (all the common verbs), eg: **hinter'gehen**, **hinter'lassen**, **hinter'legen**, **hinter'treiben**.

	Separable (some verbs in R1, especially C + S), eg: **'hintergehen**, 'to go to the back'.
miß–	This prefix is always inseparable except in the infinitive of **mißverstehen**: **mißzuverstehen**.
über–	*Only separable* (very few intransitive verbs, with the literal meaning 'over'), eg: **'überhängen**, **'überkippen**, **'überkochen**.

Only inseparable (many transitive verbs, with the following meanings), eg:

repetition:	**über'arbeiten, über'prüfen**
more than enough:	**über'fordern, über'lasten, über'treiben**
failing to notice:	**über'blicken, über'hören, über'sehen**
over:	**über'denken, über'fliegen, über'fallen**

Separable or inseparable (many verbs). The separable ones are mainly intransitive, and have the literal meaning 'over'. The inseparables are transitive and have a more figurative meaning:

	Separable	Inseparable
überfahren	to cross over	to knock sb down
überführen	to transfer	to convict sb (R3)
übergehen	to turn into sth	to leave sth out
überlaufen	to overflow; desert	to overrun sb
überlegen	to put sth over sb	to consider sth
übersetzen	to ferry across	to translate sth
überspringen	to jump over	to skip sth
übertreten	to change over	to infringe sth (ie law)
überziehen	to put sth on	to cover sth

um–

Only separable (many verbs, with the meaning of 'turning round', 'turning over', 'changing' or 'switching'), eg: **'umblicken, 'umbringen, 'umdrehen, 'umfallen, 'umkehren, 'umkommen, 'umladen, 'umlegen, 'umschalten, 'umschlagen, 'umsteigen**.

Only inseparable (many verbs, with the meaning of 'encircling' or 'surrounding'), eg: **um'armen, um'drängen, um'fassen, um'fließen, um'geben, um'kreisen, um'randen, um'ringen, um'segeln, um'zingeln**.

Separable or inseparable (many verbs, with the difference in meaning usually as given above), eg:

	Separable	Inseparable
umbauen	to rebuild	to enclose
umbrechen	to break up	to set (ie type) (R3)
umfahren	to run down	to travel round
umgehen	to circulate	to avoid
umreißen	to tear down	to outline
umschreiben	to rewrite	to paraphrase
umstellen	to rearrange	to surround (R3a)

≫→

unter–	*Only separable* (many verbs, with the literal meaning 'under'), eg: 'unterbringen, 'untergehen, 'unterkommen, 'unterkriegen, 'untersetzen.

Only inseparable (many verbs, with the following meanings), eg:

less than enough:	unter'bieten, unter'schätzen, unter'schreiten
under:	unter'drücken, unter'liegen, unter'nehmen, unter'schreiben, unter'stützen, unter'werfen (R3)
miscellaneous:	unter'bleiben (R3), unter'brechen, unter'lassen (R3), unter'laufen (R3), unter'richten (R3), unter'sagen (R3), unter'schreiben, unter'suchen

Separable or inseparable (many verbs). The separable verbs are mainly intransitive, with the literal meaning 'under'. The inseparables are all transitive, usually with a more figurative meaning, eg:

	Separable	Inseparable
unterbinden	to tie underneath	to prevent (R3)
untergraben	to dig in	to undermine
unterhalten	to hold underneath	to entertain
unterlegen	to put underneath	to underlay
unterschieben	to foist sth on sb	to insinuate (R1)
unterschlagen	to cross (ie legs)	to embezzle (R3)
unterstellen	to keep, store	to assume (R3)
unterziehen	to put on underneath	to undergo

voll–	*Only separable* (many verbs, with the meaning 'full'), eg: 'vollstopfen, 'vollschreiben, 'volltanken.

Only inseparable (a few R3 verbs meaning 'complete' or 'accomplish'), eg: voll'bringen, voll'enden, voll'führen, voll'strecken, voll'ziehen.

wider–	This prefix is always inseparable, except for: 'widerhallen (R3), 'widerspiegeln.
wieder–	This prefix is always separable, except for: wieder'holen.

2.4 Idioms

Idiomatic expressions are a notorious pitfall for the foreign learner because their overall meaning cannot be deduced from their individual parts. The learner has no way of knowing that when a German says, for instance, *schwer auf Draht* (literally: 'heavy on wire'), he means 'on the ball'. The use of expressive and racy idioms is naturally most characteristic of R1, but some are restricted to more formal registers. Even in serious newspapers idioms and what would normally be regarded as R1 expressions are used to enliven an argument or a factual account (see **1.6.6**). And much of the colloquial tone of popular newspapers derives from their wide use of idiomatic expressions. Given below is a selection of some frequent current idioms which differ markedly in phrasing from their English equivalents, or which have no simple English equivalent.

```
N  = North
C  = Central
S  = South
SW = South West
SE = South East
AU = Austria
CH = Switzerland
(see 1.2.3)
```

A

mit Ach und Krach	by the skin of your teeth
bei jdm gut/schlecht angeschrieben sein	to be in sb's good/bad books
den Anschluß verpassen	to miss the boat
sich schwarz ärgern	to get really mad
jdn auf den Arm nehmen(N)	to pull sb's leg
jdm unter die Arme greifen	to help sb out
etw aus dem Ärmel schütteln	to produce sth from nowhere
Das kann leicht ins Auge gehen	It might easily go wrong
beide Augen zudrücken	to turn a blind eye
unter vier Augen	in confidence

B

etw auf die lange Bank schieben	to put sth off
Ich fresse einen Besen	I'll eat my hat
in die Binsen gehen	to go down the tubes
den Bock zum Gärtner machen	to choose someone totally unsuitable
Das sind für mich böhmische Dörfer	I can't make head or tail of it
Ich habe ein Brett vor dem Kopf	I can't think straight
ein dicker Brocken	a tough nut

D

jdm aufs Dach steigen	to have a go at sb
die Daumen drücken	to keep one's fingers crossed
an die Decke gehen	to hit the roof
mit jdm unter einer Decke stecken	to be hand in glove with sb
auf gut deutsch	in plain English (ie bluntly)
Das geht nicht mit rechten Dingen zu	That's a bit odd
schwer auf Draht	on the ball

E

etw aus dem Effeff können	to be able to do sth standing on one's head
im Eimer	gone west; broken
jdn/etw zum alten Eisen werfen	to throw sb/sth on the scrap-heap

F

Das ist nicht mein Fall	It's not my cup of tea
Es paßt wie die Faust aufs Auge	It's totally out of place
Dann ist Feierabend	Then it's all over
ins Fettnäpfchen treten	to put one's foot in it
sich alle zehn Finger nach etw (dat) lecken	to be dying for sth
Du bist eine Flasche	You're a dead loss
zwei Fliegen mit einer Klappe schlagen	to kill two birds with one stone
die Flinte ins Korn werfen	to throw in the towel
Sei doch kein Frosch	Be a sport, join in

G

hinter schwedischen Gardinen	behind bars
Darauf kannst du Gift nehmen	You can bet your life on it
Der Groschen ist gefallen	The penny's dropped

H

Haare lassen	to come off badly
an den Haaren herbeigezogen	a bit far-fetched
der Hahn im Korbe sein	to be the only man in female company
für jdn die Hand ins Feuer legen	to vouch for sb
Da liegt der Hase im Pfeffer	There's the catch
etw über den Haufen werfen	to throw sth out
gleich mit der Tür ins Haus fallen	to say sth straight out
aus dem Häuschen sein	to be out of one's mind
aus der Haut fahren	to hit the roof
etw auf dem Herzen haben	to have sth on one's mind
Mir fällt ein Stein vom Herzen	That's a load off my mind
auf dem Holzweg	on the wrong track
mit jdm ein Hühnchen rupfen müssen	to have a bone to pick with sb
Da liegt der Hund begraben	That's the snag, the trouble
wie Hund und Katze leben	to lead a cat and dog life
Das ist ein dicker Hund	It's a bit much
Das kannst du dir an den Hut stecken	You can keep it

K

Das war für die Katz'	It was a waste of time
die Katze aus dem Sack lassen	to let the cat out of the bag
Die Katze läßt das Mausen nicht	The leopard doesn't change its spots
eine Katze im Sack kaufen	to buy a pig in a poke
wie die Katze um den heißen Brei herumgehen	to beat about the bush
Nachts sind alle Katzen grau	All cats are grey in the dark
etw auf dem Kerbholz haben	to have done sth wrong
das Kind beim Namen nennen	to call a spade a spade
Mit dem ist nicht gut Kirschen essen	It's best to stay out of his way
wie auf glühenden Kohlen sitzen	to be like a cat on a hot tin roof
jdn vor den Kopf stoßen	to antagonize sb
sich den Kopf zerbrechen	to rack one's brains
jdm einen Korb geben	to turn sb down (ie a suitor)
jdn/etw aufs Korn nehmen	to hit out at sb/sth

Jetzt geht's ihm an den Kragen	Now he's for it
Dagegen ist kein Kraut gewachsen	There's no cure for that
in Teufels Küche kommen	to get into a mess
Was macht die Kunst?	How's tricks?

L

Ich kann auch ein Lied davon singen	I can tell you a few things about that
mit dem linken Bein zuerst aufstehen	to get out of bed the wrong side
Das mache ich mit der linken Hand	I can do that with my eyes shut
auf dem letzten Loch pfeifen	to be on one's last legs
wie ein Loch saufen	to drink like a fish
Er geht gleich in die Luft	He's on a short fuse
etw unter die Lupe nehmen (R2/R3)	to look closely at sth

M

Das ging mir durch Mark und Bein	It went right through me
eine Mattscheibe kriegen	not to be able to think straight
in den Mond gucken	to go empty-handed
jdm mit gleicher Münze heimzahlen	to pay sb back in his own coin

N

die Nase (gestrichen) voll haben	to be fed up
der Nase nachgehen	to follow one's nose
jdn mit der Nase auf etw stoßen	to make sth crystal clear to sb
gelb vor Neid	green with envy
Der ist eine Niete	He's a dead loss
Null-Acht-Fuffzehn	run of the mill

O

bis über die Ohren verliebt	head over heels in love
sich (dat) etw hinter die Ohren schreiben	to be sure to remember sth
es faustdick hinter den Ohren haben	to be fly
jdm einen Floh ins Ohr setzen	to put an idea into sb's head
Der ist schwer in Ordnung	He's OK

P

Es ist keinen Pappenstiel wert	It's not worth a bean
in der Patsche/Tinte sitzen	to be in the soup
jdm den schwarzen Peter zuschieben	to leave sb holding the baby
nach seiner Pfeife tanzen	to dance to his tune
Ich pfeife darauf	I couldn't care less
Er hat die Pfoten überall drin	He's got a finger in every pie
wie ein begossener Pudel dastehen	to stand there looking pathetic
Er hat das Pulver nicht erfunden	He'll not set the Thames on fire

R

das fünfte Rad am Wagen sein	to be out of place
jdm einen Strich durch die Rechnung machen	to spoil sb's plans
aus der Rolle fallen	to act out of character
Rosinen im Kopf haben	to have big ideas
jdm in den Rücken fallen	to stab sb in the back

S

mit Sack und Pack	with bag and baggage
jdn mit Samthandschuhen anfassen	to handle sb with kid gloves
sein Schäfchen ins trockene bringen	to see oneself all right
sein Scherflein zu etw (dat) beitragen	to do one's bit towards sth
Das ist zum Schießen	That's hilarious
jdn auf die Schippe nehmen (S)	to pull sb's leg
aus dem Schneider sein	to be out of the wood
etw in den Schornstein schreiben	to write sth off
vom alten Schrot und Korn	of the old school
jdm etw in die Schuhe schieben	to put the blame for sth on sb
Wo drückt der Schuh?	What's the matter?
schwarz arbeiten	to moonlight
ins Schwarze treffen	to hit the bull's-eye
aus dem Stegreif reden	to speak impromptu
den Stier bei den Hörnern packen	to take the bull by the horns
sich an einen Strohhalm klammern	to clutch at a straw
sich zwischen zwei Stühle setzen (R2/R3)	to fall between two stools

T

Er hat nicht alle Tassen im Schrank	He's not quite all there
Hier geht's zu wie im Taubenschlag	It's like a madhouse here
Auf Teufel komm raus	Come hell or high water
den Teufel an die Wand malen	to tempt fate
unter den Tisch fallen	to go by the board
vom Regen in die Traufe kommen	to fall out of the frying-pan into the fire
zwischen Tür und Angel (R2/R3)	in passing

W

jdm auf den Wecker fallen	to drive sb up the wall
Die Weichen sind gestellt (R2/R3)	The course is set
Unter Wölfen muß man heulen (R2/R3)	When in Rome do as the Romans do
aus allen Wolken fallen	to be taken aback
jdm die Würmer aus der Nase ziehen	to extract information from sb
Jetzt geht's um die Wurst	This is the crunch

Z

jdm auf den Zahn fühlen	to sound sb out, grill sb
jdn in die Zange nehmen	to put the screws on sb
Zier dich nicht!	Don't be shy!
auf keinen grünen Zweig kommen	to get nowhere

2.5 Prepositions

R1* = vulgar
R1 = informal
  colloquial
R2 = neutral
R3 = formal
R3a = literary
R3b = non-literary
(see 1.1.5)

N = North
C = Central
S = South
SW = South West
SE = South East
AU = Austria
CH = Switzerland
(see 1.2.3)

The ability to handle prepositions confidently is a good touchstone for advanced competence in a foreign language. Although some German prepositions, such as *hinter*, *ohne*, *trotz* and *zwischen*, do have a relatively constant meaning and a clear normal English equivalent, most of the very frequent ones are extremely elusive in their meaning and purely idiomatic in use. In addition, each preposition governs a particular case, which can vary according to context or register. It is therefore even more essential than with nouns or verbs to commit prepositions to memory in context. This section gives details of the most characteristic and frequent meanings of the majority of German and English prepositions, with the usual equivalents in the other language clearly indicated. These are followed by a selection of those expressions where the choice of a particular preposition is idiomatic or arbitrary and there is no parallel between the two languages. Note that the use of prepositions with verbs, so-called 'prepositional objects', is treated separately in section **4.1.4**.

In sections **2.5.1–2.5.4** the German prepositions are arranged and treated according to the cases they govern. It should be realized, though, that as German prepositions govern particular cases, some familiar English constructions are not possible in German, for instance:

(a) The same noun cannot be made dependent on two prepositions, as it can in English. In German, the sentence would be split into separate phrases, eg:

I was rather astonished by and pleased at this sudden turn of events	**Ich war von dieser plötzlichen Wende etwas überrascht und freute mich sehr darüber**

(b) In general, two prepositions are not found with a single noun in German. The commonest way of expressing this in German is to replace one of the English prepositions with a directional adverb (ie a compound of *hin-* or *her-* plus preposition), eg:

He looked *across at* me	**Er schaute *zu* mir *herüber***
The water poured *down through* the hole	**Das Wasser strömte *durch* das Loch *hinunter***
He pulled it *from under* the bed	**Er zog es *unter* dem Bett *hervor***
She looked *in at* the window	**Sie schaute *zum* Fenster *herein***

2.5.1 German prepositions with the accusative

The common prepositions taking the accusative are:

bis, durch, für, gegen, ohne, um

Less widely used, but worth noting, are:

per, pro, wider

BIS

NOTE: *bis* is never followed by an article; it is used on its own only with names, adverbs and some time words. Otherwise it has another preposition with it and this decides the case.

(a) **bis** expressing place = *as far as, (up) to*

bis (nach) **Rostock**	*as far as* Rostock
bis **dorthin**	*(to)* there, *as far as* that
bis zu **meinem Haus** ⎫ *bis an* **mein Haus** ⎭	*up to, as far as* my house
bis aufs **Dach**	*right onto* the roof

(b) **bis** expressing time = *until, by*

von Montag *bis* **Freitag**	from Monday *to* Friday
bis **morgen**	*until* tomorrow, *by* tomorrow
bis **dahin**	*by* then, *between* now and then
bis auf **weiteres**	*until* further notice, *for* the present
Kinder *bis zu* **zehn Jahren**	children *up to* the age of ten

(c) **bis auf** can express exclusion = *but for, down to*

Der Bus war *bis auf* **den letzten Platz besetzt**	The bus was full *down to* the last seat
	The bus was full *but for* the last seat

NOTE: *bis auf* can be ambiguous, as the example shows.

DURCH

(a) **durch** expressing place = *through*

durch **das Feuer**	*through* the fire
durch **die ganze Stadt**	*throughout* the town
mitten *durch* **den Park**	*through* the middle of the park
durchs **Examen fallen** (R1)	to fail the exam

(b) **durch** expressing means, cause = *by, through* (for *durch* in passive constructions see **4.4.4**)

die Erfindung des Verbrennungsmotors *durch* **Benz und Daimler**	the invention of the internal combustion engine *by* Benz and Daimler
Ich lernte ihn *durch* **eine Freundin kennen**	I got to know him *through* a friend
durch **Betätigung des Mechanismus** (R3b)	*by* activating the mechanism

(c) **durch** expressing time = *throughout*

durch **das ganze Leben (hindurch)**	*throughout* one's whole life
das ganze Jahr *durch* (R1)	*throughout* the year

FÜR	(a)	**für** in most senses = *for*	
		für **meine kranke Schwester**	*for* my sick sister
		für **sein Alter**	*for* his age
		für **den Fall, daß...**	*in* case . . .
		ein Sinn, ein Beispiel *für* **etw**	a sense, an example *of* sth
	(b)	**für** expressing time = *for*	
		Ich habe das Haus *für* **sechs Monate gemietet**	I've rented the house *for* six months
		Tag *für* **Tag**	day *after* day
		Schritt *für* **Schritt**	step *by* step

GEGEN	(a)	**gegen** expressing place = *against, into*	
		Möbel *gegen* **die Wand stellen**	to put furniture *against* the wall
		gegen **den Strom schwimmen**	to swim *against* the current (also figurative)
		etw *gegen* **das Licht halten**	to hold sth *up to* the light
		gegen **den Tisch stoßen**	to bump *into* the table
	(b)	**gegen** expressing opposition = *against, for, compared with*	
		gegen **meinen Willen**	*against* my wishes
		ein Mittel *gegen* **Asthma**	a medicine *for* asthma
		Gegen **deinen Bruder ist er klein**	He is small *compared with* your brother
	(c)	**gegen** expressing approximation = *towards, about*	
		gegen **vier Uhr**	*towards/about* four o'clock
		Es waren *gegen* **50 000 Zuschauer im Stadion**	There were *about* 50,000 spectators in the stadium

OHNE		**ohne** = *without*	
		ohne **mein Wissen**	*without* my knowing
		ohne **Mantel**	*without* a coat, *without* his coat
		Ohne **mich!** (R1)	Count me out!

NOTE: *ohne* is used predominantly without the indefinite article or a possessive (eg with clothing).

UM	(a)	**um** expressing place = *round*	
		um **die Ecke**	*round* the corner
		(rund/rings) *um* **die Kirche**	(right) *round* the church
		um **die Stadt (herum)**	(right) *round* the town
	(b)	**um** expressing time = *at* (with clock times), *about* (with other time phrases)	
		um **zwanzig nach sechs**	*at* twenty past six
		ungefähr *um* **sieben**	*at/about* seven (o'clock)
		um **Weihnachten (herum)**	*around* Christmas
		einen Tag *um* **den anderen**	day *after* day
	(c)	**um** expressing measurement = *by*	
		um **die Hälfte teurer**	dearer *by* half
		um **nichts besser**	no better

⟫→

[UM]	(d)	**um** in the sense of 'concerning' = *for, about*	
		ein Streit *um* etw	a quarrel *about* sth
		(es ist) schade *um* etw	(it's a) pity *about* sth
		***um* nichts in der Welt**	*for* nothing in the world

A few less widely used prepositions govern the accusative.

PER

per = *by*
Mainly commercial R3b, eg:

***per* Einschreiben**	*by* registered mail
***per* 31. Dezember**	*by, for* 31 December

The following uses are R1:

***per* Auto, *per* Bahn**	*by* car, *by* train
mit jdm *per* du sein	to call sb 'du'
***per* Anhalter fahren**	to hitch-hike

PRO

pro = *per*
Essentially commercial R3b, but widely used in R1, too:

20 Pfennig *pro* Stück	20 pfennigs each
5 Mark *pro* Person	5 marks *per* person

WIDER

wider = *against*
R3a, now obsolete except in a few phrases, eg:

***wider* alles Erwarten**	*against* all expectations
***wider* Willen**	*against* my (his, her, etc) will
***wider* besseres Wissen**	*against* my (his, her, etc) better judgement

---

2.5.2   German prepositions with the dative

The common prepositions taking the dative are:

aus, außer, bei, gegenüber, mit, nach, seit, von, zu

Less widely used, but worth noting, are:

ab, binnen, gemäss, laut, zufolge

AUS	(a)	**aus** expressing place = *out of, from*	
		Er kommt *aus* Sachsen	He comes *from* Saxony (ie that is his native region)
		***aus* der Flasche trinken**	to drink *out of* the bottle
		***aus* der Nähe**	*from* close to
		***aus* erster Hand**	*at* first hand
		***aus* der Übung kommen**	to get *out of* practice
	(b)	**aus** expressing material = *(made) of*	
		***aus* Holz, Stahl, Eisen**	*made of* wood, steel, iron
		***Aus* dir wird nichts werden** (R1)	You'll never come to anything

(c) **aus** expressing cause, motive = *for, from, out of*

aus **Furcht vor etw (dat)**	*for* fear of sth
aus **diesem Grund**	*for* this reason
aus **Überzeugung**	*from* conviction
aus **Mitleid**	*out of* pity

AUSSER

(a) **außer** expressing restriction = *except (for), but for, besides, apart from*

außer **dem Gehalt bekommt er noch einen Zuschuß**	*apart from/besides* his salary he receives an allowance

(b) **außer** expressing place = *out of*

In modern usage mainly in set phrases with no article. In some of these cases the noun may be in the genitive or, after verbs of motion, in the accusative.

außer **Betrieb**	*out of* order
außer **Dienst** (a.D.)	retired/*not in* active service
etw *außer* **acht lassen**	to disregard sth
außer **Landes** (R3)	*out of* the country
Ich war *außer* **mir** (R2/R3)	I was *beside* myself
Es steht *außer* **jedem Zweifel**	It is *beyond* all doubt
etw *außer* **jeden Zweifel stellen**	to put sth *beyond* all doubt

---

BEI

(a) **bei** expressing place, etc = *by, at*

Pinneberg liegt *bei* **Hamburg**	Pinneberg is *by/near* Hamburg
bei **meinen Eltern**	*at* my parents' (house)
(dicht) *bei* **der Kirche**	(right) *by* the church
die Schlacht *bei* **Hastings**	the battle *of* Hastings
bei **Thomas Mann**	*in* Thomas Mann's works
Er ist *bei* **der Bahn**	He works *for* the railways
Wir haben Englisch *bei* **Frau Henne**	Frau Henne teaches us English

(b) **bei** expressing time = *at, by*

beim **Frühstück**	*at* breakfast
bei **Gelegenheit**	when the opportunity arises
bei **schönen Wetter**	if/when the weather is fine
bei **diesen vielen Problemen**	*with*/given these many problems
das schönste *bei* **der ganzen Sache**	the best thing *about* the whole business

(c) **bei** with verbal nouns = *on*

This usage is particularly frequent in modern R3b, though it is by no means restricted to it, see **5.2.3** and **5.3.2**.

bei **der Ankunft des Zuges** (R3)	*on* the arrival of the train
bei **näherer Betrachtung** (R3)	*on* closer observation
beim **Schlafen, Essen**	whilst sleeping, eating
bei **der Arbeit**	when working

GEGENÜBER		May precede or follow the noun. It tends to follow words for persons and always follows pronouns, otherwise it is commoner before the noun.	
	(a)	**gegenüber** expressing place = *opposite*	
		mir *gegenüber* *gegenüber* **von mir** (R1) }	*opposite* me
		gegenüber (**von** R1) **der Kirche** **der Kirche** *gegenüber*	*opposite* the church
	(b)	**gegenüber** expressing comparison = *compared with, towards*	
		ein Fortschritt *gegenüber* **den Jahren davor**	an advance *compared with* the previous years
		eine neue Politik *gegenüber* **der UdSSR**	a new policy *towards* the USSR

MIT	(a)	**mit** in most senses = *with*	
		mit **dem Schlüssel**	*with* the key
		mit **meinem Freund zusammen**	together *with* my friend
		etw *mit* **dem Fuß stoßen**	to kick sth
		mit **den Achseln zucken**	to shrug one's shoulders
		mit **anderen Worten**	*in* other words
		mit **leiser Stimme**	*in* a low voice
		mit **20 Jahren**	*at* the age of 20
		mit **der Zeit**	*in* (the course of) time
		mit **der Maschine schreiben**	to type
		etw *mit* **Absicht tun**	to do sth on purpose
	(b)	**mit** expressing means of transport = *by*	
		mit **dem Flugzeug, Schiff, Zug**	*by* aeroplane, boat, train

NACH	(a)	**nach** expressing place = *to* (**only** with names, etc – except N)	
		nach **Genf**	*to* Geneva
		nach **Süden (hin)**	*to* the south
		nach **Finnland**	*to* Finland
		nach **innen, außen, oben, unten gehen**	to go inside, outside, up, down
		nach **rechts, links gehen**	to go (*to the*) right, left
		nach **Hause gehen**	to go home
		nach **allen Seiten**	*in* all directions
		Er geht *nach* **dem Bahnhof** (N)	He is going *to* the station
	(b)	**nach** expressing time = *after, past*	
		nach **fünf Jahren**	*after* five years, five years *later*
		zehn *nach* **sieben**	ten *past* seven
		Ich bin *nach* **ihm dran** (R1)	It's my turn *after* him

(c) **nach** in the sense of 'according' = *according to, judging by*

NOTE: in this sense *nach* may follow the noun, especially in some set phrases, in R3 and in the meaning 'judging by'.

nach **dem Gesetz/dem Gesetz** *nach* (R3)	*according to* the law
meiner Meinung *nach/nach* **meiner Meinung**	*in* my opinion
der Reihe *nach*	*in* turns
allem Anschein *nach*	*to* all appearances
nach **französischer Art**	*in* the French manner
je *nach* **den Umständen**	*depending on* the circumstances
Ihrer Sprache *nach* **ist sie Schweizerin**	*Judging by* the way she speaks, she is Swiss
nach **allem, was er gesagt hat**	*from* all he said
etw *nach* **dem Gewicht verkaufen**	to sell sth *by* weight
Es sieht *nach* **Regen aus**	It looks like rain

SEIT

seit = *for* (a period of time up to now), *since* (a point in time)

Seit **drei Jahrhunderten gehört dieses Haus der Familie Falk**	This house has belonged to the Falk family *for* three centuries
seit **Anfang des Jahres**	*since* the beginning of the year
erst *seit* **kurzem**	not *for* long, only *for* a little while

VON

(a) **von** expressing place = *from*

Er kommt *von* **seiner Mutter**	He's coming *from* his mother's
von **der Brücke an**	(starting) *from* the bridge
vom **Fenster aus**	*from (out of)* the window
von **mir aus** (R1)	*as far as* I'm concerned
von **Natur aus**	*by* nature
von **Grund auf**	entirely

(b) **von** expressing time = *from*

von **Montag an**	*from* Monday
von **alters her** (R3)	*from* time immemorial
von **Zeit zu Zeit**	*from* time to time, occasionally

(c) **von** expressing possession, etc = *of*

NOTE: for the use of *von* or the genitive see **4.2.2**.

ein Stab *von* **dieser Länge**	a bar *of* this length
der Verkauf *von* **Diamanten**	the sale *of* diamonds
Das war nett *von* **dir**	That was nice *of* you

(d) **von** in passive constructions = *by* (see **4.4.4**)

eine Oper *von* **Verdi**	an opera *by* Verdi
Das wird *von* **ihm erwähnt**	That is mentioned *by* him

ZU

(a) **zu** expressing place = *to*

Dieser Bus fährt *zum* Rathaus	This bus goes *to* the town hall
Er geht *zu* seiner Nichte	He is going *to* his niece's
***zur* Decke (hin) blicken**	to glance *towards* the ceiling
***zur* Schule gehen**	to go *to*/attend school
***zu* Hause**	*at* home
***zu* beiden Seiten**	*on* either side
Setz dich *zu* uns	Sit down *with* us
Er sang *zur* Gitarre	He sang *to* the guitar

(b) **zu** expressing time = *at*

***zur* Zeit/*zurzeit** (CH, AU)	*at* the moment
***zur* Zeit des letzten Kaisers**	*at* the time of the last emperor
***zu* Ende**	*at* an end
***zu* Weihnachten**	*at/for* Christmas
die Nacht *zum* Donnerstag	Wednesday night
***Zu* meinem Geburtstag hat sie mir eine Platte geschenkt**	She gave me a record *for* my birthday
***zum* Schluß**	finally
***zu* Mittag essen**	to eat lunch

(c) **zu** expressing purpose = *for*

***zu* diesem Zweck**	*for* this purpose
***zu* früh *zum* Aufstehen**	too early *for* getting up/*to* get up
Stoff *zu* einem Kleid	material *for* a dress
Es ist *zum* Heulen (R1)	It's enough to make you weep
***zum* Spaß**	*for* fun, *for* a joke
***zum* Glück**	fortunately
***zum* Andenken an jdn**	*in* memory of sb
***zu* Fuß**	*on* foot
***zur* Not**	if need be, at a pinch

(d) **zu** expressing change

***zu* nichts werden**	to become nothing
jdn *zum* Präsidenten wählen	to elect sb president
Das ist *zum* Sprichwort geworden	That has become proverbial

(e) **zu** expressing quantity

zehn Stück Seife *zu* je zwei Mark	ten pieces of soap *at* two marks each
***zur* Hälfte fertig**	half finished
***zum* Teil**	partially
drei *zu* zwei gewinnen	to win three *to* two

A number of less widely used prepositions govern the dative.

AB	**ab** = *from*

Essentially R3b, but widely used in R1 for R2 and R3a *von . . . an*. In time expressions it may be followed by the accusative, especially in R1.

ab **allen deutschen Bahnhöfen**	*from* all stations in Germany
ab **nächste(r) Woche**	*from* next week
ab **Dienstag, dem/den 19. Mai**	*from* Tuesday, 19 May

BINNEN	**binnen** = *within*

Restricted to R3. It may occur with the genitive in old–fashioned R3a.

binnen **einem Jahr** }	*within* a year
binnen **eines Jahres** (R3a) }	

GEMÄSS	**gemäß** = *in accordance with, according to*

It may precede or (more commonly) follow the noun. It is mainly used in R3, but if it is used in R2 or R1 it is sometimes found with the genitive.

gemäß **den Anweisungen** }	*in accordance with* the
den Anweisungen *gemäß* }	instructions

LAUT	**laut** = *according to* (verbatim)

Followed by the dative or, in R3 only, the genitive, but even in R3 the genitive is never used with names or single nouns.

laut **unseres Berichtes** (R3) }	*according to* our report
laut **unserem Bericht** }	
Laut **Hans-Joachim will er nicht**	*According to* Hans-Joachim (what Hans-Joachim says is:), he doesn't want to

ZUFOLGE	**zufolge** = *according to*

This usage is frowned on by purists, but very frequent in the R3b of newspapers. *zufolge* follows the noun.

unbestätigten Berichten *zufolge*	*according to* unconfirmed reports
einem Regierungssprecher *zufolge*	*according to* a government spokesman

2.5.3   German prepositions with the dative or the accusative

These are:

an, **auf**, **entlang**, **hinter**, **in**, **neben**, **über**, **unter**, **vor**, **zwischen**

These prepositions are followed by the dative when expressing position, but by the accusative when expressing movement. In this context 'movement' means movement in relation to the object or person indicated by the noun following the preposition. In *er setzte sich neben seine Frau* we have the accusative because he is moving in relation to his wife. However, in *er ging neben seiner Frau* the dative appears because his position is unchanged relative to that of his wife.

Even so, there are constructions where the choice of case seems rather illogical. In particular, the dative is used in combination with verbs of arriving, appearing and disappearing, eg:

Wir sind um fünf *am* **Rathaus angekommen**
Die Delegation traf heute mittag *in* **der Hauptstadt ein**
Er erschien/verschwand *hinter* **dem Berg**

It will be obvious that this rule can only apply when these prepositions are used to express place. In other, mainly figurative senses one of the two cases tends to be used to the exclusion of the other. With *auf* and *über* the accusative is usual, with the others the dative.

AN (dat)	(a)	**an** expressing position = *on, at, by*

an der Grenze	*on/at* the border
an der Universität Marburg	*at* the University of Marburg
Er stand *an* **der Wand**	He was standing *by* the wall
Das Bild hängt *an* **der Wand**	The picture is hanging *on* the wall
am **Rathaus**	*at/by* the town hall
nahe *am* **Hotel**	near *(to)* the hotel
unten *am* **Fluß**	down *by* the river(side)
an **einem Buch arbeiten**	to be working *on* a book

(b)   **an** expressing time = *on*

am **31. Oktober**	*on* 31 October
am **Sonntag**	*on* Sunday(s)
am **nächsten Tag/***am* **Tag darauf**	the next day/the following day
am **Anfang**	*in* the beginning
am **Ende**	finally

(c)   **an** used in other expressions

arm/reich *an* **Bodenschätzen**	poor/rich *in* mineral resources
Es ist was *dran* (R1)	There's something to it
Jetzt ist's *an* **ihm**	It's *up* to him now
Es lag *an* **der Kälte**	It was *because of* the cold
sieben *an* **der Zahl**	seven *in* number

AN (acc)	**an** expressing movement = *to, on*	
	an **die Grenze fahren**	to go, drive *to* the border
	an **die Tür klopfen**	to knock *on* the door
	ein Bild *an* **die Wand hängen**	to hang a picture *on* the wall
	eine Bitte *an* **seinen Onkel**	a request *to* his uncle
	an **das Klavier heran**	(right) *up to* the piano

AUF (dat)	**auf** expressing position = *on, at* (with public buildings, events)	
	Das Buch liegt *auf* **dem Tisch**	The book is *on* the table
	auf **dem Mond landen**	to land *on* the moon
	auf **dem Feld**	*in* the field
	auf **dem Rathaus**	*at* the town hall
	auf **dem Land(e)**	*in* the country
	auf **einer Tagung**	*at* a conference
	auf **dem Weg nach Erfurt**	*on* the way to Erfurt
	blind *auf* **einem Auge**	blind *in* one eye
	Das hat nichts *auf* **sich** (R1)	There's nothing *in* it

AUF (acc)	(a)	**auf** expressing movement = *on(to), to* (with public buildings, events)
		Sie legte das Buch *auf* **den Tisch**	She put the book *on* the table
		Er kletterte *auf* **die Mauer**	He climbed (up) *on to* the wall
		Ich gehe *auf* **das Rathaus**	I'm going *to* the town hall
		Ich gehe *auf* **eine Tagung**	I'm going *to* a conference
		auf **die Tür zu**	*towards* the door
	(b)	**auf** expressing time = *for* (a length of time from now)
		Sie fährt *auf* **vier Monate in die Schweiz**	She's going to Switzerland *for* four months
		von heute *auf* **morgen**	from one day *to* the next, at a moment's notice
		Das Taxi ist *auf* **acht bestellt**	The taxi has been ordered *for* eight
		auf **unbestimmte Zeit**	indefinitely
	(c)	**auf** used in other expressions
		auf **spanisch**	*in* Spanish
		aufs **angenehmste** (R3)	most pleasantly
		auf **meinen Brief hin**	*following* my letter
		auf **diese Weise**	*in* this way
		auf **den ersten Blick**	*at* first sight
		auf **keinen Fall**	*on* no account
		auf **eigene Kosten**	*at* one's own expense
		auf **den Gedanken kommen**	to get an/the idea
		Auf **Ihr Wohl!**	Your health!
		etw *auf* **Raten kaufen**	to buy sth *by* instalments
		Es kommt *darauf* **an**	It all depends

⟫→

ENTLANG	**entlang** = *along*	
	The commonest usage nowadays is:	
	expressing rest – comes before a noun in the dative (R3 also genitive)	
	expressing movement – comes after a noun in the accusative (CH: dative)	
	an (dat) *entlang* is a common alternative for either rest or movement but is not used for 'along the middle' (eg of roads, rivers, etc)	

	Wir flogen die Küste *entlang* ⎫ **Wir flogen an der Küste** ⎬ *entlang* ⎭	We flew *along* the coast
	Entlang **der Küste wachsen** ⎫ **hohe Palmen** ⎬ **An der Küste** *entlang* **wachsen** ⎭ **hohe Palmen**	Tall palm-trees grow *along* the coast
	Wir kamen die Straße *entlang*	We came *along/up/down* the street

HINTER (dat)	**hinter** expressing position = *behind*	
	Er stand *hinter* **der Garage**	He was standing *behind* the garage
	20 Kilometer *hinter* **der Grenze**	20 kilometres *beyond* the border
	Er ging *hinter* **mir her**	He was walking *behind* me/following me
	hinter **meinem Rücken**	*behind* my back

HINTER (acc)	**hinter** expressing movement = *behind*	
	Er lief *hinter* **die Garage**	He ran *behind* the garage
	hinter **die Wahrheit kommen**	to get to the truth

IN (dat)	(a)	**in** expressing position = *in*	
		im **Kühlschrank**	*in* the refrigerator
		in **der Hütte drin** (R1)	*inside* the hut
		im **Norden**	*in* the north
		in **der Schweiz**	*in* Switzerland
		in **der Nähe**	near by
		im **Ausland**	abroad
	(b)	**in** expressing time = *in*	
		in **einer Woche**	*in* a week (ie 'in a week's time' or 'within a week')
		heute *in* **acht Tagen**	a week today
		im **Winter**	*in* (the) winter
		in **der Nacht**	*in* the night
		in **der nächsten Woche**	*(during)* the following week
		im **vergangenen Jahr**	last year
		in **der Zeit nach dem Krieg**	*in* the time after the war
		im **voraus**	*in* advance
		im **letzten Augenblick**	*at* the last moment

	(c)	**in** used in other expressions	
		nicht *im* **geringsten/ entferntesten**	not *in* the slightest
		im **Durchschnitt**	*on* average
		etw *im* **Vorbeigehen bemerken**	to mention sth *in* passing
		in **dieser Weise**	*in* this way
		in **gewissem Maße**	*to* a certain extent
		im **höchsten Grad**	extremely
		im **allgemeinen**	*in* general
		In **der Anlage erhalten Sie . . .** (R3b)	Please find enclosed . . .
		in **dieser Hinsicht**	*in* this respect
		eine Frau *in* **den Dreißigern**	a woman *in* her thirties

IN (acc)		**in** expressing movement = *in(to), to*	
		Sie hat es *in* **den Kühlschrank gestellt**	She put it *in* the refrigerator
		Wir gehen *ins* **Theater**	We're going *to* the theatre
		in **die Schweiz fahren**	to go *to* Switzerland
		etw *ins* **Deutsche übersetzen**	to translate sth *into* German
		in **die Arbeit vertieft**	engrossed *in* one's work
		in **einen weißen Anzug gekleidet**	dressed *in* a white suit
		sich *in* **Bewegung setzen**	to begin to move, start moving
		etw *in* **die Länge ziehen**	to drag sth out, prolong sth

NEBEN (dat)	(a)	**neben** expressing position = *next to, beside*	
		Er saß *neben* **mir**	He was sitting *next to/beside* me
		Das Buch steht *neben* **dem Radio**	The book is *next to* the radio
		Er ging *neben* **ihr her**	He was walking *beside* her
	(b)	**neben** expressing exclusion = *besides, apart from*	
		Neben **einigen Deutschen kommen die meisten Touristen aus Japan**	*Apart from* a few Germans most of the tourists come from Japan
	(c)	**neben** expressing comparison = *compared with*	
		Neben **seinem Bruder ist er groß**	He is tall *compared with* his brother

NEBEN (acc)		**neben** expressing movement = *next to, beside*	
		Er setzte sich *neben* **mich (hin)**	He sat down *next to/beside* me
		Er stellte das Buch *neben* **das Radio**	He put the book *next to* the radio

⤷

ÜBER (dat)   **über** expressing position = *over, above, across, beyond*

Das Bild hängt *über* dem Schreibtisch	The picture is hanging *over/above* the desk
Die Sonne ging *über* den Bergen auf	The sun rose *over* the mountains
3000 Meter *über* dem Meeresspiegel	3000 metres *above* sea-level
Es lag (quer) *über* dem Weg	It lay *across* the path
Er wohnt *über* der Grenze	He lives *over/across/beyond* the border

ÜBER (acc)   (a)   **über** expressing movement = *over, across, via, beyond*

Er hing das Bild *über* den Schreibtisch	He hung the picture *over* the desk
die Gänse flogen *über* das Watt (hin)	The geese flew *over* the mud-flats
Er ging *über* die Straße	He went *across* the road/he crossed the road
Er ist *über* die Grenze geschwommen	He swam *across/over* the border
Der Baum fiel uns (quer) *über* den Weg	The tree fell *across* our path
einen Pullover *über* die Bluse ziehen	to put a sweater on *over* one's blouse
Wir sind *über* Calais gekommen	We came *via* Calais
Es lief mir kalt *über* den Rücken	A cold shiver went *down* my spine
***über* Leichen gehen** (R1)	to be utterly ruthless
***über* etw hinwegsehen**	to ignore sth

(b)   **über** expressing time = *over*

***über* Nacht**	*over*night
***übers* Wochenende**	*over* the weekend
***über* kurz oder lang**	sooner or later

(c)   **über** expressing quantity = *over*

Es kostet *über* 1000 Mark	It costs *more than* 1000 marks
ein Scheck *über* 100 Mark	a cheque for 100 marks
***über* alle Maßen** (R3a)	*beyond* all measure

(d)   **über** in the sense of 'concerning' = *about*

ein Buch *über* das Rheintal	a book *about* the Rhine valley
***über* deine Mutter sprechen**	to talk *about* your mother
meine Freude *über* ihren Erfolg	my delight *at* her success

UNTER (dat)   (a)   **unter** expressing position = *under, below, beneath, among*

Der Hund liegt *unter* dem Tisch	The dog is lying *under* the table
***unter* der Erde**	*beneath* the ground, dead and buried

		unter der Herrschaft der Kaiserin	*under* the rule of the empress
		Es gab Streit *unter* den Kindern	There was quarrelling *among* the children
		unter uns (gesagt)	*between* ourselves
		unter vier Augen	privately
		unter anderem	*among(st)* other things
	(b)	**unter** expressing circumstances = *with, on, in, amid*	
		unter größten Schwierigkeiten	*with* the greatest difficulty
		unter diesen Umständen	*in* these circumstances
		unter diesen Bedingungen	*on* these conditions
		unter tosendem Beifall	*amid* thunderous applause
		Sie gestand *unter* Tränen	She confessed *amid* tears
	(c)	**unter** expressing quantity = *under, below*	
		ein Fahrrad *unter* 300 Mark	a bicycle *under*/for *less than* 300 marks
		unter 20 Grad Kälte	*below* −20 degrees (Celsius)
UNTER (acc)		**unter** expressing movement = *under, below, among*	
		Der Hund kroch *unter* den Tisch	The dog crawled *under* the table
		Er ging *unter* die Erde	He went *below* the ground
		Er lief *unter* die Kinder	He ran *among(st)* the children
VOR (dat)	(a)	**vor** expressing position = *in front of, ahead of*	
		Er wartet *vor* dem Kino	He is waiting *in front of* the cinema
		Der Pazifik lag *vor* uns	The Pacific lay *before* us
		vor mir in der Dunkelheit	*ahead of* me in the darkness
		Er schlenderte *vor* mir her	He was strolling *ahead* of me
		Es liegt *vor* der Küste	It is *off* the coast
	(b)	**vor** expressing time = *before, ago*	
		ein Tag *vor* ihrer Ankunft	a day *before* their arrival
		zehn Minuten *vor* fünf	ten minutes *to* five
		heute *vor* acht Tagen	a week *ago* today
		erst *vor* einer Woche	not until a week *ago*
	(c)	**vor** expressing cause	
		NOTE: in this sense of 'involuntary' cause *vor* is used without a following article.	
		blaß *vor* Furcht	pale *with* fear
		aus Furcht *vor* jdm/etw (dat)	for fear *of* sb/sth
		Vor Nebel war nichts zu sehen	Nothing could be seen *for* the fog
		Vor ihm ist keiner sicher	Nobody is safe *from* him

⟫⟫→

VOR (acc)	**vor** expressing movement = *in front of*	
	Er fuhr *vor* das Kino	He drove up *in front of* the cinema
	***vor* sich hin**	*to* oneself
	Was geht hier *vor* sich? (R1)	What's going on here?

ZWISCHEN (dat)	**zwischen** expressing position = *between, among*	
	Sie saß *zwischen* mir und meiner Frau	She was sitting *between* me and my wife
	***zwischen* drei und halb vier**	*between* three and half-past

ZWISCHEN (acc)	**zwischen** expressing motion = *between, among*	
	Sie setzte sich *zwischen* mich und meine Frau	She sat down *between* me and my wife
	Sie pflanzte Schneeglöckchen *zwischen* die Sträucher	She planted snowdrops *among* the bushes

2.5.4 German prepositions with the genitive

There are four relatively common prepositions which take the genitive:

(an)statt, trotz, während, wegen

However, in R1 and CH they usually take the dative, and the dative is always used in all registers if the following noun is plural and has no article. Other prepositions which take the genitive are listed below the table.

(AN)STATT	**(an)statt** = *instead of*	
	NOTE: the longer alternative *anstatt* is restricted to R3.	
	***(an)statt* eines Radios** (R2/R3) ***statt* einem Radio** (R1) }	*instead of* a radio
	***statt* Bildern**	*instead of* pictures

TROTZ	**trotz** = *despite, in spite of*	
	***trotz* des Regens** (R2/R3) ***trotz* dem Regen** (R1) }	*despite* the rain
	***trotz* Einwänden**	*in spite of* objections
	NOTE: the dative is used in a few set phrases:	
	***trotz* allem/*trotz* alledem**	*in spite of* everything/*for* all that

WÄHREND	**während** = *during*	
	***während* meines Urlaubs** (R2/R3) ***während* meinem Urlaub** (R1) }	*during* my holiday
	***während* zweier Tage** (R3) ***während* zwei Tagen** (R1/R2) }	*for* two (whole) days
	NOTE: *während*, unlike *during*, is not normally used with nouns such as *Tag, Abend, Nacht, Jahr*, etc in the singular, see **2.5.5**.	

WEGEN

wegen = *because of*

In R3 *wegen* occasionally follows the noun, but in all modern usage it is much more usual for it to precede the noun.

wegen **des schlechten Wetters**
  (R2/R3)
des schlechten Wetters *wegen*
  (R3)
} *because of* the bad weather

wegen **Unfällen** — *because of* accidents
wegen **Umbau(s) geschlossen** — closed *for* alterations

meinet*wegen* { *because of* me (R2/R3)
                   I don't mind (R1)

wegen **mir** (R1)
wegen **meiner** (SE) } *because of* me

(a) Specific place prepositions with the genitive

These are normally found in R3:

außerhalb	*outside*	**unterhalb**	*below*
innerhalb	*inside*	**diesseits**	*on this side of*
oberhalb	*above*	**jenseits**	*on that side of*

If they are used in R2 or R1 they are followed by *von*, eg:

innerhalb **dreier Tage** (R3)
innerhalb **von drei Tagen**
  (R1/R2)
} *within* three days

(b) Other prepositions with the genitive

There are a large number of these. They are restricted to R3b and are quite typical of that register, eg:

anläßlich **seines siebzigsten Geburtstages**	*on the occasion of* his seventieth birthday
kraft **seines Amtes**	*by virtue of* his office
mittels **eines Kranes**	*by means of* a crane
angesichts **dieser Schwierigkeiten**	*in view of* these difficulties
hinsichtlich **dieses Briefes**	*with regard to* this letter

2.5.5 English prepositions

In this section the most common German equivalent of each English preposition is given first, with one or more examples. In most cases further examples are given of idiomatic equivalents in certain contexts.

ABOUT	(a)	*about* in the sense of 'concerning' = **über** (acc)	
		a book *about* the war	**ein Buch *über* den Krieg**
		He knows all *about* it	**Er weiß *darüber* Bescheid**
		He doesn't understand anything *about* it	**Er versteht nichts da*von***
	(b)	*about* in the sense of 'approximately' = **etwa, ungefähr**	
		about fifty people	***etwa/ungefähr* fünfzig Leute**
		she is *about* thirty	**sie ist *etwa* dreißig/um die dreißig herum**
		(at) *about* seven	***gegen* sieben/so *um* sieben** (R1)
	(c)	*about* expressing place = **. . . herum**	
		to walk *about* the garden	**im Garten umher-/herumgehen**
		to sit *about* the house	**im Haus herumsitzen**
ABOVE		*above* = **über** (dat), **oberhalb** (R3)	
		above the village	***über* dem Dorf**
		the Rhine *above* the town of Schaffhausen	**der Rhein *oberhalb* der Stadt Schaffhausen** (R3)
		above all	***vor* allem**
ACCORDING TO		*according to* = **nach** – may follow noun in R3	
		laut – direct quotation	
		entsprechend, gemäß, zufolge – all these are typically R3b and follow or, less commonly, precede the noun	
		according to the regulations	**nach den Vorschriften/den Vorschriften nach** (R3)
		according to (what) Hans (says)	***laut* Hans**
		according to the law (as written)	***laut* Gesetz**
		according to expectations	**den Erwartungen *entsprechend*** (R3b)
		according to our principles	**unseren Prinzipien *gemäß/zufolge*** (R3b)
		according to foreign press reports	**ausländischen Pressemeldungen *zufolge*** (R3b)

ACROSS		*across* = **über** (acc) – movement **über** (dat) – rest	
		to walk *across* the bridge	*über* die Brücke gehen
		to fall *across* the path (diagonally)	(*quer*) *über* den Weg fallen
		to go *across* the meadows	*durch* die Wiesen gehen
		to lie *across* the bed (diagonally)	(*quer*) *auf* dem Bett liegen
		She lives *across* the street	Sie wohnt *gegenüber*
AFTER	(a)	*after* expressing time = **nach**	
		after the party	*nach* dem Fest
		the week *after* next	übernächste Woche
		the day *after* tomorrow	übermorgen
		day *after* day	Tag *für/um* Tag
	(b)	*after* expressing place = **hinter** (dat)	
		She ran *after* him	Sie lief *hinter* ihm her
		to shout *after* sb	*hinter* jdm herrufen
AGAINST		*against* = **gegen** **wider** (R3) – mainly in a few idioms	
		against our decision	*gegen* unseren Beschluß
		to sail *against* the wind	*gegen* den Wind segeln
		against expectations	*wider* Erwarten
		to be leaning *against* the wall	*an* der Wand lehnen
		to lean sth *against* the wall	etw *an* die Wand lehnen
ALONG		*along* = **entlang** (dat) – rest (acc) **entlang** – movement **an** (dat) **entlang** – movement or rest	
		He is coming *along* the road	Er kommt die Straße *entlang/lang* (R1)
		We flew *along* the coast	⎰ **Wir flogen die Küste** *entlang* ⎱ **Wir flogen an der Küste** *entlang*
		Trees stood *along* the bank	⎧ *Entlang* **dem Ufer standen Bäume** ⎨ **Am Ufer** *entlang* **standen Bäume** ⎩ **Längs des Ufers standen Bäume** (R3)
		Along the coast the weather is fine	*An* der Küste ist das Wetter schön
		along the floor	*am* Boden hin
		I went *along* beside her	Ich ging *neben* ihr her
AMONG		*among* = **unter** (dat), **zwischen** (dat)	
		among the crowd	*unter* der Menge
		among other things	*unter* anderem
		among the trees	*unter/zwischen* den Bäumen
		among the hills	*in* den Bergen
		She is *among* the best	Sie gehört *zu* den besten

AT

(a)   *at* expressing place = **an** (dat)
                      bei – esp 'vaguely in the vicinity of'
                          – 'at sb's house'
                      auf (dat) – with public buildings

at the corner	**an der Ecke**/*bei* **der Ecke**
at the station	**am Bahnhof**/*an* **der Bahn** (R1)/*auf* **dem Bahnhof** (R3)
at the town hall	*auf* **dem Rathaus**
at the butcher's	*beim* **Metzger**
at our house	*bei* **uns**
at university	**an** (R3 *auf*) **der Universität**
at the office	*im* **Büro**
at the bank, the post office	*auf* **der Bank**/ *auf* **der Post**
at home	*zu* **Hause**/**daheim** (S)
at school	*in* **der Schule**
at a distance of 400 metres	*in* **einer Entfernung von 400 Metern**

(b)   *at* expressing time = **um** – with precise clock times

at five (o'clock)	*um* **fünf (Uhr)**
at 7.20 pm	*um* **19.20 Uhr** (R3)
at about seven	*gegen* **sieben**/**ungefähr** *um* **sieben**/**so** *um* **sieben** (R1)
at present, *at* the moment	*zur* **Zeit**/**zurzeit**
at the same time	**zugleich**/*zur* **gleichen Zeit**
at the end of April	**Ende April**
at the weekend	*am* **Wochenende**
at Christmas	*zu* (R1 *an*, AU *auf*) **Weihnachten**
at night	*in* **der Nacht**/**nachts**
at this time tomorrow	**morgen** *um* **diese Zeit**

(c)   *at* used in other expressions

at a speed of 100 kilometres per hour	*mit* **einer Geschwindigkeit von 100 Stundenkilometern**
at −40 degrees (Celsius)	*bei* **40 Grad Kälte**
at any rate	*auf* **alle Fälle**
at two marks a pound	*zu* **zwei Mark das Pfund**
at all costs	*um* **jeden Preis**
at first sight	*auf* **den**/*beim* **ersten Blick**
at bottom	*im* **Grunde (genommen)**
to begin *at* the beginning	*von* **vorn(e) anfangen**
at his expense	*auf* **seine Kosten**

BEYOND

beyond = **über** (dat), **jenseits** (R3)
       über (acc) . . . **hinaus** – 'surpassing'

beyond the hills	⎰ *über* **den Bergen** ⎱ *jenseits* **der Berge** (R3)
20 kilometres *beyond* Frankfurt	**20 Kilometer** *hinter* **Frankfurt**

		beyond human understanding	*über* den Menschenverstand *hinaus*
		nothing *beyond* that	nichts *außerdem*/sonst nichts
		beyond doubt	*außer* Zweifel

BY	(a)		*by* expressing place = **an** (dat) 'right by' **bei** 'in the vicinity of'	
			by the window	*am* Fenster/*beim* Fenster
			by my side	*an* meiner Seite
			to sit *by* sb	*neben* jdm sitzen
			to take sb *by* the hand	jdn *an* die Hand/*bei* der Hand nehmen
			to lead sb *by* the hand	jdn *an* der Hand führen
			We went *by* his house	Wir gingen *an* seinem Haus *vorbei*
	(b)		*by* expressing time = **bis**	
			by Friday	*bis* Freitag
			by then, (in future)	*bis* dann/*bis* dahin
			by then (in past), *by* now	inzwischen
	(c)		*by* expressing measure = **um**	
			taller *by* a head	*um* einen Kopf größer
			by the hour, metre	stunden*weise*, meter*weise*
			by far	*bei* weitem
	(d)		*by* expressing means = **mit**	
			by train, bus, car	*mit* dem Zug, dem Bus, dem Wagen
			to pay *by* cheque	*mit* Scheck bezahlen
	(e)		*by* expressing cause = **durch**	
			NOTE: for *by* in passive constructions see **4.4.4**.	
			the discovery of America *by* the Vikings	die Entdeckung Amerikas *durch* die Wikinger
			by pressure on the button	*durch* einen Druck auf den Knopf
			by accident, *by* chance	*durch* Zufall, zufällig
			by mistake	*aus* Versehen
			a play *by* Frisch	ein Stück *von* Frisch
	(f)		*by* used in other expressions	
			one *by* one	einer *nach* dem anderen
			to know sb *by* sight	jdn vom Sehen her kennen
			side *by* side	nebeneinander
			by heart	auswendig
			by request	*auf* Wunsch
			not *by* any means	keineswegs/noch lange nicht (R1)

DOWN	*down =* . . . **hinab**, . . . **hinunter** – 'away from one' . . . **herab**, . . . **herunter** – 'towards one' . . . **'runter** (R1) – 'away from one' or 'towards one'

We went *down* the street	**Wir gingen die Straße** *hinab/hinunter*
She came *down* the street	**Sie kam die Straße** *herab/herunter*
He lives *down* the street	**Er wohnt etwas weiter (unten)**
down the side of the house	**seitlich am Haus** *entlang*
down the centuries	*durch* **die Jahrhunderte (hindurch)**
Tears rolled *down* her cheeks	**Tränen rollten ihr** *über* **die Wangen**

DURING	*during =* **während**

during the war	*während* **des Krieges** (R2/R3) *während* **dem Krieg** (R1) *im* **Krieg**
during the day	*am* **Tag**
during the night	*in* **der Nacht**

EXCEPT (FOR)	*except (for) =* **außer**, **bis auf** (acc), **abgesehen von**

except for me	*außer* **mir**
The flat is finished *except for* the kitchen	*Bis auf* **die Küche ist die Wohnung fertig**
except for a few little things	*außer/bis auf/abgesehen von* **ein paar Kleinigkeiten**

FOR	(a)	*for* expressing benefit = **für**

room *for* us	**Platz** *für* **uns**
a present *for* her husband	**ein Geschenk** *für* **ihren Mann**
a reward *for* sth	**eine Belohnung** *für* **etw**

NOTE: with verbs, the person benefiting may be in the dative, but a phrase with *für* is being used increasingly, especially in R1 (see **4.1.2**), eg:

He bought a book *for* me	**Er hat** *mir* **ein Buch gekauft** **Er hat ein Buch** *für* **mich gekauft**

	(b)	*for* expressing purpose = **zu**

for this purpose	*zu* **diesem Zweck**
What's it *for*, then?	**Wo**z**u dient es denn?**
for pleasure	*zum* **Vergnügen**
for breakfast	*zum* **Frühstück**

(c)   *for* expressing time = **seit** – period up to now
  = **für/auf** (acc) – period from now (R1 often
     simply acc phrase)
  = acc phrase (often with **lang**) – simple length of
     time

I have been sitting here *for* three hours	**Ich sitze** *seit* **drei Stunden hier**
I had been sitting there *for* three hours	**Ich saß** *seit* **drei Stunden dort**
I am going to Kiel *for* three weeks	**Ich fahre** *für* **drei Wochen/***auf* **drei Wochen/drei Wochen** (R1) **nach Kiel**
I sat there *for* two hours	**Ich habe zwei Stunden (lang) dort gesessen**
He won't be back *for* a month	**Erst** *in* **einem Monat ist er wieder da**
I'll do it *for* Monday	**Ich mache es** *bis* **Montag fertig**
for years on end	**jahrelang/Jahre hindurch** (R3)
for the first time	*zum* **erstenmal**
for hours on end	**stundenlang**

(d)   *for* expressing place

change *for* Dortmund	*nach* **Dortmund umsteigen**
leave *for* Bochum	*nach* **Bochum abfahren**
bends *for* 5 kilometres ahead	**Kurven** *auf* **5 Kilometer**

(e)   *for* used in other expressions

not see anything *for* fog	*vor* **Nebel nichts sehen**
thirst *for* knowledge	**Drang** *nach* **Wissen**
for example	*zum* **Beispiel**
as *for* me	**was mich angeht**
a cheque *for* 110 marks	**ein Scheck** *über* **DM110**
to do sth *for* love	**etw** *aus* **Liebe tun**
for this reason	*aus* **diesem Grund**

FROM   (a)   *from* expressing place = **von** – coming from a place one has been 'at',
  with the idea of direction from (the
  opposite of *zu*)
  = **aus** – coming from, or out of a place one has
  been 'in', with the idea of origin (the
  opposite of *in* (acc))

She comes *from* Ireland (ie that is her native land)	**Sie kommt** *aus* **Irland**
She is coming *from* Ireland (ie travelling from there)	**Sie kommt** *von* **Irland**
the train *from* Berne	**der Zug** *aus* **Bern**
the train *from* Berne to Basle	**der Zug** *von* **Bern nach Basel**
20 kilometres *from* the coast	**20 Kilometer** *von* **der Küste entfernt**
to drink *from* a glass	*aus* **einem Glas trinken**
from top to bottom	*von* **oben bis unten**
Where did you get that *from*?	**Wo hast du das her?** (R1)

[FROM]	(b)	*from* expressing time = **von ... an**	
			ab (R3b) – with precise times
		from today	*von* **heute** *an*/*ab* **heute** (R3b)
		from 1 May	*vom* **1. Mai** *an*/*ab* **1. Mai** (R3b)
		from the start	*von* **Anfang** *an*
		from (last) January	*seit* **Januar**
		from (next) January	*von* **Januar** *an*/*ab* **Januar** (R3b)
		from morning till night	*von* **morgens bis abends**
		from childhood	*von* **Kind** *auf*/*an*, *von* **klein** *auf*
	(c)	*from* used in other expressions	
		from 50 marks	*ab* **50 Mark**
		from experience	*aus* **(der) Erfahrung**
		from what I've heard	*nach* **dem, was ich gehört habe**
		from the outset	*von* **vornherein**
		She was trembling *from* the cold	**Sie zitterte** *vor* **Kälte**

IN	(a)	*in* expressing place = **in** (dat) – position in	
			in (acc) – movement into
		It is *in* his pocket	**Es ist** *in* **seiner Tasche**
		He put it *in* his pocket	**Er steckte es** *in* **die Tasche**
		in Brunswick	⎰ *in* **Braunschweig**
			⎱ *zu* **Braunschweig** (R3a)
		in town	*in* **der Stadt**
		in the country	*auf* **dem Lande**
		in the picture	*auf* **dem Bild**
		in the sky	*am* **Himmel**
		in heaven	*im* **Himmel**
		in the direction of the station	(*in*) **Richtung Bahnhof**
		to go *in* that direction	*in* **diese(r) Richtung gehen**

NOTE: both accusative and dative are used but dative is more frequent.

		in the fields	*auf* **dem Feld**/*auf* **der Wiese**
		in (among) the trees	*unter* **den Bäumen**
		wounded *in* the arm	*am* **Arm verletzt**
		in your place	*an* **deiner Stelle**
	(b)	*in* expressing time = **in** (dat)	
		in autumn	*im* **Herbst**
		in May	*im* **Mai**
		in mid-May	**Mitte Mai**
		in ten days	*in* **zehn Tagen**
		in earlier times	*in* **früheren Zeiten**
		in 1983	**1983**, *im* **Jahre 1983**
		in the evening(s)	*am* **Abend**/**abends**
		later *in* the day	**später** *am* **Tag**
		in the days when ...	*zu* **der Zeit, wo**/**als** ...
		in the long run	*auf* **die Dauer**
		in advance	*im* **voraus**

(c) *in* used in other expressions

in any case	*auf* jeden Fall
in that case	*in* dem Fall
just *in* case	*für* alle Fälle
in German	*auf* deutsch
in my opinion	{ meiner Meinung *nach* meines Erachtens (R3)
in a loud voice	*mit* lauter Stimme
in vain	umsonst, vergeblich
in this way	{ *auf* diese Weise *in* dieser Weise
to write *in* ink	*mit* Tinte schreiben
in all respects	*in* jeder Hinsicht
deaf *in* one ear	*auf* einem Ohr taub
four *in* number	vier *an* der Zahl
all *in* all	alles *in* allem
not *in* the least	nicht *im* geringsten

INSIDE

inside = **in** (dat), **innerhalb** (R3) – rest
    in (acc) – movement
    in (dat), **innerhalb** (R3), **binnen** (R3) – time

inside the house	{ *im* Haus/*im* Haus drin (R1) *innerhalb* des Hauses (R3)
He went *inside* the house	**Er ging *ins* Haus (hinein)**
inside four days	{ *in* vier Tagen *innerhalb*/*binnen* vier Tagen (R3) *innerhalb* von vier Tagen (R2/R3)

INSTEAD OF

instead of = **(an)statt, anstelle von**

instead of flowers	{ (*an*)*statt* Blumen *anstelle von* Blumen
instead of his brother	{ *statt* seines Bruders (R2/R3) *statt* seinem Bruder (R1)
instead of me	{ *statt* meiner (R3) *statt* mir (R1) *an* meiner Stelle

---

INTO

into = **in** (acc)

She went *into* the room	**Sie ging *ins* Zimmer (hinein)**
to translate *into* Spanish	*ins* Spanische übersetzen
to drive *into* a tree	*gegen* einen Baum fahren

⟫⟫→

OF

(a) *of* expressing possession, etc = genitive or **von** (see **4.2.2**)

| the roof *of* the house | { das Dach des Hauses
{ das Dach *vom* Haus (R1/R2) |
| the discovery *of* America | die Entdeckung *von* Amerika |

(b) *of* expressing quantity = apposition (gen or **von** (see **4.2.2**))

a stack *of* old newspapers	ein Haufen alter Zeitungen
a piece *of* wood	ein Stück Holz
all *of* them	sie alle
the five *of* us	wir fünf
a friend *of* mine	ein Freund *von* mir

(c) *of* with names = apposition

the city *of* Cologne	die Stadt Köln
the month *of* February	der Monat Februar
the University *of* London	die Universität London

(d) *of* expressing material = **aus**

| a house *of* straw | ein Haus *aus* Stroh |
| a table *of* beechwood | ein Tisch *aus* Buchenholz |

(e) *of* used in other expressions

of course	selbstverständlich, natürlich
point *of* view	Gesichtspunkt
of its own accord	*von* selbst
today *of* all days	ausgerechnet heute
to die *of* hunger	*vor* Hunger sterben
north *of* Kassel	nördlich *von* Kassel
the battle *of* Lützen	die Schlacht *bei* Lützen
an example *of* sth	ein Beispiel *für* etw
typical, characteristic *of* sb/sth	typisch, charakteristisch *für* jdn/etw

OFF

off = **von . . . (her-/hinunter)**

He jumped *off* the train	Er sprang *vom* Zug (hinunter)
He took it *off* the shelf	Er nahm es *vom* Regal (herunter)
off the peg	*von* der Stange
10 kilometres *off* the main road	10 Kilometer *von* der Hauptstraße *weg*
off the south coast of England	*vor* der englischen Südküste

ON

(a) *on* expressing place = **auf** (dat) – 'on (top of)' (rest)
     = **auf** (acc) – 'on/onto (the top of)' – movement
     = **an** (dat) – 'on (the side of)' (rest)
     = **an** (acc) – 'on/onto (the side of)' – movement

The book is *on* the table	Das Buch liegt *auf* dem Tisch
He put the book *on(to)* the table	Er legte das Buch *auf* den Tisch
The picture hung *on* the wall	Das Bild hing *an* der Wand
He hung the picture *on* the wall	Er hängte das Bild *an* die Wand

on the river	{ *auf* dem **Fluß** (on it, eg in a boat) / *am* **Fluß** (beside it) }
We are sitting *on* the floor	**Wir sitzen** *am* **Boden**/*auf* dem **Boden**
on the ceiling	*an* der **Decke**
on stage	*auf* der **Bühne**
on top of the mountain	**oben** *auf* dem **Berg**
to kiss sb *on* the mouth	**jdn** *auf* den **Mund küssen**
on the violin, *on* the trumpet	*auf* der **Geige**, *auf* der **Trompete**
on the piano, *on* the drums	*am* **Klavier**, *am* **Schlagzeug**
on the way	*auf* dem **Weg**/**unterwegs**
on the left	*auf* der **linken Seite**/**links**
on the wall	*an* der **Wand**/*auf* der **Mauer**
on the coast	*an* der **Küste**
on the telephone	*am* **Telefon**
a house *on* the main road	**ein Haus** *an* der **Hauptstraße**
on board	*an* **Bord**
on the train	*im* **Zug**
to go *on* the train	*mit* dem **Zug fahren**
on his face	*im* **Gesicht**
on the second floor	*im* **zweiten Stock**
it says *on* the poster that . . .	*auf* dem **Plakat steht, daß** . . .

As the last example shows, *auf* is used for *on* for any kind of writing 'on' paper, etc, irrespective of its position.

(b)   *on* expressing time = **an** (dat)
  bei 'on the occasion of' (esp with verbal nouns in R3b)

on Sunday	*am* **Sonntag**
on Sundays	**sonntags**/*am* **Sonntag**
on weekdays	*an* **Wochentagen**
on the morning of 4 July	*am* **Morgen des 4. Juli**
on the following evening	*am* **Abend darauf**
on this occasion	*bei* **dieser Gelegenheit**
on his arrival	*bei* **seiner Ankunft**

(c)   *on* in the sense of 'concerning' = **über** (acc)

a book *on* German history	**ein Buch** *über* **deutsche Geschichte**

(d)   *on* used in other expressions

cash *on* delivery	*per* **Nachnahme**
to go *on* a journey	*auf* **eine Reise gehen**
on the radio, the television	*im* **Radio**, *im* **Fernsehen**
on no account	*auf* **keinen Fall**
on average	*im* **Durchschnitt**
on purpose	*mit* **Absicht**/**absichtlich**
on one condition	*unter* **einer Bedingung**
It was improved *on* her suggestion	**Es wurde** *auf* **ihren Vorschlag hin verbessert**

OPPOSITE	*opposite* = **gegenüber**	
	opposite me	{ **mir** *gegenüber* (R2/R3) { *gegenüber* **von mir** (R1)

	opposite the hospital	{ **dem Krankenhaus** *gegenüber*
		  (R2/R3)
		gegenüber **dem Krankenhaus**
		gegenüber **vom Krankenhaus**
		  (R1)

OUT OF **OUTSIDE**	*out of, outside* = **nicht in** (dat), **außerhalb** – rest **aus** – movement	
	to be *out of* town	{ *nicht in* **der Stadt sein** { *außerhalb* **der Stadt sein** (R3)
	It is *outside* the city	**Es liegt** *vor* **der Stadt**
	to go *out of* the room	*aus* **dem Zimmer hinaus-** **gehen**
	out of the door	*zur* **Tür** *hinaus*
	out of breath, danger, sight	*außer* **Atem, Gefahr, Sicht**
	out of control	*außer* **Kontrolle**
	outside office hours	*außerhalb* **der Dienstzeit**

OVER	*over* = **über** (dat) – rest **über** (acc) – movement	
	Clouds hung *over* the city	**Wolken hingen** *über* **der Stadt**
	We flew *over* the city	**Wir flogen** *über* **die Stadt** **(hin)**
	the bridge *over* the Neckar	**die Brücke** *über* **den Neckar**
	children *over* ten years old	**Kinder** *über* **zehn Jahre alt**
	over and above that	*darüber* **hinaus**
	over a year ago	{ **gut ein Jahr her** { **vor gut einem Jahr**
	over dinner	*beim* **Abendessen**
	over the years	*im* **Laufe der Jahre**

PAST	(a)	*past* expressing place = **an** (dat) . . . **vorbei** **hinter** (dat) – 'beyond'	
		past the house	*am* **Haus** *vorbei*
		just *past* the barn	**gleich** *hinter* **der Scheune**
	(b)	*past* expressing time = **nach**	
		twenty *past* seven	**zwanzig** *nach* **sieben**

ROUND	*round* = **um**	
	round the corner	*um* **die Ecke**
	right *round* the lake	{ *um* **den ganzen See herum** { **rings/rund** *um* **den See**
	all *round* the house	{ *um* **das Haus herum** (outside) { *im* **ganzen Haus** (inside)
	all *round* Belgium	*durch* **ganz Belgien**

THROUGH	*through* = **durch**	
	through the tunnel	*durch* **den Tunnel**
	through the city	*durch* **die Stadt**

to go *through* a red light	**bei Rot** *durchfahren*
cancelled *through* illness	*wegen* **Krankheit ausgefallen**
all *through* her life	**ihr ganzes Leben** *lang*
all *through* the night	**die ganze Nacht** *hindurch*
all *through/throughout* the city	{ *in* **der ganzen Stadt** *überall in* **der Stadt**

TO   (a)   *to* expressing direction = **an** (acc), **auf** (acc), **in** (acc) – with most nouns referring to place we use either *an*, *auf* or *in* with the **dative** case when we want to say we are 'in' or 'at' that place. The preposition chosen depends on the noun, eg *Ich bin an der Kirche, auf dem Markt, im Büro*. To express direction, we use the same prepositions with the same nouns, but with the **accusative** case, eg *Ich gehe an die Kirche, auf den Markt, ins Büro*

= **zu** – this expresses direction as much as arrival and is the opposite of *von*; it is always used for people (ie 'to sb's house'); it is also very commonly used in R1 and R2 for *auf* (acc), *an* (acc) or *in* (acc), although in the last case it will never be used if the final destination is inside a building

= **nach** – this is only used, without an article, with neuter names of countries, towns, etc, and with some adverbs; it is widely used in N in place of *zu*

I go *to* university (ie to study there)	**Ich gehe** *an* **die Universität**
I am going *to* the university (ie that is my destination)	**Ich gehe** *zur* **Universität**
She walked (up) *to* the window	**Sie trat** *an* **das Fenster**
(up) *to* the castle	*auf* **das Schloß**
(up) *to* my room	*auf* **mein Zimmer**
to the toilet	{ *auf* **die Toilette** *aufs* **Klo** (R1)
to town	*in* **die Stadt**
to the office	*ins* **Büro**
to the Isle of Wight	*auf* **die Insel Wight**
I've been *to* Hof	**Ich bin** *in* **Hof gewesen**
to go *to* bed	*ins* **Bett** (R3 *zu* **Bett**) **gehen**
close *to* sth	**nahe** *bei/an* **etw (dat)**
a visit *to* my friend	**ein Besuch** *bei* **meiner Freundin**
to the butcher's	*zum* **Metzger**
This bus goes *to* the station	**Dieser Bus fährt** *zum* **Bahnhof**
the door *to* the yard	**die Tür** *zum* **Hof** (hin)
parallel *to* the wall	**parallel** *zur* **Mauer**
to Italy	*nach* **Italien**

⟫⟫→

[TO]		to Switzerland	*in* die Schweiz
		to the south	*nach* Süden
		to the right	*nach* rechts
		to the front	*nach* vorn(e)

(b) *to* expressing indirect object = dative

an (acc) – *if* the notion of direction is stressed

He gave it *to* me	**Er hat es mir gegeben**
She has been a good friend *to* me	**Sie ist mir eine gute Freundin gewesen**
I wrote *to* her	**Ich habe ihr/*an* sie geschrieben**
serving drinks *to* minors	**der Alkoholausschank** *an* **Jugendliche** (R3b)
He told that *to* his friend	**Das hat er seinem Freund gesagt**
This is what he said *to* me, . . . (followed by quoted speech)	**Das hat er** *zu* **mir gesagt:** . . .

(c) *to* expressing time = **vor** (dat) – in telling time

ten *to* six	**zehn** *vor* **sechs**
punctual *to* the minute	**pünktlich** *auf* **die Minute**

(d) *to* used in other expressions

to hold sth *to* the light	**etw** *gegen* **das Licht halten**
What's that *to* you?	**Was geht dich das an?** (R1)
HSV won three *to* one	**Der HSV hat drei** *zu* **eins gewonnen**
to my delight	*zu* **meiner Freude**
200 inhabitants *to* the square kilometre	**200 Einwohner** *pro* **Quadratkilometer**
to my knowledge	**meines Wissens**
to work *to* rule	*nach* **Vorschrift arbeiten**
to a great extent	*in* **hohem Grad,** *in* **hohem Maße**
related *to* sb	*mit* **jdm verwandt**
restricted *to* sth	*auf* **etw beschränkt**
an answer *to* your question	**eine Antwort** *auf* **Ihre Frage**

TOWARDS	**(a)**	*towards* expressing place = **auf** (acc) . . . **zu**	
		towards the door	*auf* **die Tür** *zu*
		towards Oldenburg	*nach* **Oldenburg** *hin*
		towards the north	*nach* **Norden** *hin/zu*
		She came *towards* me	**Sie kam mir entgegen**

	(b)	*towards* expressing time = **gegen**	
		towards the end of the last century	*gegen* **Ende des vorigen Jahrhunderts**

UNDER	*under* = **unter** (dat) – rest **unter** (acc) – movement

He parked the car *under* the bridge	**Er hat den Wagen *unter* der Brücke geparkt**
She put the money *under* the mattress	**Sie hat das Geld *unter* die Matratze gesteckt**
children *under* 12 years old	**Kinder *unter* 12 Jahren**
under construction	*im* **Bau**

UNTIL/TILL	*until/till* = **bis** – in positive sentence = **erst** + appropriate preposition – in negative sentence

until 1988	*bis* **1988**
until then	*bis* **dahin**
until the end of the month	*bis* (*zum*) **Monatsende**
until his death	*bis zu* **seinem Tod**
until after his death	*bis nach* **seinem Tod**
not until tomorrow	*erst* **morgen**
not until three hours ago	*erst vor* **drei Stunden**
not until the 20th century	*erst im* **20. Jahrhundert**
not until the late evening	*erst am* **späten Abend**
not until after his death	*erst nach* **seinem Tod**

UP	*up* = . . . **hinauf** – away from one . . . **herauf** – towards one . . . **'rauf** (R1) – away from or towards one

They went *up* the street	**Sie gingen die Straße *hinauf***
They came *up* the street	**Sie kamen die Straße *herauf***
We live *up* the street	**Wir wohnen etwas *weiter* die Straße *entlang***
He lives *up* the mountain	**Er wohnt (oben) *auf* dem Berg**
up one's nose	*in* **der Nase**
further *up* this page	**weiter oben *auf* dieser Seite**

WITH	*with* = **mit**

with a hammer	*mit* **einem Hammer**
with his girlfriend	*mit* **seiner Freundin**
with a trembling hand	*mit* **zitternder Hand**
He lives *with* his mother	**Er wohnt *bei* seiner Mutter**
She lives *with* her boyfriend	**Sie wohnt *mit* ihrem Freund** (*zusammen*)
I've no money *with* me	**Ich habe kein Geld *bei* mir**
35 years *with* the firm	**35 Jahre *bei* der Firma**
Do you want to go *with* us?	**Willst du *mit*?**
Put it *with* the others	**Leg's *zu* den anderen**
to tremble *with* cold	*vor* **Kälte zittern**
with a hat and coat on	*in* **Hut und Mantel**

2.6 Modal particles

One of the most characteristic features of German R1 is the extensive use of modal particles, and a foreigner's command of German can often be gauged from an appropriate use of *auch, doch, ja, schon*, etc. However, their meanings are very elusive and their use is extraordinarily difficult to paraphrase or explain concisely. Their function is broadly to clarify or emphasize to the listener the speaker's attitude to what he or she is saying. They act as a kind of lubrication in dialogue – indeed they are infrequent outside spoken German in general and conversation in particular – making sure that the speaker's intentions and attitudes are not misunderstood. By using them one can appeal for agreement, express surprise or annoyance, soften a blunt question or sound reassuring. In English we tend to use other means to these ends, in particular changes in tone of voice or intonation, which are difficult to describe. The best way to learn how to use these particles is to become familiar with as many examples as possible and try to assess the meaning as they are used. Included in this section are some typical uses of the common particles together with an indication of possible English equivalents. These must *not* be taken as standard translations; their purpose is only to convey some idea of the force of the German particle.

NOTE: in the examples below the stressed syllable is indicated by a stress mark when it is crucial to the meaning in both languages.

ABER	(a)	In statements, **aber** expresses surprise.

Possible English equivalents: *Oh!*, rhetorical question, negative tag, exclamation.

Das Bier ist aber 'kalt	Oh! This beer 'is cold
Das ist aber 'stark	That's a bit 'much, isn't it?
Das ist aber 'schön	Isn't that 'nice? (rather pejorative)
'Das war aber eine Reise!	What a journey 'that was!

(b) In statements, **aber** expresses contradiction or insistence (rather weaker than *jedoch*).

Possible English equivalents: *but, though*.

Mein Freund 'kam aber nicht	My friend didn't 'come, though
Sie muß uns aber ge'sehen haben	But she must have 'seen us

(c) In commands, **aber** qualifies a previous statement.

Possible English equivalents: *but, though*.

Du kannst ruhig etwas weiter nach links gehen ... Paß aber an der 'Tür auf!	Don't worry, you can go a bit further to the left ... Look out by the 'door, though!

AUCH

(a) In statements, **auch** confirms the case and often gives reasons for a contradiction.

Possible English equivalents: *too*, *you know*.

Das 'ist er auch	He 'is, too
Wir können's auch 'lassen	We can 'drop it, you know

(b) In yes/no questions, **auch** asks for verification, as the speaker is uncertain.

Possible English equivalents: positive statement followed by negative tag, *are you sure that . . .?*

Hast du auch die 'Rechnung bezahlt?	You've paid the 'bill, haven't you?
Haben Sie's auch ver'standen?	You 'did understand it, didn't you?
Hast du auch deine 'Socken eingepackt?	Are you sure you put your 'socks in?

(c) In answers or responses, **auch** agrees and explains.

Possible English equivalents: *well, . . ., but then, ...*

Speaker A:
Die Straßen sind aber trocken	The roads are dry, though

Speaker B:
Es hat auch wenig ge'regnet	Well, it hasn't 'rained much
Sein Vater hat auch viel 'Einfluß	But then, his father 'does have a lot of influence

(d) In wh-questions, **auch** expects a negative answer.

Possible English equivalent: *well, . . .*

Was kann man auch dazu 'sagen?	Well, what can you 'say to that?
Warum mußte er auch 'wegfahren?	Well, why did he have to go a'way?

(e) In commands, **auch** reinforces.

Possible English equivalent: *Make sure . . .*

Aber schreib ihm auch 'morgen	But make sure you write to him to'morrow
Sei auch schön 'brav!	Make sure you be'have!

(f) **auch** with a noun.

Possible English equivalent: *even*.

Auch 'Manfred kann sich geirrt haben	Even 'Manfred may have been wrong

≫→

| [AUCH] | (g) | The combination **auch nur** expresses a restriction. |

Possible English equivalents: *even, so much as.*

| **Es war unmöglich, auch nur 'Brot zu kaufen** | It was impossible even to buy 'bread |
| **Ich weigerte mich, sie auch nur 'anzuschauen** | I refused to so much as 'look at them |

| DENN | (a) | In yes/no questions, **denn** expresses surprise and mildly requests confirmation. |

Possible English equivalent: *then* (at end of sentence).

| **Hast du denn die Re'nate gesehen?** | Did you see Re'nate, then? |
| **Willst 'du sie denn fragen?** | Are 'you going to ask her, then? |

| | (b) | In wh-questions, **denn** is added (almost automatically) to tone down the question. |

Possible English equivalent: *then* (at end of sentence).

| **Wie bist 'du denn gekommen?** | How did 'you get here, then? |
| **Wie lang 'fährt man denn nach Ulm?** | How long does it 'take to get to Ulm, then? |

NOTE: in informal R1 *denn* is usually shortened to *'n* and placed straight after the verb, eg: *Hast'n du die Renate gesehen?*

| DOCH | | NOTE: in most senses *doch* conveys a note of insistence on the part of the speaker that he/she is right or going to get his/her own way. |

| | (a) | In statements, **doch** contradicts (if heavily stressed) or appeals for agreement (if more lightly stressed). |

Possible English equivalents: stressed verb (possibly *do* form), *though, after all,* negative tag, initial *but.*

Es hat 'doch geschneit	It 'did snow
Ich habe 'doch recht gehabt	I 'was right after all, wasn't I?
Wir müssen 'doch morgen nach Trier	We 'have got to go to Trier tomorrow, though
Er 'hat doch gesagt, daß er kommt	But he 'said he was coming
Das 'mußt du doch zugeben	You've 'got to admit it, though
Es ist doch 'schön hier	It 'is nice here, isn't it?

| | (b) | In commands, **doch** may sound impatient or advising. |

Possible English equivalents: stressed *do,* negative tag, *why not . . .?*

Kommen Sie doch 'morgen vorbei	'Do call in tomorrow, won't you?
Hör doch 'auf!	'Do stop it, won't you?
'Mach doch nicht immer so ein Gesicht	'Don't keep on making a face like that
Leg dich doch zwei Stunden 'hin!	'Why not go and lie down for a couple of hours?

(c) **doch** makes a statement into a question expecting the answer 'yes'.

Possible English equivalent: negative tag.

Den Wagen kann ich doch morgen früh 'abholen?	I'll be able to col'lect the car tomorrow morning, won't I?
Das schaffst du doch bis 'Montag?	You'll have it finished by 'Monday, won't you?
Er ist doch nicht 'krank?	He's not 'ill, is he?

(d) In wh-questions, the combination **doch gleich** asks for an answer to be repeated.

Possible English equivalent: *again*.

Wie 'war das doch gleich?	'What was that again?
Wie 'hieß sie doch gleich?	'What was her name again?

EBEN

NOTE: mainly N + C, replaced by *halt* in S.

(a) In statements, **eben** emphasizes an inescapable conclusion.

Possible English equivalents: *well, . . . just*.

Du mußt eben zu 'Hause bleiben	Well, you'll just have to stay at 'home
Dann müssen wir eben den 'Zug nehmen	We'll just have to take the 'train, then
Er hätte eben nicht 'kommen sollen	Well, he just ought not to have 'come
Es ist eben 'kalt heute	Well, it is 'cold today

(b) In commands, **eben** stresses lack of alternative.

Possible English equivalents: *well, just . . . then*.

Bleib eben dort 'sitzen	Well, just stay 'sitting there, then
Fahr eben durch die 'Stadt	Well, just drive through the 'town, then

EIGENTLICH (a) **eigentlich** tones down questions and makes them sound casual, often with *denn*.

Possible English equivalents: *actually, tell me . . .*

Kommt er eigentlich 'oft zu Besuch?	Tell me, does he visit you 'often?
Wie 'spät ist es eigentlich?	What 'time is it, actually?
Was 'hältst du denn eigentlich davon?	Tell me, what do you 'think of it(, actually)?

(b) In replies, **eigentlich** moderates a refusal or an objection.

Possible English equivalents: *well, actually/really . . .*

Wir haben eigentlich schon 'zu	Well, really, we're already 'closed
Ich wollte eigentlich eine neue 'Bluse	Well, actually, I 'did want a new blouse

⟫→

| [EIGENTLICH] | (c) | In statements, **eigentlich** tentatively raises an objection. |

Possible English equivalents: *really*, *strictly speaking*.

| **Eigentlich 'darfst du das nicht** | Strictly speaking, you are not al'lowed to |
| **Wir haben eigentlich schon ver'loren** | Really, we've already 'lost |

ERST

(a) Referring to time, **erst** suggests it is earlier than expected or desired.

Possible English equivalents: *only*, *not before/until*.

Wir kommen erst recht 'spät in München an	We shan't get to Munich till very 'late
Sie können den Film leider erst 'morgen abholen	I'm afraid you'll not be able to collect the film before to'morrow
Es ist erst halb 'fünf	It's only half past 'four

(b) In statements, **erst** is equivalent to English *only*, but suggests that more is to follow.

Possible English equivalent: *only . . . (as yet)*.

| **Ich habe erst zehn Seiten geschrieben** | I've only written ten pages (as yet) |
| **Erst drei Schiffe haben den Hafen verlassen** | Only three ships have left port (as yet) |

(c) In statements, **erst** carries the idea of going one better.

Possible English equivalents: *nothing less than*, *only*.

| **Erst mit einer Stelle bei 'Braun wird er sich zufriedengeben** | He'll not be satisfied with anything less than a job at 'Braun's |

(d) Especially in exclamations, **erst** emphasizes that sth is the ultimate (often in the combination *erst recht*).

Possible English equivalents: *really*, *simply*.

Dann ging's erst 'recht los	Then things 'really got going
Das konnte sie erst 'recht nicht	She 'simply couldn't manage that
Das macht es erst 'recht schlimm	That really 'does make it bad

---

ETWA

(a) In yes/no questions, **etwa** expresses fear that the answer might be positive.

Possible English equivalents: negative statement with positive tag, *don't tell me*.

Habt ihr etwa ge'schlafen?	You haven't been a'sleep, have you?
Ist das etwa 'dein Wagen?	That's not 'your car, is it?
Hast du es etwa ge'lesen?	Don't tell me you've 'read it?

(b) In statements or questions, **etwa** makes a tentative suggestion.

Possible English equivalents: *say*, *for instance*, *perhaps*.

Sie wollte ihn nicht etwa 'kränken	She didn't want to 'hurt him, for instance
Willst du etwa 'Sonntag kommen?	Do you want to come on 'Sunday, say?
Bist du sicher, daß du den Karl gesehen hast, und nicht etwa seinen Bruder 'Jürgen?	Are you sure it was Karl you saw and not his brother 'Jürgen, perhaps?

JA

(a) In statements, **ja** may confirm or check or appeal for agreement.

Possible English equivalents: stressed verb (*do*-form), *really*, *you know*, *of course*, *it's all right*, ...

Gestern hat's ja ge'regnet	It 'did rain yesterday, you know
Das ist ja eine Ge'meinheit	That really 'is mean
Er ist ja schon 'längst im Ruhestand	He's been retired for a 'long time now, you know
Sie 'wissen ja, daß es keiner geschafft hat	You 'do know, of course, that nobody's managed it
Die Prüfung ist ja 'bald vorbei	The exam will 'soon be over
Ich 'komme ja schon	It's all right, I'm on my 'way

(b) In commands (usually stressed), **ja** expresses threat.

Possible English equivalents: stressed pronoun, *just ...*, *or else*.

Sei 'ja vorsichtig	'You just be careful (, or else)
Mach mir 'ja keine Dummheiten	Just 'don't do anything silly, or else

MAL

NOTE: in N often *man*.

(a) Especially in commands or requests, **mal** has a toning-down effect; it encourages by implying the lack of difficulty.

Possible English equivalents: *just*, *won't you*, etc.

Lies den 'Brief mal durch	Just read the 'letter through
Hol mal schnell die 'Milch	Just go and fetch the 'milk, would you?
Komm mal 'Montag vorbei	Just pop in on 'Monday, won't you?
Würden Sie mir mal 'helfen?	Would you just give me a 'hand?

NOTE: the combination *doch mal* makes a command even more casual and less imperative, cf English: *Why don't you ...?*, *Why not ...?*

Nimm doch mal ein neues 'Blatt!	Why don't you get another piece of 'paper?
Komm doch mal mit ins 'Kino!	Why not come to the 'cinema with us?

⟫⟫→

| [MAL] | (b) | In statements, the combination **nun mal** emphasizes a lack of alternative. |

Possible English equivalents: *just*, stressed verb.

Kinder 'sind nun mal so	Children are just 'like that
Es wird nun mal 'lange dauern	It's just going to take a 'long time
Da es nun mal pas'siert ist …	As it 'has happened …

NUR

NOTE: *bloß* is a common alternative, most often used in R1.

(a)   In statements, **nur** limits agreement or expresses qualification.

Possible English equivalents: *only*, *but*.

| **Die Mittelmeerküste ist sehr schön. Sie ist nur etwas 'dreckig** | The Mediterranean coast is very lovely. It's just rather 'dirty |
| **Sie möchte gern Medizin studieren. Ihre 'Noten sind nur etwas schwach** | She would like to study medicine. But – her 'marks are rather weak |

(b)   In conditionals, **nur** expresses a wish (may be strengthened by *doch*).

Possible English equivalent: *only*.

| **Wenn er 'doch nur geschrieben hätte** | If 'only he'd written |
| **Wenn sie nur 'anrufen würde** | If 'only she'd ring |

(c)   In wh-questions, **nur** stresses the importance of sth.

Possible English equivalents: *-ever*, *… on earth*.

Wo 'bleibt er nur?	Where on 'earth is he?
Wie 'kann er sich nur so einen Wagen leisten?	How on 'earth can he afford a car like that?
Was ist nur mit 'ihm los?	What'ever's up with him?

(d)   In negative commands, stressed, **nur** expresses a warning.

Possible English equivalents: *you* added to command, *just*, *better*.

| **Komm 'nur nicht zu spät** | { Just 'don't be late
 { You'd 'better not come too late |
| **Fahr 'nur nicht so schnell** | { Just 'don't drive so fast
 { 'Don't you drive so fast |

(e)   In commands, unstressed, **nur** expresses tentative suggestion with, at times, a hint of impatience.

Possible English equivalent: *just*.

> ' stressed syllables are preceded by a stress mark

Kommen Sie nur he'rein	'Do just come in
Laß mich nur 'machen	Just 'let me get on with it
'Sagen Sie nur	Just 'say the word

RUHIG		In commands or requests, **ruhig** gives a reassuring tone.

Possible English equivalents: *I don't mind*, *don't disturb yourself*, etc.

Bleib 'ruhig sitzen	Don't get up for 'me
Mach 'ruhig weiter	Carry on, don't dis'turb yourself
Sie können 'ruhig Ihre Jacke ausziehen	You can take your jacket off, it's 'OK by me
Sie können mir 'ruhig die Wahrheit sagen	You can tell me the truth, 'I don't mind

SCHON   (a)   Referring to time, **schon** suggests that sth is earlier than expected or desired, or that sth has happened on occasions.

Possible English equivalents: *already*, *as early as*, *sometimes*.

Bist du schon 'fertig?	Have you 'finished already?
Sie kommen schon heute 'abend	They're coming to'night (I know we hadn't expected them so soon)
Ich habe ihn 'auch schon im Kino gesehen	'I've sometimes seen him at the cinema, too
Das habe ich schon 19'60 geahnt	I suspected that as early as 19'60
Warst du schon mal 'dort?	Have you ever 'been there?
Da ist sie schon 'wieder	There she is a'gain (I know we didn't want to see her so soon)

(b)   In statements in the future tense, **schon** expresses reasonable expectation that sth will happen. It can be reassuring or sometimes threatening.

Possible English equivalents: *all right*, *don't worry*.

Ich werde schon 'aufpassen	I'll watch 'out all right
Er wird's schon 'hinkriegen	He'll 'manage it, don't worry
Dir werde ich's schon 'zeigen	I'll (soon) 'show you all right
'Den werde ich schon kriegen	I'll (soon) get 'him, don't worry

(c)   In statements, **schon** concedes agreement in principle, but implies reservation. It is often followed by *aber* (or implies a following *aber*).

Possible English equivalents: stressed verb (*do*-form), *well*, . . .

Pa'ris ist schon eine schöne Stadt (aber . . .)	Paris 'is a lovely city(, but . . .)
Ich wollte schon 'kommen(, aber . . .)	Well, I 'did want to come(, but . . .)
Das 'schon, aber . . .	Well, 'may be, but . . .

⟫⟫→

[SCHON]   (d)   Qualifying a noun, **schon** expresses restrictions.

Possible English equivalents: *mere(ly)*, *even*, *very*.

Schon der Ge'danke machte ihn stutzig	The very/mere 'thought made him suspicious
Wenn ich das schon 'sehe, ...	If I even 'see that, ...
Schon 'vor dem Krieg war es schwierig	Even be'fore the war it was difficult

(e)   In wh-questions, **schon** expects a negative answer.

Possible English equivalent: negative statement, positive tag.

Wer 'wird ihm schon helfen?	'Nobody's going to help him, are they?
Was heißt 'das schon?	'That's not supposed to mean anything, is it?

(f)   **schon** gives commands a tone of urgency and emphasis.

Possible English equivalents: *do* ...(*,please*).

Be'eile dich schon	'Do hurry up(, please)
'Sag mir schon, was du denkst. Ich werde dir's nicht übelnehmen	'Do tell me what you think. I shan't take offence

In combination with *nun*, *schon* can sound impatient, cf English: *well*, *..., then*.

Nun, gib's schon 'her	Well, 'give it to me, then
Nun, 'fahr schon	Well, get a 'move on, then

ÜBERHAUPT   (a)   **überhaupt** makes statements more general.

Possible English equivalents: *anyhow*, *anyway*, *... at all*, *all in all*, *in any case*.

London is über'haupt eine gräßliche Stadt	London is a dreadful city 'anyhow
Er sagt über'haupt sehr wenig	He says very little 'anyway
Ich mag sie über'haupt nicht	I don't like her at 'all
Das ist über'haupt eine gefährliche Angelegenheit	That's a risky business in 'any case

(b)   In questions, **überhaupt** casts doubts on a basic assumption.

Possible English equivalent: *... at all*.

Trinkt er denn überhaupt 'Wein?	Does he drink 'wine at all, then?
Kann er überhaupt 'deutsch sprechen?	Can he speak 'German at all?

VIELLEICHT	(a)	In statements, **vielleicht** expresses surprise. It is synonymous in this sense with *aber* (a).

Possible English equivalents: stressed verb, *really*, *not half*.

'Ich habe vielleicht einen Hunger	I (really) 'am hungry
'Du bist vielleicht ein Idiot	You (really) 'are an idiot
'Der hat vielleicht einen langen Bart gehabt	He (really) 'did have a long beard
'Ich habe vielleicht gestaunt	I wasn't 'half surprised

    (b)   In yes/no questions, **vielleicht** expects a negative answer.

Possible English equivalents: negative statement with positive tag, *really*.

Willst du mir vielleicht er'zählen, daß . . . ?	You 'don't mean to tell me that . . ., do you?
Soll ich vielleicht bis abends um 'sieben arbeiten?	Am I really supposed to work till 'seven at night?

WOHL	**wohl** expresses probability or supposition, turning a question into a statement.

Possible English equivalents: future tense (see **4.3.1**), *probably*, *I suppose/presume . . .*, negative tag, *no doubt*.

Der Franz ist wohl schon 'wieder krank	Franz will be 'ill again, I suppose
Die Sabine ist wohl gestern 'abend angekommen	Sabine will have arrived last 'night, no doubt
Sie sind wohl der 'letzte	I presume you're the 'last
Du bist wohl ver'rückt geworden	You must be 'mad, mustn't you?

The combination *ja wohl* sounds more certain, cf English *certain(ly)*.

Sie wird ja wohl noch in 'Essen sein	She's pretty certainly still in 'Essen

The combination *doch wohl* sounds rather less certain, but the speaker hopes it is the case, cf English *surely . . .* with a negative tag.

Er hat doch wohl noch einen 'Schlüssel	Surely, he's got another 'key, hasn't he?
Die An'gelika wird doch wohl das Abitur schaffen	Surely, An'gelika will get through the Abitur, won't she?

2.7 Greetings and forms of address

2.7.1 Greetings

The choice of formula for greeting and leave-taking is a matter of register, determined by the relationship between the people involved. It is important in an area of usage governed so much by social convention that the English-speaking learner should be aware that more conventional greetings are used in Germany than is now usual in Britain. Not only are there in German greetings such as *Mahlzeit* and *Feierabend* which have no equivalent in English, but other standard forms of greeting are used more frequently. It is, for instance, quite unthinkable to enter or leave a small shop in Germany without the customary *guten Tag* and *auf Wiedersehen*. The following table shows a progression from informal greetings (used to friends) to formal ones (showing respect to the person addressed).

Situation	R1	R1/R2	R2
meeting	Hallo! Grüß dich! Moin! (N) Servus! (SE)	(Gu'n) Morgn! (Gu'n) Tag! (Gu'n) Ahmt!	Guten Morgen! Guten Tag! Guten Abend!
		←——— Grüß Gott! (S) ———→	
	Grüezi! (CH)		
leave-taking	Tschüß! Ade! (SW) Salü!, Tschau! (SW, CH) Servus!, Pfiati! (SE) Mach's gut! Bis gleich! Bis bald!	(uf) Wiedersehn! (uf) Wiederschaung! (AU)[†] (uf) Wiederluege! (CH)	Auf Wiedersehen! Auf Wiederschauen! (AU)[†]

[†] *Auf Wiederschauen* has become rather fashionable in Germany, whilst in Austria *auf Wiedersehen* is nowadays often regarded as more refined.

Situation	R1	R2
at table	Laß es dir schmecken!	Guten Appetit!
lunchtime	←——————— Mahlzeit! ———————→	
end of week	←——— Schönen Sonntag! ———→ ←——— Schönes Wochenende! ———→	
end of work	←——————— Feierabend! ———————→	

Situation *contd*	R1 *contd*	R2 *contd*
Good luck	Toi toi toi! Hals- und Beinbruch!	Viel Glück!
Have a good time!	Viel Spaß!	Viel Vergnügen!
bedtime	Schlaf gut!	Angenehme Ruhe! (very formal)
journey	←——————— Gute Reise! ———————→	
going home	Komm gut nach Hause!	Gute Heimfahrt!

2.7.2   *du* and *Sie*

This is a summary of the use of *du* and *Sie*. Fuller accounts of current usage may be found in Clyne (1984), pp. 124–8, and G. Augst, *Sprachnorm und Sprachwandel*, Wiesbaden, 1977, pp. 13–60.

Broadly speaking, *du* (or *ihr* in the plural) is used in the following situations:

Speaking to . . .

> children (up to about 14; in schools to the end of the *Mittelstufe* – tenth school year)
> animals and inanimate objects
> oneself
> God

Between . . .

> family members and close relatives
> close friends
> all schoolchildren and students
> workmates (blue collar)
> non-commissioned soldiers

In all other instances, *Sie* is used, especially to strangers and generally in white-collar employment (eg to colleagues in an office or a bank).

However, matters are often less clear-cut, and with changing social attitudes and conventions the usage of *du* and *Sie* is in a state of flux, so that many Germans feel insecure about which one to use in unfamiliar surroundings. Nevertheless, consciousness of the need to use the 'right' one is as strong as ever. In the 'wrong' situation *du* sounds too familiar, condescending, patronizing and signals a lack of respect verging on rudeness, whilst *Sie* in the 'wrong' situation sounds stand-offish, pompous, haughty, with a hint of arrogance verging on rudeness.

du shows intimacy, affection and solidarity; people who use *du* to one another are conscious of belonging to the same group or standing together. The modern move towards *du*, especially among young people, reflects this clearly. *du* has become much more frequent since the late sixties, and the old ceremony of *Brüderschaft trinken* associated with the switch from *Sie* to *du* between

R1* = vulgar
R1 = informal
    colloquial
R2 = neutral
R3 = formal
R3a = literary
R3b = non-literary
(see 1.1.5)

N = North
C = Central
S = South
SW = South West
SE = South East
AU = Austria
CH = Switzerland
(see 1.2.3)

acquaintances and friends is practised less. It is certainly no longer true that '*wenn ein Mann und eine Frau sich duzen, dann ist was passiert*'. Nevertheless, this trend towards *du* shows signs of slowing down now, and the use of *du* is still much less widespread, especially in middle–class circles, than is the use of first names in Britain or North America. In a bank or a shop, with a fairly formal, professional atmosphere, people who work together every day can be on *Sie* terms for 30 years or more. By and large *Sie* is associated with using the formal title, eg *Herr Meyer*, *Frau Wimmer*, etc, and the shift to *du* involves the corresponding shift to the use of the first name. But the use of *Sie* with the first name may be an intermediate stage (usually very transient) before moving to *du*. It is common, though, when parents are speaking to their (older) children's friends.

Finally, *ihr* deserves special mention, as it is not invariably used as the simple plural of *du*. It is quite common, especially in R1, when speaking to any group of people even if one might address individuals among them by *Sie*. And in S, particularly in rural areas, it is still used as a mark of respect to persons of standing in the community, eg the priest or the schoolmaster.

2.8 Letters

The whole layout of letters in the German-speaking countries differs in several respects from English conventions.

(a) Name and address on the envelope

Herrn Prof. Dr. Albert Schröder Waldstraße 27 W-3550 Marburg/Lahn

Frau Angelika Trautmann Korinthstraße 39 O-7013 Leipzig

R1* = vulgar
R1 = informal
    colloquial
R2 = neutral
R3 = formal
R3a = literary
R3b = non-literary
(see 1.1.5)

To a couple:

To a family with children:

Herrn und Frau Manfred und Ute Schwenk Josefgasse 5 A-1080 Wien

Fam. Andreas Wernli Säckinger Allee 7 CH-3010 Bern

N = North
C = Central
S = South
SW = South West
SE = South East
AU = Austria
CH = Switzerland
(see 1.2.3)

Note the position of titles, the underlining of the town name and the lack of indentation. The street name is placed above the town. The country prefixes before the postcode may be omitted in internal mail except in Germany, where W and O should be used to distinguish between former West and East Germany.

NOTE: *Fräulein* tends now to be used only to young girls. Any adult woman, irrespective of whether she is married or single, will be addressed as *Frau*.

(b) The sender's name and address

On personal letters, these are written as one line on the back of the envelope, preceded by *Abs.* (= *Absender*), eg:

Abs.: Susana Jellinek, Traklgasse 9, 1084 <u>Wien</u>

This information is not repeated at the top of the letter, where just the place and date are given, eg:
Wien, den 7. September 1992

(c) Formulae for opening and closing

The choice of these will depend on one's relationship to the person addressed. The following table shows the most common.

NOTE: unlike English *Dear*, German *Liebe(r)* is not used in business correspondence to strangers, or to persons with whom one is on formal terms.

Openings

R3 (most formal) **Sehr geehrte Damen und Herren!**
Sehr geehrte Herren!
Sehr geehrter Herr Professor Dr. Schröder!

(less formal) **Lieber Herr Pedersen!**
Liebe Frau Havemann!

R2 (least formal) **Lieber Wolfgang!**
Liebe Uschi!
Liebe Mutter!

NOTE: in writing to more than one person the adjective is repeated, eg:
Lieber Wolfgang, liebe Uschi!

Older practice has always been to follow these with an exclamation mark as given above, but it is increasingly usual to find a comma, in which case the first word of the letter should *not* start with a capital.

Closings

R3 (most formal) **Hochachtungsvoll** ⎫
Mit freundlichen Grüßen ⎬
followed by ⎰ **Ihr(e)**
⎱ **Ihr(e) sehr ergebene(r)**

(less formal) **Mit herzlichen Grüßen** followed by **Ihr(e)**

R2 (least formal) **Von ganzem Herzen** ⎫
(Viele) liebe Grüße ⎬ followed by **Dein(e)**
Herzlich/Herzlichst ⎭

The least formal phrases will be used only to a person addressed as *du*. In correspondence, *Du* (*Dich*, *Dein*, etc) and *Ihr*, (*Euch*, etc) are always written with capital letters.

3 Words and forms

3.1 Nouns: genders and plurals

Inflection for gender, number and case is central to the way German functions as a language and is at the root of much of its difference from English in the way things are expressed. It is vital to know the gender of nouns and how they form their plurals in order to be able to express yourself properly in German.

In principle every German noun has an arbitrary gender and an arbitrary way of forming the plural, and both of these must be learnt separately for each noun. The meaning of a noun, aside from the general tendency for names of male beings to be masculine, those of female beings to be feminine, rarely gives any indication of gender. In practice, though, there are many helpful regularities – in particular there is often a close link between the gender of a noun, its structure (ie what suffixes it has) and its plural. In this section we survey the most important regularities and the most common exceptions to them.

3.1.1 Suffixes as indicators of gender and plural

Most suffixes are almost invariably linked to a particular gender and a particular plural.

(a) Feminines

Suffix	Plural	Examples
-anz, -ei, -enz -heit, -ie, -ik, -ion -keit, -schaft, -tät -ung, -ur	-en	die Bücherei, die Residenz die Panik, die Revolution die Eitelkeit, die Mannschaft die Bedeutung, die Natur
-in	-nen	die Freundin

Exceptions: **der** Papagei (-en), **das** Genie (-s), **der** Atlantik, **der** Pazifik, **der** Katholik (-en, -en), **das** Stadion (-ien), **das** Abitur

(b) Masculines

Suffix	Plural	Examples
-ler, -ner -er (from verbs)	–	der Tischler, der Redner der Lehrer, der Bäcker
-an, -än, -är, -eur -ich, -ig, -ling -or (stressed)	-e	der Kapitän, der Friseur der König, der Lehrling der Maj'or

Suffix	Plural	Examples
-and, -ant, -ent -et, -graph, -ist } -krat, -loge, -nom	**-en, -en**	der Komödiant, der Student der Athlet, der Komponist der Demokrat, der Astrologe
-or (unstressed)	**-s, -en**	der Prof'essor

NOTE: the stress shift in plural: die Profess'oren

Suffix	Plural	Examples
-ismus	**-ismen**	der Organismus

Exceptions: **das** Organ, **das** Porzellan, **das** Militär, **das** Restaurant (-s), **das** Talent, **das** Transparent, **das** Prozent, **der** 'Korridor(-e), **das** Labor

<table><tr><td>' stressed syllables are preceded by a stress mark</td></tr></table>

(c) Neuters

Suffix	Plural	Examples
-chen, -lein, -sel, -tel	–	das Mädchen, das Viertel
-tum	¨er	das Eigentum
-at, -ett, -il } -ment	**-e**	{ das Format, das Ventil das Dokument
-um	**-en**	das Datum

NOTE: *-um* is replaced by *-en* in the plural, eg *die Daten*

Exceptions: **der** Reichtum, **der** Irrtum, **der** Zement, **der** Moment,[4] **das** Regiment (-er), **der** Apparat, **der** Automat (-en, -en), **der** Salat, **der** Senat

(d) Masculine if persons, neuter if things

Suffix	Plural	Examples
-al, -ar, -ier [iːr] } -on [oːn] (stressed)	**-e**	{ der General,[5] das Regal der Bar'on, das Mikro'phon
-on [on] (unstressed)	**-en, -en**	der 'Dämon, das E'lektron

NOTE: the stress shift in pl: die Dä'monen, Elek'tronen

Exceptions: **der** Kanal (¨e), **der** Karneval, **die** Moral, **der** Skandal, **der** Kommentar, **der** Singular, **die** Manier(-en), **das** Lexikon (-ika), **die** Person (-en)

<table><tr><td>NOTE: in this section nouns with variant forms are marked as follows:
[1] Other plural form possible, see 3.1.4
[2] Different plural exists with different meaning, see 2.2.3
[3] Doublet exists, see 2.2.4
[4] Also has another gender with different meaning, see 2.2.2
[5] Gender variable, see 3.1.7</td></tr></table>

3.1.2   Suffixes or prefixes as clues to gender and plural

For all other nouns, the link between gender, suffix (or, in one case, prefix) and plural is more a matter of tendency than rule, but the tendencies are worth knowing.

(a)   Nouns in **-nis** and **-sal** (pl: **-nisse**, **-sale**)

Mainly neuter (70%)	das Ergebnis, das Hindernis, das Zeugnis, das Scheusal (R3a), das Schicksal, etc
Some common feminines	die Bedrängnis, die Besorgnis, die Betrübnis, die Erkenntnis, die Erlaubnis, die Finsternis (R3), die Kenntnis, die Wildnis, die Mühsal (R3), die Trübsal (R3)

(b)   Nouns in **Ge-** (pl usually **-e** if no suffix, otherwise **–**)

Mainly neuter (90%)	das Gebet, das Gebiet, das Gebirge, das Gehör, das Gesindel (R3), etc
Six neuters have plural in ¨ er	das Gehalt,[4] das Gemüt (R3), das Geschlecht, das Gesicht,[2] das Gespenst, das Gewand (R3)
Some masculines (pl ¨e except where indicated)	der Gebrauch, der Gedanke (-ns,-n), der Gehalt[4](-e), der Gefallen (–), der Gehorsam, der Genosse (-n,-n), der Genuß, der Geruch, der Gesang, der Geschmack, der Gewinn
*Some feminines (pl **-en** or **-n**)*	die Gebühr, die Geburt, die Geduld, die Gefahr, die Gemeinde, die Geschichte, die Gestalt, die Gewalt, die Gewähr

(c)   Nouns in **-el**, **-en**, **-er**

*Nouns in **-er** from verbs are all masculine if they denote persons (see **3.1.1(b)**)*	der Bäcker, der Fahrer, der Lehrer, der Redner, der Unternehmer

Most of the rest are masculine (60%), with plural –	der Flügel, der Löffel, der Schatten, der Schuppen, der Adler, der Fehler, etc
Some feminines (25%), with plural -n	die Gabel, die Kugel, die Regel, die Butter, die Kiefer, die Ziffer, etc
Some neuters (15%), with plural –	das Segel, das Kabel, das Kissen, das Zeichen, das Fenster, das Messer, etc

Exceptions:

Several masculines have plural ¨	der Apfel, der Boden, der Bogen,[1] der Bruder, der Faden, der Garten, der Graben, der Hafen, der Hammer, der Kasten, der Laden,[1] der Mangel, der Mantel, der Nagel, der Ofen, der Schaden, der Vater, der Vogel
A few masculines have plural -n	der Bauer[4](-n, -n), der Muskel, der Pantoffel, der Stachel, der Vetter
One masculine has plural -e	der Char'akter (NOTE: the stress shift in pl: *die Charak'tere*)
Two feminines have plural ¨	die Mutter,[2] die Tochter
Two neuters have plural ¨	das Abwasser, das Kloster

(d)   **Nouns in -e (all have plural -n)**

Mainly feminine (90%)	die Fichte, die Gabe, die Lampe, die Reise, etc
Some masculines denoting male beings (all -n, -n)	der Bote, der Franzose, der Gatte (R3), der Kunde, der Riese, etc (see **3.2.1**)
Eight masculines with genitive in -ns (eg des Namens)	der Buchstabe, der Friede,[3] der Funke,[3] der Gedanke, der Glaube, der Name, der Same,[3] der Wille (see **3.2.2**)
One other masculine (plural usually Käsesorten)	der Käse
Seven neuters	das Auge, das Ende, das Erbe, das Image, das Interesse, das Prestige, das Regime

NOTE: in this section nouns with variant forms are marked as follows:

[1] Other plural form possible, see 3.1.4
[2] Different plural exists with different meaning, see 2.2.3
[3] Doublet exists, see 2.2.4
[4] Also has another gender with different meaning, see 2.2.2
[5] Gender variable, see 3.1.7

(e) Remaining cases

- **Masculine** (60%) – equally split between plural in **-e** and in **¨e**

Plural in -e	der Arm, der Besuch, der Hund, etc
Plural in ¨e	der Arzt, der Bach, der Gast, etc

Exceptions:

Some names of male beings have **-en, -en**	der Bär, der Fürst, der Graf, der Held, der Herr(-n,-en), der Hirt, der Mensch, der Prinz, der Tor[4] (R3), etc (see **3.2.1**)
A few have plural ¨er	der Geist, der Gott, der Mann,[2] der Rand, der Ski, der Wald, der Wurm
A few have plural -en	der Dorn, der Fels,[3] der Mast, der Nerv, der Schmerz, der Schreck,[3] der See,[4] der Staat, der Strahl, der Typ,[3] der Zeh[3]

- **Neuter** (25%) – 75% of these have plural in **-e**, 25% have plural in **¨er**

Plural in -e	das Beil, das Gas, das Jahr, etc
Plural in ¨er	das Bad, das Buch, das Ei, das Volk, etc

Exceptions:

A few have plural -en	das Bett, das Hemd, das Insekt, das Ohr, das Verb, das Herz (-ens, -en, see **3.2.2**)
One with plural ¨e	das Floß

- **Feminine** (15%) – 75% of these have plural in **-en**, 25% have plural in **¨e**

Plural in -en	die Arbeit, die Form, die Frau, etc
Plural in ¨e	die Gans, die Hand, die Kuh, die Luft, die Maus, die Stadt, etc

Exception:

One with plural ¨en	die Werkstatt

NOTE: in this section nouns with variant forms are marked as follows:

[1] Other plural form possible, see 3.1.4
[2] Different plural exists with different meaning, see 2.2.3
[3] Doublet exists, see 2.2.4
[4] Also has another gender with different meaning, see 2.2.2
[5] Gender variable, see 3.1.7

3.1.3 Plurals in -s

A large and increasing number of nouns of all genders have a plural in *-s*. It is of relatively recent, or regional origin and tends to be looked down on in R3, but its use is spreading rapidly in R1, even to native words, though it is found particularly with very new words, especially loans from French and English.

It is current in the following examples:

- *Words ending in a vowel other than -e* — das Auto → die Autos
  die Mutti → die Muttis, etc

- *Abbreviations, names of letters, shortened words* — der LKW → die LKWs
  das L → die Ls, etc
  die Lok → die Loks (R1)

- *Other parts of speech (esp in R1)* — das Aber → die Abers
  das Blau → die Blaus, etc

- *Some N nautical words* — das Deck → die Decks
  das Dock → die Docks
  der Kai → die Kais
  das Wrack → die Wracks

- *To refer to families* — die Müllers, Schmidts, Werners, etc

- *With words for persons (R1 in N only)* — der Bengel → die Bengels
  das Fräulein → die Fräuleins
  der Onkel → die Onkels
  der Junge → die Jungs, etc

- *In French words pronounced in (semi-) French way* — das Atelier → die Ateliers
  das Amendement → die Amendments, etc

- *In all words recently adopted from English* — das Baby → die Babys (!)
  die Band → die Bands
  der/das Essay → die Essays, etc

- *With the following words, the plural in -s is now the most frequent; other plural forms are old-fashioned or restricted to R3:*

der Balkon	das Labor
der Ballon	das Parfüm
das Etikett	der Park
das Kabarett	das Porträt
der Karton	der Schal
das Karussell	der Scheck
das Kotelett	der Streik

3.1.4 Nouns with alternative plurals

A number of other words have alternative ways of forming the plural. These are often associated with regional or register differences:

der Admiral	**-e**	(occ ¨e)	der Laden	¨	(N – 'shutters')
das Bett	**-en**	(CH **-er**)	das Lager	–	(S, R3b ¨)
der Bogen	¨	(N –)	das Mädel	–	(N **-s**; S **-n**)
das Ding	**-e**	(R1 **-er**)	der Magnet	**-en, -en**	(occ **-e**)
der Erlaß	**-e**	(AU ¨e)	der Pastor	**-en**	(N ¨e)
der Fasan	**-en**	(occ **-e**)	das Roß	**-e**	(S ¨er)
der General	**-e**	(occ ¨e)	das Scheit	**-e**	(AU, CH **-er**)
der Geschmack	¨e	(R1 ¨er)	der Stiefel	–	(S **-n**)
die Kartoffel[5]	**-n**	(R1 –)	das Stück	**-e**	(S **-er**)
der Koffer	–	(CH **-n**)	der Wagen	–	(S ¨)
der Kragen	–	(S ¨)	der Ziegel	–	(S **-n**)
der Kran	¨e	(occ **-e**)			

NOTE: das Regime [reʒiːm], die Regime [reʒiːmə]

3.1.5 Foreign words with unusual plurals

Many words taken from the classical languages have kept an original or deviant plural, if sometimes only in R3. Some of the commonest are given below, with variant forms where these exist:

das Album → Alb**en** (R1 **-s**)
der Atlas → Atla**nten** (R1 **-asse**)
das Drama → Dram**en**
das Epos → Ep**en**
das Examen → Exam**ina** (R1/R2 –)
die Firma → Firm**en**
das Fossil → Fossil**ien**
der Kaktus → Kakt**een** (R1 **-usse**)
das Komma → Komma**ta** (R1/R2 **-s**)
das Konto → Kont**en** (R1 **-s**)
das Lexikon → Lexik**a** (R1 **-iken**)
das Material → Material**ien**
das Mineral → Mineral**ien** (rare: **-e**)
der Mythos → Myth**en**
das Prinzip → Prinzip**ien**
das Reptil → Reptil**ien**
das Risiko → Risik**en** (also: **-s**)
das Schema → Schema**ta** (R1 **-men/-s**)
die Villa → Vill**en**
das Virus[5] → Vir**en**
das Visum → Vis**en** (also: **Visa**)

NOTE: in this section nouns with variant forms are marked as follows:

[1] Other plural form possible, see 3.1.4
[2] Different plural exists with different meaning, see 2.2.3
[3] Doublet exists, see 2.2.4
[4] Also has another gender with different meaning, see 2.2.2
[5] Gender variable, see 3.1.7

3.1.6 Differences in plural usage between German and English

(a) In many cases German uses a singular word where English has a plural:

der Anfang *beginning(s)*
der Arbeitsanzug *overalls*
das Archiv *archives*
die Asche *ashes*
das Aussehen *looks*
das Benehmen *manners*
der Besitz *possessions*
der Bodensatz *dregs*
die Brille *glasses, spectacles*
der Dank *thanks*
der Darm *intestines, guts*
das Einkommen *earnings*
die Eisenbahn *railways*
das Fernglas *binoculars*
das Feuerwerk *fireworks*
die Gebrauchsanweisung
   instructions
der Gewinn *winnings*
der Hafer *oats*
das Hauptquartier *headquarters*
das schottische Hochland
   the Highlands
der Hopfen *hops*
die Hose *trousers, pants*
der Inhalt *contents*
die Kaserne *barracks*
der Kehrricht *sweepings*
die Kundschaft *customers*
der Lohn *wages*

die Lunge *lungs*
das Mittel *means*
das Mittelalter *the Middle Ages*
die Mühe *pains*
die Pension *lodgings*
die Physik *physics*
die Politik *politics*
das Protokoll *minutes*
der Pyjama[5] *pyjamas*
der Reichtum *riches*
der Schadenersatz *(legal) damages*
die Schere *scissors*
das Schilf *reeds*
der Schlüpfer *knickers*
die Schutzbrille *goggles*
der Stadtrand *outskirts*
die Statistik *statistics*
die Stehleiter *steps*
die Treppe *stairs, steps*
die Umgebung *surroundings*
das Unkraut *weeds*
die Unterhose *underpants*
die Waage *scales*
die Wahl *election(s)*
der Wald *wood(s)*
die Zange *pliers, tongs*
der Ziegenpeter *mumps*
der Zirkel *compasses*
der Zoll *customs*

All the above must of course be used with a verb in the singular, eg:
   Meine Brille **ist** kaputt *My glasses **are** broken*

The same applies to singular collective nouns, which are often used with a plural verb in English, but never in German, eg:
   Die Polizei **kommt** *The police **are** coming*

Similarly with *die Mannschaft, das Publikum, die Regierung, das Volk*, etc.

(b) In a few instances German uses a plural word for an English singular:

die Flitterwochen *honeymoon*
die Kosten *cost(s)*
die Lebensmittel *food*
die Möbel *furniture*
die Pocken *smallpox*

die Ränke (R3) *intrigue*
die Trümmer *rubble*
die Wirren *turmoil*
die Zinsen *interest*

(c) In certain instances English and German differ as to whether some nouns can have a plural:

Singular	Plural
der Atem *breath*	die Atemzüge *breaths*
die Auskunft *(piece of) information*	die Auskünfte *information*
das Brot *bread, loaf*	die Brote *loaves*
das Essen *meal*	die Mahlzeiten *meals*
der Fortschritt *advance*	die Fortschritte *progress*
die Hausaufgabe *(piece of) homework*	die Hausaufgaben *homework*
die Kenntnis *(piece of) knowledge*	die Kenntnisse *knowledge*
die Liebe *love*	die Liebschaften *loves*
die Nachricht *(piece of) news*	die Nachrichten *news*
das Obst *fruit*	die Obstsorten *fruits*
der Rasen *lawn*	die Rasenflächen *lawns*
der Schaden *damage*	die Schäden *instances of damage*
die See[4] *sea*	die Meere *seas*
das Spielzeug *toy*	die Spielwaren *toys*
der Sport *sport*	die Sportarten *sports*
der Tod *death*	die Todesfälle *deaths*
das Versprechen *promise*	die Versprechungen *promises*

(d) Other instances of difference in the use of singular and plural

Masculine and neuter nouns of measurement used with numerals keep their singular form:

  vier **Pfund** Rindfleisch
  sechs **Paar** Schuhe
  zwei **Glas** Bier

With words denoting clothes and parts of the body the singular is used if each person has one of each:

  alle hoben **die** rechte **Hand** . . . *their right **hands***
  sie redete die Leute nie mit **dem Namen** an . . . *by their **names***
  NOTE ALSO:
  manche haben **ein** leichtes **Leben** . . . *easy **lives***

NOTE: in this section nouns with variant forms are marked as follows:

[1] Other plural form possible, see 3.1.4
[2] Different plural exists with different meaning, see 2.2.3
[3] Doublet exists, see 2.2.4
[4] Also has another gender with different meaning, see 2.2.2
[5] Gender variable, see 3.1.7

3.1.7 Nouns with variable gender

- The gender of a number of nouns is not fully fixed and a sample of these is given below. The variation is often linked to regional and register differences.

der (occ **die**) Abscheu	**die** (S **der**) Kartoffel
der (CH **das**) Aperitif	**der** (AU **das**) Keks
der (also **das**) Barock	**das** (also **der**) Knäuel
der (S **das**) Bonbon	**das** (CH, R1 **der**) Liter
die (S **der**) Butter	**der** (also **das**) Meteor
das (occ **der**) Dossier	**das** (AU **der**) Polster
der (also **das**) Dotter	**der** (CH **das**) Pyjama
der (occ **das**) Dschungel	**das** (S **der**) Radio
das (occ **der**) Gulasch	**der** (also **das**) Sims
der (R1 **das**) Gummi	**das** (CH **der**) Taxi
der (also **das**, R1 **die**) Joghurt	**das** (R1 **der**) Virus

- A few words are rather more problematic:

Meter is nowadays more often masculine, but, especially in old-fashioned R3, is not infrequently neuter. Most compounds have the same variation, but there are exceptions:
> *always masc:* der Kilometer, der Gasometer
> *always neuter:* das Barometer, das Thermometer

Mut is masculine, but some of its compounds are feminine, cf:
> *masc:* Freimut, Gleichmut, Hochmut, Kleinmut, Übermut, Unmut
> *fem:* Anmut, Armut, Demut, Großmut, Sanftmut, Schwermut, Wehmut

Teil is nowadays always masculine in all its meanings, except in a few set phrases, ie:
> ich für **mein** (also **meinen**) Teil
> er hat **sein** (also **seinen**) Teil getan
> NOTE: also in the sense 'part of a whole' – **jedes Teil** DM3

Its compounds are also predominantly masculine, but note the following exceptions:
> **das** Abteil, **das** Einzelteil, **das** Ersatzteil, **das** Gegenteil, **das** Urteil
> **das** (also **der**) Oberteil
> **das** (legal R3b **der**) Erbteil

- With many recent loan-words from English, no gender has yet become established. The majority (60%) are masculine, most of the rest are neuter, but many show variation, eg:
> *masc or neuter:* Curry, Display, Essay, Filter, Layout, Lunch, Match, Script, Service, Terminal, etc
> *masc or fem:* Couch, Jet, Lobby, Speech, etc
> *neuter or fem:* Aerobic, Coke, Trademark, etc

3.2 Nouns: case

Case in German is most often shown through article and/or adjective endings. For most nouns the only endings in modern German are:
(i)   Masculine and neuter nouns add -*(e)s* in the genitive singular.
(ii) -*n* is added in the dative plural if possible (ie if the nominative plural does not end in -*n* or -*s*).
However, there are a few exceptions to this pattern, and these are outlined in **3.2.1–4**.

3.2.1 'Weak' masculines

About 10% of masculine nouns (mostly denoting living beings) take -*(e)n* in the plural *and* in the genitive, dative and accusative singular.

- Most end in -*e*.

der Kollege	die Kollegen
des Kollegen	der Kollegen
dem Kollegen	den Kollegen
den Kollegen	die Kollegen

- Those that do not end in -*e* often decline regularly in the singular in R1.

R1	**R2/R3**
der Bär	der Bär
des Bärs	des Bären
dem Bär	dem Bären
den Bär	den Bären

  Similarly: *Automat, Bauer, Bursch, Fürst, Graf, Held, Hirt, Kamerad, Mensch, Planet, Prinz, Soldat, Typ* and many nouns ending in -*ant*, -*ent*, -*ist*.

  NOTE: *Nachbar* and *Oberst* always have -*n* in the genitive singular in all registers, eg *des Nachbarn*, but often lack it in the dative and accusative singular, especially in R1, eg *dem, den Nachbar* (for R2/R3 *dem, den Nachbarn*).

- The singular endings are omitted in R2 and R3 *if* the noun has no article or adjective with it, eg:
  die Gemeinsamkeit zwischen Mensch und Tier
  eine Herde ohne Hirt

- Some nouns have now switched entirely to a regular singular in all registers, though older R3a may use weak endings, eg:
  Nerv, Papagei, Pfau, Spatz, Vetter

- *Herr* has the ending -*n* in singular but -*en* in the plural:
  des, dem, den Herrn
  die, der, den Herren

3.2.2 'Mixed' nouns

Eight masculine nouns have a mixture of weak and regular endings, eg:

der Name	die Name**n**
des Name**ns**	der Name**n**
dem Name**n**	den Name**n**
den Name**n**	die Name**n**

The others are:

Buchstabe, Friede [3], Funke [3], Gedanke, Glaube, Same [3], Wille

The neuter noun *Herz* has a similar irregular pattern:

das Herz	die Herz**en**
des Herz**ens**	der Herz**en**
dem Herz**en**	den Herz**en**
das Herz	die Herz**en**

3.2.3 Dative -*e*

Masculine and neuter nouns of one syllable may add -*e* in dative singular, eg:

dem Mann**e**, dem Kind**e**, dem Bild**e**, dem Tisch**e**

This is restricted to R3a and it has become rather unusual even there over the last 50 years. However, it is still normal in a few set phrases and idioms, eg:

- Always **-e**:

im Grund**e** genommen	unter Tag**e** arbeiten
bei Licht**e** betrachtet	zu Werk**e** gehen
am Rand**e** bemerkt	im Zug**e** sein
jdn zu Rat**e** ziehen	

- Usually **-e** in R2/R3, but often no **-e** in R1:

im Fall**e**	auf dem Land**e**
bis zu einem gewissen Grad**e**	im Lauf**e** des Tages
in hohem Grad**e**	im Licht**e**
zum Hals**e** heraushängen	in gewissem Maß**e**
nach Haus**e**, zu Haus**e**	im Sand**e** verlaufen
von Haus**e** aus	im Schwung**e** sein
aus dem Jahr**e** 1897	in diesem Sinn**e**
im Jahr**e** 1983	zum Zug**e** kommen

3.2.4 Genitive singular -*(e)s*

(a) -*es* or -*s*?

- Nouns ending in -*s*, -*ß*, -*sch*, or -*z* always add -*es*, eg:

  des Haus**es**, des Fuß**es**, des Tisch**es**, des Netz**es**

- Nouns of more than one syllable or ending in a vowel add -*s*, eg:

  des König**s**, des Bürgertum**s**, des Lehrer**s**, der Auto**s**, des Bau**s**

>>>→

- Nouns of one syllable ending in a consonant add *-es* in R3, eg:
  des Tag**es**, des Buch**es**
  But they often just add *-s* in R1/R2, eg:
  des Tag**s**, des Buch**s**

(b)   **The genitive singular ending is omitted in:**

- Foreign nouns ending in *-s*, eg:
  des Organismus, des Atlas (NOTE: des Bus**ses**)

- Adverbs, pronouns, etc used as nouns; also abbreviations
  (NOTE: sometimes *-s* in R3), eg:
  des Ich, des Aber, des LKW, des EKG (R3: des Ich**s**, des LKW**s**, etc)

- Many foreign words and names, especially in R3b, eg:
  des britischen Establishment
  die Werke des Barock

- Foreign geographical names, eg:
  die Berge des High Peak

- With months, eg:
  des Januar, des Mai

- With days of the week, eg:
  des Montag, des Mittwoch

- With prepositions if no article (NOTE: R3a *always* has *-s*), eg:
  wegen Geldmangel
  R3a: wegen Geldmangel**s**

- Names preceded by article (NOTE: R1/R2 increasingly has *-s*), eg:
  des modernen Deutschland
  R1/R2: des modernen Deutschland**s**

(c)   **Usage with personal names**

- Personal names have *-s* and precede, eg:
  Sabine**s** Fahrrad, Vati**s** Auto

- Multiple names: last one has *-s*; the genitive phrase may precede or
  follow, eg:
  Helmut Kohl**s** Politik OR die Politik Helmut Kohl**s**

- Noun + name: name has *-s*; the genitive phrase may precede or
  follow, eg:
  der Sieg Kaiser Wilhelm**s** OR Kaiser Wilhelm**s** Sieg

- *Herr* + name: both decline, eg:
  Herr**n** Pauli**s** Einladung

- Article + noun + name: noun and article decline, eg:
  der Sieg **des** Kaiser**s** Wilhelm

- Name + article + adjective: all decline, eg:
  der Sieg Wilhelm**s** **des** Zweite**n**

3.3 Verbs: strong and weak

There are two main classes of verb in German, the 'weak' verbs, which have a *-t-* suffix in the past tense and past participle, and 'strong' verbs, which have vowel changes. The weak verbs are far more numerous, but the strong verbs account for a good proportion of the really common verbs.

3.3.1 Strong verb classes

Although there is no way of telling from the infinitive whether a verb is strong or weak, and so no real alternative to learning which verbs are strong, the strong verbs with their principle parts do fall into recognizable groups which can help them to be remembered.

(a) Present tense in -ei-

bl**ei**ben	bl**ie**b	gebl**ie**ben
b**ei**ßen	b**i**ß	geb**i**ssen

(i) Like *bleiben* are:
gedeihen (R3), leihen, meiden, preisen, reiben, schneiden, schreien, schreiben, schweigen (R3), steigen, treiben, verzeihen, weisen

(ii) Like *beißen* are:
erbleichen, gleiten, greifen, kneifen, pfeifen, reißen, scheißen (R1*), schleichen, schmeißen (R1), schreiten (R3), streichen, streiten, vergleichen, weichen

Exceptions:

l**ei**den	l**i**tt	gel**itt**en
h**ei**ßen	h**ie**ß	geh**ei**ssen
schn**ei**den	schn**itt**	geschn**itt**en

(b) Present tense in -i-

b**i**nden	b**a**nd	geb**u**nden
schw**i**mmen	schw**a**mm	geschw**o**mmen

(i) Like *binden* are:
dringen, gelingen, klingen, ringen, singen, sinken, springen, stinken, trinken, verschwinden, zwingen

(ii) Like *schwimmen* are:
beginnen, gewinnen, rinnen, sinnen, spinnen

Exception:

s**i**tzen	s**a**ß	ges**ess**en

R1* = vulgar
R1 = informal colloquial
R2 = neutral
R3 = formal
R3a = literary
R3b = non-literary
(see 1.1.5)

N = North
C = Central
S = South
SW = South West
SE = South East
AU = Austria
CH = Switzerland
(see 1.2.3)

(c) **Present tense in -ie-**

biegen   bog   gebogen

Like *biegen* are:
   bieten, fliegen, fliehen, fließen, frieren, gießen, kriechen, riechen,
   schieben, schießen, schließen, verlieren, wiegen

Exceptions: liegen   lag   gelegen
               ziehen   zog   gezogen

(d) **Present tense in -e-**

helfen   half   geholfen
geben   gab   gegeben
fechten   focht   gefochten

(i)   Like *helfen* are:
     befehlen, bergen, bersten, brechen, empfehlen, erschrecken,
     gelten, sprechen, stechen, stehlen, sterben, treffen, verderben,
     werben, werfen

(ii) Like *geben* are:
     fressen, genesen[†], geschehen, lesen, messen, sehen, treten,
     vergessen

(iii) Like *fechten* are:
     bewegen[†] (R3), flechten, heben[†], scheren[†], schmelzen,
     schwellen, weben

Exceptions: essen   aß   gegessen
              nehmen   nahm   genommen
              werden   wurde (R3a: ward) geworden

NOTE: all the verbs in **-e-** *except* those marked [†] change the vowel in
the second and third person singular of the present tense and the
second person imperative, eg:
   helfen: du hilfst, er hilft, hilf!
In most cases the vowel is **-i-**, eg:
   er bricht, spricht, gibt
     NOTE: er nimmt, tritt, wird
Some verbs with a long **-e-** change this to **-ie-**, eg:
   er befiehlt, es geschieht, er liest, sieht, stiehlt

(e) **Present tense in -a-**

fahren   fuhr   gefahren
fallen   fiel   gefallen

(i) Like *fahren* are:
     backen, graben, laden, schaffen, tragen, wachsen, waschen

(ii) Like *fallen* are:
     blasen, braten, halten, lassen, raten, schlafen

Exception: fangen   fing   gefangen

All these verbs (with the exception of *schaffen*) have Umlaut in the
second and third person singular of the present tense, eg:
   du fährst   er fährt
     NOTE: er hält, lädt, rät

(f) Other strong verbs

These do not fit into any of the above groups.

betrügen	betrog	betrogen	
erlöschen (R3)	erlosch	erloschen	(er erlischt)
gehen	ging	gegangen	
hängen	hing	gehangen	
kommen	kam	gekommen	
laufen	lief	gelaufen	(er läuft)
lügen	log	gelogen	
rufen	rief	gerufen	
saufen	soff	gesoffen	(er säuft)
schwören	schwor	geschworen	
stehen	stand	gestanden	
stoßen	stieß	gestoßen	(er stößt)
tun	tat	getan	

3.3.2 Deceptive weak verbs

Of course, any compound or derivative of a strong verb follows the strong pattern. There are, however, a few verbs which look deceptively like strong verbs, but are in fact weak and quite regular, eg:

veranlassen   veranlaßte   veranlaßt

Other examples:

beantragen, beauftragen, begleiten (R3), beinhalten, fehlen, handhaben, verleiden

3.3.3 Irregular weak verbs

brennen	brannte	gebrannt
kennen	kannte	gekannt
nennen	nannte	genannt
rennen	rannte	gerannt
senden	sandte	gesandt (see **3.3.4(b)**)
wenden	wandte	gewandt (see **3.3.4(a)**)
bringen	brachte	gebracht
denken	dachte	gedacht
mahlen	mahlte	gemahlen
salzen	salzte	gesalzen
spalten	spaltete	gespalten
wissen	wußte	gewußt

NOTE: *wissen* is irregular in the present:

ich weiß	wir wissen
du weißt	ihr wißt
er weiß	sie wissen

3.3.4 Verbs with strong and weak forms

Some verbs have both strong (or irregular) and weak forms. In some instances there is no distinction in meaning (but then usually with regional or register differences), but there is in others.

(a) Strong and weak forms without a meaning difference

backen	buk (R3) backte	gebacken	er bäckt er backt (R1, S)
fragen	frug (N, R3) fragte	gefragt	er frägt (R1) er fragt
hauen	hieb (R3) haute	gehauen gehaut (S)	
melken	molk (R3a) melkte	gemolken gemelkt (R1)	
saugen	sog saugte	gesogen gesaugt	(both equally frequent; weak forms especially in R1 and R3b)
schmelzen	schmolz schmelzte (R3a)	geschmolzen geschmelzt (R3a)	
stecken	stak (R3a) steckte	gesteckt	(*stak* only if intransitive)
weben	wob (R3) webte	gewoben (R3) gewebt	
wenden	wandte (R3) wendete	gewandt (R3) gewendet	

(b) Strong and weak forms with a meaning distinction

hängen **hängen**	hing hängte	gehangen gehängt	*to hang* (itr) *to hang sth* (tr)
erlöschen (R3)	erlosch	erloschen	*to go out* (eg fire, light)
löschen	löschte	gelöscht	*to put sth out* (eg fire, light)
schaffen **schaffen**	schuf schaffte	geschaffen geschafft	*to create* *to manage* (SW also = *to work*)
scheren **scheren**	schor scherte	geschoren geschert	*to shear, shave* *to concern*
schleifen **schleifen**	schliff schleifte	geschliffen geschleift	*to sharpen* *to drag*
erschrecken (R3) **erschrecken**	erschrak erschreckte	erschrocken erschreckt	*to be frightened* (itr) *to frighten sb* (tr)

senden (R3)	sandte	gesandt	*to send*
senden	sendete	gesendet	*to broadcast*
bewegen (R3)	bewog	bewogen	*to induce sb*
bewegen	bewegte	bewegt	*to move*
weichen	wich	gewichen	*to yield*
weichen	weichte	geweicht	*to soak*

3.4 Determiners and adjectives

The inflection of articles and adjectives seems the most daunting area of German grammar to the native speaker of English. However, it is central to the way in which German works, and acquiring confidence in using these inflections correctly is a crucial aspect of mastering the language. Without this, it is very difficult to express oneself properly in German or to be taken seriously by German speakers as having an adequate command of the language. They are presented below as simply and concisely as possible, concentrating on areas of difficulty and uncertainties in usage, but they can be assimilated only through practice in real phrases and sentences, not through tables. Article endings in particular are absolutely vital, because, more than any endings on the noun itself, they show gender, case and number and so provide the clues as to how the sentence is constructed and what it means.

> R1* = vulgar
> R1 = informal
>   colloquial
> R2 = neutral
> R3 = formal
> R3a = literary
> R3b = non-literary
> (see 1.1.5)

> N = North
> C = Central
> S = South
> SW = South West
> SE = South East
> AU = Austria
> CH = Switzerland
> (see 1.2.3)

An important principle is that if the determiner has an unambiguous suffix to show gender, case and number, then a following adjective can have a 'weaker' ending (*-e* or *-en*). If there is no determiner, or it has no ending, then the adjective has to have the most distinctive endings (often called 'strong'). Determiners and adjectives thus back each other up in making it clear what gender, case and number we are dealing with.

3.4.1 Basic determiner endings

The basic set of unambiguous endings is best seen on the demonstrative *dieser*:

	Masc	*Fem*	*Neuter*	*Plural*
Nom	dies**er**	dies**e**	dies**es**	dies**e**
Acc	dies**en**	dies**e**	dies**es**	dies**e**
Gen	dies**es**	dies**er**	dies**es**	dies**er**
Dat	dies**em**	dies**er**	dies**em**	dies**en**

All articles and similar words have endings related to this basic set. Many decline like *dieser*:

> **aller, einiger, etlicher, folgender, irgendwelcher, jeder, jener, mancher, sämtlicher, solcher, welcher**

A few are only used in the plural:

> **beide, mehrere, viele, wenige**

The definite article is rather like *dieser*:

	Masc	Fem	Neuter	Plural
Nom	der	die	das	die
Acc	den	die	das	die
Gen	des	der	des	der
Dat	dem	der	dem	den

The indefinite articles *ein* and *kein* and the possessives *mein, dein, sein, unser, euer* and *ihr* decline like *dieser except* that they have *no ending* in the nominative singular masculine and neuter and the accusative singular neuter, eg:

	Masc	Fem	Neuter	Plural
Nom	mein	meine	mein	meine
Acc	meinen	meine	mein	meine
Gen	meines	meiner	meines	meiner
Dat	meinem	meiner	meines	meinen

3.4.2 Basic adjective endings

- Adjectives not preceded by a determiner have endings like *dieser* in **3.4.1** (so-called strong endings):

  starker Wein, klare Luft, brave Kinder
  in hohem Grad, mit größter Vorsicht
  durch tadelloses Benehmen

  except that the genitive singular masculine and neuter ends in *-en* (R3):

  starken Weines, frohen Herzens

- Adjectives preceded by a determiner which has no ending also have these endings:

  manch braver Mann (R3a)
  solch hartes Los (R3a)
  mit viel kaltem Wasser

  This is so with the endingless *ein, mein*, etc:

  ein solcher Tisch, ein kleines Schiff
  mein neuer Mantel, sein krankes Herz
  unser treuer Hund, ihr rotes Kleid

- On the other hand, when the adjective is preceded by a determiner with a full ending, the endings are:

  -e in the nominative singular (all genders) and the accusative singular feminine and neuter
  -en in **all** other cases

  These are usually called weak endings. For example:

	Masc	Fem	Neuter	Plural
Nom	der neue Tag	die blaue Luft	das weite Tal	die weiten Täler
Acc	den neuen Tag	die blaue Luft	das weite Tal	die weiten Täler
Gen	des neuen Tages	der blauen Luft	des weiten Tals	der weiten Täler
Dat	dem neuen Tags	der blauen Luft	dem weiten Tal	der weiten Tälern

3.4.3 Uncertainties and variation in current usage

In certain instances usage is not fixed and there are variants and alternatives.

- *aller, mancher, solcher, welcher* nowadays usually have *-en* in genitive singular masculine and neuter **if** the noun has the ending *-(e)s* (in practice found in R3 only), eg:

    trotz all**en** Eifers
    sich manch**en** Tages erinnern
    solch**en** Gedankens
    welch**en** Fortschritts

    jeder is tending to follow the same pattern, if not always, eg:

    am Ende jed**en** Abschnitts
    OR
    am Ende jed**es** Abschnitts

- When there is more than one adjective before a noun they all have the same ending, eg:

    bei nachhaltend**er**, andauernd**er** Wirkung

    However, in the dative singular masculine and neuter, a second adjective often has *-en* in R3, eg:

    mit unverantwortlich**em** individuell**en** Fehlverhalten (frequent R3)
    mit unverantwortlich**em** individuell**em** Fehlverhalten (more usual)

- After a pronoun the strong endings are the rule, eg:

    du arm**er** Bursch
    mit mir jung**em** Kerl

    However, *-en* is now usual after *wir* and *ihr*, eg:

    wir fremd**en** Leute
    ihr lieb**en** Kinder

    uns and *euch*, though, are usually followed by *-e*, eg:

    das geht uns Deutsch**e** an
    gegen euch arm**e** Leute

- Colour adjectives from nouns are not usually declined in R2 and R3, eg:

    ein rosa Kleid
    ein lila Hemd

    But they often are in R1, usually with an *-n-* after the vowel, eg:

    ein rosa**nes** Kleid
    ein lila**nes** Hemd

- Adjectives in *-er* from city names are never declined, eg:

    die Frankfurter Messe
    die Berliner Autobahn

The declension of adjectives after some of the indefinite determiners and pronouns is particularly subject to variation and uncertainty in all registers. Current usage in the plural, where these words are most often found, is as follows:

- *alle*, *beide*, *sämtliche* are usually followed by weak endings, eg:
  alle fremd**en** Truppen
  aller fremd**en** Truppen
  allen fremd**en** Truppen
  In R3 the genitive plural is occasionally strong, eg:
  aller fremd**er** Truppen

- *solche* and *irgendwelche* may be followed by weak or strong endings. Weak endings are more common, eg:
  solche gut**en** (gute) Freunde
  solcher gut**en** (gut**er**) Freunde
  solchen gut**en** Freunden

- *manche* may be followed by weak or strong endings. Strong endings are more common, eg:
  manche gut**e** (gut**en**) Freunde
  mancher gut**er** (gut**en**) Freunde
  manchen gut**en** Freunden

- *einige*, *etliche*, *folgende*, *mehrere*, *viele*, *wenige* are usually followed by strong endings, eg:
  viele gut**e** Freunde
  vieler gut**er** Freunde
  vielen gut**en** Freunden

- In R3 the genitive plural is occasionally weak, eg:
  vieler gut**en** Freunde

Some determiners may be used in combination with others, and when this occurs the second of them will usually decline like an adjective. The following such combinations are common:

die beiden . . .	die beiden Postkarten
both . . ., the two . . .	diese beiden Postkarten
die folgende . . .	die folgende Erläuterung
the following . . .	die folgenden Worte
ein jeder (. . .)	eines jeden Pastors
*any (. . .) (see **3.5.6**)*	einer jeden Mutter
der meine, etc	das meine, dem deinen
*mine, etc (see **3.5.3**)*	der Ihre, den unseren
der sämtliche . . .	das sämtliche Geld
all the . . .	mein sämtliches Geld
ein solcher . . .	ein solches Wetter
*such a . . . (see **3.5.6**)*	einem solchen Betrüger
viele solche . . .	viele solche Menschen
many such . . .	vieler solcher Versuche

die vielen . . .	die vielen Anwesenden
the many . . .	dieser vielen Reisen
die wenigen . . .	die wenigen Besucher
the few . . .	der wenigen Schallplatten
einige wenige . . .	einiger weniger Großstädte
a few . . .	einigen wenigen Stunden

With declined *alle*, however, the second word keeps its own declension (see **3.5.6**):

alle die . . .	alle die Bände
all the . . .	alle diese Operationen
alle meine . . ., etc	alle meine Freunde
all my . . ., etc	allen Ihren Träumen

3.4.4 Adjectives as nouns

In German almost any adjective may be used as a noun. This is not possible in English, and these forms often create confusion for English learners. We have to use adjectives with 'dummy' nouns such as *man, woman, person, people, one, things* to express the same idea, eg:

der Alte	*the old man*
die Alte	*the old woman*
das Wichtige	*the important thing*
Wichtiges	*important things*
Abwesende	*people absent*
die Zuhörenden	*the people listening*
ein Singender	*someone singing*
das Grüne	*the green one*

In all instances the adjective used as a noun retains its adjective endings. This is always a major source of error even for advanced learners and is worth illustrating fully:

der Beamte	*the civil servant*	die Beamten	*the civil servants*
des Beamten		die Beamten	
dem Beamten		den Beamten	
den Beamten		die Beamten	

ein Beamter	*a civil servant*	Beamte	*civil servants*
eines Beamten		Beamter	
einem Beamten		Beamten	
einen Beamten		Beamte	

Similarly: *einige Beamte, alle Beamten, solche Beamte(n)*, etc.

Many of these adjectives used as nouns are the equivalent of ordinary nouns in English, and the following are very frequent. In most instances they can be used as masculine or feminine with an appropriate article, eg: *der Fremde*, 'the (male) stranger', *die Fremde*, 'the (female) stranger'. The exception to this is *die Beamtin*, 'the (female) civil servant'.

der/die Abgeordnete	*representative*
Angehörige	*member*
Angestellte	*employee*
Arbeitslose	*unemployed person*
Bekannte	*acquaintance*
Deutsche	*German*
Einheimische	*local*
Erwachsene	*adult*
Farbige	*black person*
Freiwillige	*volunteer*
Fremde	*stranger*
Gefangene	*prisoner*
Geistliche	*clergyman*
Gelehrte	*scholar*
Gesandte (R3)	*emissary*
Geschworene	*jury member*
Heilige	*saint*
Industrielle	*industrialist*
Jugendliche (R3b)	*young person*
Reisende	*traveller*
Verlobte	*fiancé(e)*
Verwandte	*relative*
Vorbeigehende	*passer-by*
Vorgesetzte	*superior*
Vorsitzender	*chairman*

A few are always feminine:

die Diagonale	*diagonal*
Horizontale	*horizontal*
Illustrierte	*magazine*
Linke	*left (side), left hand, (political) left*
Moderne (R3)	*modern times*
Rechte	*right (side), right hand*

A few are always neuter:

das Äußere	*outside*
das Freie	*open (air)*
Gehacktes	*mince*
das Innere	*inside*

In R1, the names of German regions are often given by using a neuter adjective:

das Bayerische	*Bavaria*
im Hessischen	*in Hesse*

Note the neuter adjectives with *alles*, *etwas*, *viel* and *nichts*:

alles Gute	*all good things*	**dat**: allem Guten
etwas Gutes	*something good*	**dat**: etwas Gutem
viel Gutes	*many good things*	**dat**: viel Gutem
nichts Gutes	*nothing good*	**dat**: nichts Gutem

Names of languages usually appear in the form of a neuter adjective which is in most cases not declined, eg:

Wir lernen **Spanisch, Französisch, Russisch, Englisch**
In Hannover soll man das beste **Deutsch** sprechen
der Unterschied zum heutigen **Deutsch**
die Aussprache des modernen **Deutsch**

But with a definite article and no other adjective it *is* declined, eg:

Das Englische ist **dem Deutschen** verwandt.
eine Übersetzung aus **dem Italienischen**

Names of colours are very similar and do not usually decline, eg:

das **Grün** der Wiesen
in **Blau** gekleidet
von einem glänzenden **Rot**
ein häßliches **Gelb**

Only in a few set phrases with the definite article is this colour adjective declined, eg:

ins **Grüne** fahren
das **Blaue** vom Himmel herunter versprechen
ins **Schwarze** treffen

3.5 Other words that decline: forms and uses

3.5.1 Demonstratives

The common demonstrative pronoun and determiner in spoken R1 and R2 is *der*. As a determiner it declines like the definite article. As a pronoun it declines as follows:

	Masc	*Fem*	*Neuter*	*Plural*
Nom	der	die	das	die
Acc	den	die	das	die
Gen	dessen	deren	dessen	deren
Dat	dem	der	dem	denen

- In spoken German *der* can be used for *this* AND *that*, eg:
  der Tisch   *this table* OR *that table*
  den mag ich nicht   *I don't like this one/that one*

- In R1 *da* and *hier* may be added for clarity or emphasis, eg:
  der Tisch **hier**   *this table*
  der Tisch **da**   *that table*
  der da, **der hier**   *that one, this one*

- In R1 *der* is often used for a personal pronoun, eg:
  die macht es nicht (R2 **sie** macht es nicht)

- In R1 the genitive can be used for any possessive, eg:
  deren Kleid (R2 **ihr** Kleid)

- In R3, the genitive may replace an ambiguous possessive, eg:
  sein Freund und **dessen** Bruder *(ie the friend's brother)*

- In the genitive, *derer* 'ought' only to be used before a relative pronoun (R3 only, but see **3.5.2**):
  die Ansichten **derer**, die nicht anwesend waren
  Otherwise *deren* is normal, eg:
  ihre Freunde und **deren** Kinder

- In written R2 and R3 the determiner *der* might be confused with the definite article, and so it is used less, although it is not unknown. There, the common demonstrative is *dieser* (see **3.4.1**).

- *dieser* is used for both *this* AND *that*, eg:
  dieser Tisch   *this table* OR *that table*

- *jener*, 'that', is restricted to R3, and is not common even there. It has two major uses:
  (i) To draw contrast with *dieser*, eg: Herr Schröder wollte nicht dieses altes Buch kaufen, sonder **jenes**.
  (ii) For something well known, especially if a relative pronoun follows, eg: die erhabenen Ruinen **jener** Paläste, welche die deutschen Kaiser bauten

- For emphatic *that*, *derjenige* is increasingly frequent, especially in R3b, either as a pronoun or an adjective. Both parts decline.

  It is used most when a relative clause follows, eg:
  diejenigen, die ich traf
  . . . von **denjenigen** Büchern, **die** ich in der Schule lesen mußte

- Note the usage with a following relative (= *that which*, etc).

  Common R2 and R3 despite repetition, eg:
  die, die ich kaufen wollte
  . . . von **denen, die** gekommen sind

  Old-fashioned R3a (nowadays rare), eg:
  die, welche ich kaufen wollte

  Frequent R3b, eg:
  diejenigen, die ich kaufen wollte

3.5.2   Relative pronouns

The usual relative pronoun (= English *who*, *which*, *that*) in all registers is *der*. Its declension is identical to that of the demonstrative pronoun (see **3.5.1**). The following points of usage are worth noting:

- *welcher* is only found in R3 and is scarce even there, except in CH, eg:
  Usual R3:   der Herr, **der** gestorben war
  Infrequent R3: der Herr, **welcher** gestorben war

- In the genitive plural, *deren* is in practice less common than *derer*, which purists consider incorrect, eg:
  'Correct' R3:   statt **deren** . . . ⎫
  More frequent R3: statt **derer** . . . ⎭ *instead of which*

- After *alles, etwas, nichts, viel, das*, neuter adjectives used as nouns and to refer to whole clauses, the relative pronoun is *was*, eg:
  alles, **was** er hörte
  das Beste, **was** sie gesehen hatte
  etwas, **was** ihm fehlte
  Er sah mich nie direkt an, **was** ich nicht leiden konnte

- In R1 *das* and *was* are often used interchangeably, eg:
  das Zeug, **was** (R2: **das**) man da kriegt
  etwas, **das** (R2: **was**) nicht stimmt

- With prepositions, *der* is now the usual relative in all registers referring to things, eg:
  das Haus, **in dem** wir wohnten
  der Tisch, **auf dem** das Buch lag

- R1 often has *wo* with the prepositional adverb, eg:
  der Tisch, **wo** die Blumen drauf stehen

- The compound *wo* + preposition is found only in old-fashioned R3a, eg:
  das Haus, **worin** wir wohnten
  der Tisch, **worauf** das Buch lag

  Except that *wo* + preposition is used where the simple relative pronoun would be *was*, eg:
  alles, **worüber** sie sprach
  etwas, **womit** er uns schlagen konnte

- *wo* is commonly used after time and place words in R1 and R2, although R3a may prefer other possibilities, eg:
  das Land, **wo** wir wohnen (R3a **in dem**)
  am Tag, **wo** er gekommen ist (R3a **da** OR **an dem**)
  zu einer Zeit, **wo** der Kaiser noch mächtig war (R3a **zu der** OR **da**)
  jetzt, **wo** er fort ist (R3a **da**)

  For English *what* after a preposition, German needs to insert an appropriate form of the demonstrative *das*, eg:
  Er wußte nichts **von dem**, **was** mich dorthin geführt hatte.
  *He knew nothing of **what** had led me there.*

3.5.3 Possessive pronouns

The form selected depends on register:

R1 and R2:   **meiner, deiner**, etc

R3: $\begin{cases} \textbf{der meine, der deine, etc} \\ \textbf{der meinige, der deinige, etc} \end{cases}$

Note that *meiner* declines like *dieser* (see **3.4.1**) and has suffixes in the nominative singular masculine and neuter and the accusative singular neuter, eg:

Das ist nicht mein Koffer, sondern **seiner**.

Ist das Ihr Fahrrad oder **sein(e)s**?

Wollen wir mit eurem Wagen fahren oder mit **unserem**?

The second parts of *der meine, der meinige*, etc decline like adjectives, eg:

mit **der ihrigen**

durch **das meine**

von **den unseren**

3.5.4 Interrogatives

WER?	*wer?*, 'who?', declines for case:
	Nom **wer?** *who?*
	Acc **wen?** *whom?*
	Dat **wem?** *to whom?*
	Gen **wessen?** *whose?*
WESSEN?	*wessen?* is limited to R3 and is scarcely used even there, eg:
	R3 (rare): **Wessen** Bücher sind das?
	R2: $\begin{cases} \textbf{Wem gehören diese Bücher?} \\ \textbf{Von wem sind diese Bücher?} \end{cases}$
WO?	*wo?* + preposition is normally used in R2 for English preposition + *what*, although R1 does use preposition + *was*, eg:
	womit? (R1 **mit was?**) *with what?*
	worin? (R1 **in was?**) *in what?*
	NOTE: **wozu?** (R1 **zu was?**) *what . . . for?*
	For English *where?*, German always distinguishes place (*wo?*) from direction to (*wohin?*) and direction from (*woher?*). *wohin?* and *woher?* are often split in R1, eg:
	Place: **Wo** wohnen Müllers?
	Direction towards: **Wohin** muß ich es stellen? (R1 **Wo** muß ich es **hin**stellen?)
	Direction from: **Woher** kann ich es nehmen? (R1 **Wo** kann ich es **her**nehmen?)
WAS FÜR EIN?	The equivalent of *what sort of?*, eg:
	Er hat einen neuen Wagen. Was für **einer** ist es?
	Mit was für **einem** Zug ist er gekommen?
	Note that the case of *ein* does not depend on *für*.

In R1 *was* is often separated from *für ein*, eg:
  Was hat sie **für einen** Mantel gekauft?

In R1 *was für?* and *welcher?* are used interchangeably, eg:
  Was für ein Hemd ziehst du an? (*which?*; R2 **welches**)
  Welcher Vogel ist das? (*what sort of?*; R2 **was für ein?**)

In N *was für welcher?* is current for 'what sort of?', eg:
  Hast du die Vögel gesehen?
  Was für welche? (*what kind?*; standard German **was für Vögel?**)

3.5.5   *man, einer, jemand*

MAN

man, 'one', unlike its English equivalent, is common in all registers.

In the dative and accusative we find *einem* and *einen*, eg:
  Man weiß nie, ob sie es gut mit **einem** meint

As a possessive, *sein* is used, eg:
  Man kann **sein** Schicksal nicht ändern

It is *never* referred back to by *er*, but always repeated, eg:
  Man dürfte meinen, daß **man** (*not* **er**) jetzt weiterkommen sollte

EINER
KEINER

einer, 'one', and *keiner*, 'none', used as pronouns (ie without a noun following), decline like *dieser* (see **3.4.1**). They thus have an ending in the nominative singular masculine and nominative/accusative singular neuter, unlike the indefinite article, eg:
  eines von diesen wenigen modernen Häusern
  einer der schnellsten Züge
  mit **keinem** ihrer Freunde

They are often used to mean 'somebody' and 'nobody', especially in R1 and S, eg:
  Sie hat wohl **keinen** gesehen (R2 **niemand**)
  Es wird schon **einer** kommen (R2 **jemand**)

JEMAND
NIEMAND

jemand, 'somebody', and *niemand*, 'nobody', have dative and accusative forms *jemandem/niemandem* and *jemanden/niemanden*. However, these do not have to be used.
  The endingless forms are more common in the dative and accusative in all registers, eg:
  Ich habe **niemand** gesehen (less common **niemanden**)
  Sie wird **jemand** geholfen haben (less common **jemandem**)

The declension of *jemand* (*niemand*) *anders*, 'somebody (nobody) else', varies regionally:

	Nom	*Acc*	*Dat*
N + C	jemand anders	jemand(**en**) anders	jemand(**em**) anders
S	jemand ander**er**	jemand(**en**) ander**en**	{ jemand ander**em** { jemand**em** ander**en**

For 'somebody' and 'nobody' *einer* and *keiner* are very common in S. In R1, *wer* is a frequent alternative to *jemand*, eg:
  Es ist **wer** an der Tür

3.5.6 Some indefinites

ALL-	• *alle* = 'everybody', eg:
	    Alle sind gekommen
	NOTE: *alle* also = 'all gone' in R1, eg:
	    Mein Geld ist **alle**

	• *alles* = 'everything'
	    Wir wollen **alles** wissen
	NOTE: in R1, with *wer* or *was*, *alles* emphasizes quantity, eg:
	    Wer will denn **alles** mit?
	    Was will er **alles** gesehen haben?

	• *das alles* OR *alles das* = 'all that', eg:
	    Das alles/alles das geht uns nichts an
	NOTE: in the dative we have *dem allen* (R3 *allem*) OR *all(em) dem*, eg:
	    Von **dem allen/all(em) dem** wissen wir ja gar nichts

	• *aller* = 'all'. It declines like *dieser* (see **3.4.1**): ein Hotel mit **allem** modernen Komfort

	• *all der* = 'all the'. In most instances *all* does not have any endings, eg:
	    all das Geschwätz
	    nach **all** der Mühe

	Similarly with *dieser* and the possessives, eg:
	    nach **all** dieser Mühe
	    nach **all** meiner Mühe

	An exception is that in the nominative/accusative plural *alle* or *alle die* is common for 'all the' besides *all die*, eg:
	    alle (die) Kinder
	    all die Kinder

	Similarly 'all these', 'all my', eg:
	    alle diese Kinder
	    alle meine Kinder
	NOTE: in R1 *die ganzen* = 'all the':
	    die ganzen Kinder

JEDER	*jeder* = 'everybody', 'anybody', eg:
	    Das weiß doch **jeder**
	
	In R1 and R2 *ein jeder* is a more emphatic alternative, eg:
	    Da könnte **ein jeder** kommen

MANCH	*mancher* declines like *dieser* (see **3.4.1**) = 'some', 'many a', eg:
	    Mancher will es nicht wahrhaben
	    manche Arbeitslose
	
	Undeclined *manch*, with *ein* or an adjective, is limited to R3a, eg:
	    Manch einer hatte Mühe
	    manch reiches Land

SOLCH
The German equivalents of English 'such (a)' vary with register.

Singular
R1:	**so ein** (**so'n**), eg:	**so ein** Wetter
R2:	**(ein) solcher**, eg:	**(ein) solches** Wetter
R3:	**solch ein**, eg:	**solch ein** Wetter

Plural
| R1: | **so**, eg: | **so** Gerüchte |
| R2/R3: | **solche**, eg: | **solche** Gerüchte |

solcher declines like *dieser* (see **3.4.1**); *ein solcher* declines as indefinite article plus adjective, eg:
bei **einem solchen** Wetter

VIEL/WENIG
Most frequently these are not declined in the singular, eg:
viel Lärm, **viel** Wasser
wenig Mühe, **wenig** Geld
But they are declined in the plural, eg:
viele Bauern, **wenige** Politiker

Declined forms are found in the singular:
(i)   In nominative and accusative feminine and neuter (older R3 only), eg: **vieles** Rauchen, **viele** Hoffnung
(ii) In a few idioms and phrases, eg: **vielen** Dank, mit **vielem** Fleiß

WELCH
Undeclined *welch* occurs in exclamations in R3 (for R1 *Was für ein . . . !*), eg:
Welch fürchterlicher Tag!

Declined *welcher* is used as an interrogative pronoun or determiner, eg:
Welches Buch nimmst du?
Da sind die Bücher – **welches** willst du nehmen?

In R1 and, less frequently, in R2, it is used as an indefinite pronoun (= 'some', 'any'), eg:
Ich habe schon **welche**
Soll ich dir Brot reichen? – Danke, ich habe **welches**

4 Grammar: cases, tenses and moods

4.1 Verbs and cases

In German, the link between the verb and the other parts of the sentence is provided mainly through the use of cases. Realizing how cases work to form the framework of a sentence is an important step in being able to use German effectively.

With different verbs we find different ways of expressing these links to the rest of the sentence. Some verbs, such as *schlagen*, have an accusative object, some, such as *dienen*, have a dative object, some, such as *geben*, have both an accusative (direct) object and a dative (indirect) object, whilst others, such as *warten*, have a construction with a preposition rather than a case. We can usefully classify verbs in German in terms of what cases, etc, they 'govern' and this is often linked to the meaning of the verb. However, meaning is no sure guide. German provides many examples of verbs which have very similar meanings but govern different cases, eg:

to impress sb	{ **jdn** beeindrucken **jdm** imponieren
to congratulate sb	{ **jdn** beglückwünschen **jdm** gratulieren
to damage sth	{ **etw** (dat) schaden **etw** beschädigen
to laugh at sb	{ **jdn** auslachen **über jdn** lachen

As German uses cases to make the connections between the various parts of the sentence clear, German verbs are often less flexible than their English counterparts and more frequently restricted to use in certain constructions only. It is not unusual to find that whilst an English verb can be used either transitively or intransitively, or with a person or a thing as object, this is not always possible in German, where we may have to use different verbs or different sentence constructions. The following common examples illustrate this:

answer	She answered her friend	Sie antwortete ihrem Freund
	She answered the letter	{ Sie beantwortete den Brief Sie antwortete auf den Brief
climb	The plane climbed (itr)	Das Flugzeug stieg
	We climbed the mountain	Wir bestiegen den Berg
cut	He cut the meat	Er schnitt das Fleisch
	The paper cuts easily (itr)	Das Papier läßt sich leicht schneiden

drop	I dropped the biro	Ich ließ den Kuli fallen
	The stone dropped (itr)	Der Stein fiel
feel	She felt the pain	Sie fühlte den Schmerz
	She feels ill	Sie fühlt sich krank
force	He forced us to do it	Er zwang uns, es zu tun
	He forced it from us	Er erzwang es von uns
grow	The child is growing (itr)	Das Kind wächst
	He grows flowers	Er züchtet Blumen
keep	We kept the book	Wir behielten das Buch
	These apples will keep (itr)	Diese Äpfel halten sich gut
leak	The boat leaks (itr)	Das Boot leckt
	It is leaking water	Es läßt Wasser durch
leave	He left today (itr)	Er fuhr heute ab
	He left the town	Er verließ die Stadt
open	They opened the door	{ Sie machten die Tür auf (R1/R2)
		{ Sie öffneten die Tür (R2/R3)
	The door opened (itr)	{ Die Tür ging auf (R1/R2)
		{ Die Tür öffnete sich (R2/R3)
pour	He poured wine into the glass	Er goß Wein ins Glas
	The wine poured out of the glass (itr)	Der Wein strömte aus dem Glas
sell	We sold the books quickly	Wir verkauften die Bücher schnell
	The books sold quickly (itr)	Die Bücher verkauften sich schnell
sink	The ship sank (itr)	Das Schiff sank
	We sank the ship	Wir versenkten das Schiff
stand	It is standing in the corner (itr)	Es steht in der Ecke
	She stood it in the corner	Sie stellte es in die Ecke
wake up	We woke up (itr)	Wir wachten auf/erwachten (R3)
	He woke us up	Er weckte uns/erweckte uns (R3)
walk	We walked home (itr)	Wir gingen nach Hause
	He walked her home	Er brachte (R3 begleitete) sie nach Hause
wash	I washed at seven (itr)	Ich habe mich um sieben gewaschen
	I washed the dog	Ich habe den Hund gewaschen

Many further similar examples may be found in section **2.1.1**. In a great number of cases a transitive verb can be formed from an intransitive with the prefix *be-* (see **2.3.3**).

   In the remainder of this section we shall give lists of common verbs classified according to the cases or prepositions they govern, concentrating particularly on those which cause difficulty because of their difference from their usual English equivalents, and on those which have different constructions with different meanings. It should be clear that, for the foreign learner, it is vital to commit German verbs to memory in typical constructions (eg *einem etwas mitteilen, auf den Hans warten*, etc). For this reason all German verbs in this book are given with an indication of their usual constructions.

NOTE: throughout this section, [†] indicates a verb with which more than one construction is possible (see **4.1.6**).

4.1.1   Verbs governing the dative

A large number of German verbs have a dative as their only object; in many cases this dative object is a person who in some way benefits from or is disadvantaged by the action expressed in the verb. The following are typical examples:

antworten[†]:	Der Junge hat **mir** auf meine Frage geantwortet
begegnen (R3):	Sie ist **einem älteren Herrn** begegnet
danken:	Ich danke **Ihnen** sehr für Ihre Mühe
drohen:	Er drohte **dem kleinen Jungen** mit einem Stock
einfallen:	Zu diesem Thema fiel **dem Mädchen** nichts ein
gehören[†]:	Dieser Wagen gehört **dir** doch nicht
gratulieren:	Sie wollte **ihrer Freundin** zum Geburtstag gratulieren
helfen:	Er hilft **seiner Mutter** bei der Arbeit
nutzen:	Das nutzt **ihnen** doch gar nichts
raten:	Er wollte **seinem Sohn** raten, lieber in Gießen zu studieren
schmeicheln:	Damit hat sie natürlich **dem Professor** schmeicheln wollen

> [†] verb with which more than one construction is possible

Other common verbs which govern the dative are:

jdm absagen	jdm imponieren
jdm ähneln	jdm kündigen[†]
etw (dat) angehören	etw (dat) lauschen (R3)
jdm auffallen	jdm/etw (dat) mißtrauen
jdm/etw (dat) ausweichen	jdm passen[†]
jdm befehlen	jdm passieren[†]
jdm bekommen[†] (R3)	jdm/etw (dat) schaden
jdm bevorstehen (R3)	jdm/etw (dat) trauen
jdm dienen[†]	jdm/etw (dat) trotzen
jdm einfallen	jdm/etw (dat) unterliegen
jdm einleuchten	jdm vertrauen
jdm/etw (dat) folgen	etw (dat) vorbeugen
jdm gehorchen	etw (dat) vorstehen
jdm gelten	jdm wehtun
jdm genügen	jdm ziemen (R3)
jdm geschehen	jdm zürnen (R3)
jdm/etw (dat) gleichen	jdm zustoßen
jdm helfen	jdm/etw (dat) zuvorkommen

Apart from these, it can be taken as a rule that verbs with the following prefixes have an object in the dative (though some have an object in the accusative as well, see **4.1.2**):

bei-, ent-, entgegen-, nach-, wider-, zu-

For example:

---

jdm **bei**stehen (R3)
etw (dat) **ent**sprechen
jdm **entgegen**kommen
jdm **nach**schauen
jdm **wider**fahren (R3)
jdm/etw (dat) **zu**hören

- In a few verbs the German dative corresponds to the subject of the most obvious equivalent verb in English.

etw entfällt *mir*	*I* forget sth
es fällt *mir* **leicht, schwer**	*I* find sth easy, difficult
etw fehlt/mangelt *mir*	
es fehlt/mangelt *mir* **an etw** (dat)	*I* lack sth
etw gefällt *mir*	*I* like sth
etw geht *mir* **auf**	*I* realize sth
etw gelingt *mir*	*I* succeed in sth
es liegt[†] *mir* **viel an etw** (dat)	*I* am keen on sth
etw liegt[†] *mir*	*I* fancy sth
es reicht *mir*	*I* have had enough
etw schmeckt[†] *mir*	*I* like sth (food)

- With the following impersonal verbs, the dative corresponds to an English subject. Unless indicated, they are restricted to R3a.

mir **bangt vor etw** (dat)	*I* am afraid of sth
mir (OR *mich*) **ekelt vor etw** (dat)	*I* am disgusted by sth
mir (OR *mich*) **graut vor etw** (dat)	*I* am terrified by sth
mir (OR *mich*) **schaudert vor etw** (dat)	*I* tremble at sth
mir **schwindelt** (R2)	*I* feel dizzy

4.1.2   Verbs governing the dative and the accusative

- In the main, the important group of *jdm etw* verbs typically includes verbs of giving and taking, informing, and doing something to somebody's advantage or disadvantage. The accusative object is a thing, the dative a person, eg:

anbieten:	Die Firma hat **mir eine Stelle** angeboten
empfehlen:	Ich kann **dir diesen Film** sehr empfehlen
geben:	Er hat **seinem Freund das Buch** gegeben
gönnen:	Ich will **mir** jetzt **etw Ruhe** gönnen

⟫→

kaufen:	Sie will **ihrer Mutter Blumen** kaufen
leihen[†]:	Mein Bruder hat **ihr sein Fahrrad** geliehen
mitteilen:	Ich habe **Ihnen meine neue Adresse** mitgeteilt
nehmen:	Wir haben **ihr die Tasche** genommen
verweigern:	Ich kann **dir diese Bitte** nicht verweigern

The German dative thus commonly corresponds to an English prepositional phrase with *to* or *from*, or to an English indirect object (eg *he gave **his friend** the book*).

- The group is far too large to allow anything approaching a comprehensive listing. Some typical common verbs are:

anvertrauen	ersetzen	nehmen	verschaffen
beibringen	erzählen	reichen[†]	verzeihen
besorgen	gewähren	schenken	vorlegen
beweisen	liefern	schulden	wünschen
bringen	melden	stehlen	zeigen
erlauben	nahelegen	verkaufen	

- With some verbs the German dative and accusative construction is rather different from that of the nearest English equivalent:

etw einem Brief beifügen (R3b)	to enclose sth with a letter
etw etw (dat) **entnehmen**[†] (R3)	to infer/gather sth from sth
jdm etw ermöglichen	to make sth possible for sb
jdm etw erschweren	to make sth difficult for sb
jdm etw mitteilen	to inform sb of sth
jdm etw nachmachen	to copy sth from sb
jdm etw umbinden	to tie sth round sb
jdm etw verschweigen	not to tell sb about sth

- Where the dative is some kind of beneficiary (ie = English *for*) it is increasingly common in German in all registers to use a phrase with *für* rather than a dative, eg:
    Sie will **ihr/für sie** Blumen kaufen
    Er hat **uns/für uns** die Tür aufgemacht
    Die Mutter hat **ihm/für ihn** eine Wurst gekocht
This is especially the case if there is ambiguity:
    Er hat **seinem Vater** einen Brief geschrieben
Does this mean '*to* his father' or '*for* his father'?
But the following is quite clear:
    Er hat **für seinen Vater** einen Brief geschrieben

- With some verbs of sending, etc, a phrase with *an* (acc) may be used rather than a dative. The effect is to emphasize the person on the receiving end, eg:
    Er schickte das Manuskript **an** die Universität Passau
    Er verkaufte sein altes Fahrrad **an** meinen Freund Peter
    Er schrieb einen langen Brief **an** seine Großmutter
This may also have the side effect of resolving an ambiguity.

- Many verbs governing dative and accusative may be used with a dative reflexive, eg:

  Ich will **mir** Ruhe gönnen
  Du erlaubst **dir** aber viel
  Das hat er **sich** aber nicht verweigern wollen

- With the following verbs a dative reflexive with an accusative object is the usual construction in the given meaning:

sich (dat) etw aneignen	to acquire sth
sich (dat) etw anmaßen (R3)	to claim sth
sich (dat) etw einbilden	to imagine sth
sich (dat) etw verbitten	to refuse to tolerate sth
sich (dat) etw vornehmen	to intend to do sth
sich (dat) jdn vornehmen (R1)	to have a word with sb
sich (dat) etw vorstellen	to imagine sth

- With others the reflexive is accusative and the object dative:

sich jdm/etw (dat) anpassen	to adapt to sb/sth
sich jdm/etw (dat) anschließen	to join sb/sth
sich jdm/etw (dat) ergeben†	to give in to sb/sth
sich jdm/etw (dat) fügen	to bow to sb/sth
sich jdm/etw (dat) nähern	to approach sb/sth
sich jdm/etw (dat) widersetzen	to oppose sb/sth

> † verb with which more than one construction is possible

4.1.3 Verbs governing the genitive

The use of the genitive with verbs is very limited in modern German and totally restricted to R3. Many are peculiar to legal R3b. We give here a list of those verbs still widely found with a genitive in R3, together with their usual equivalents in R2.

	R3	R2
Verbs governing a genitive object alone	jds/etw (gen) bedürfen jds/etw (gen) gedenken jds/etw (gen) harren	jdn/etw brauchen an jdn/etw denken auf jdn/etw warten
Verbs governing a genitive and an accusative object	jdn etw (gen) anklagen jdn etw (gen) befreien jdn etw (gen) berauben jdn etw (gen) beschuldigen ⎫ jdn etw (gen) überführen ⎬ jdn etw (gen) verdächtigen ⎭ jdn etw (gen) entbinden jdn etw (gen) überzeugen jdn etw (gen) versichern	jdn wegen etw (gen) (R1: etw (dat)) anklagen jdn von etw (dat) befreien jdm etw rauben legal terms used with acc object only in R2 jdn von etw (dat) entbinden jdn von etw (dat) überzeugen jdm etw versichern

≫→

Reflexive verbs governing a genitive	sich jds/etw (gen) annehmen	sich um jdn kümmern
	sich etw (gen) bedienen†	etw benutzen
	sich jds/etw (gen) bemächtigen	jdn/etw in seine Gewalt bringen
	sich jds/etw (gen) entsinnen	sich an jdn/etw entsinnen
	sich jds erbarmen	mit jdm Mitleid haben
	sich etw (gen) erfreuen	etw genießen
	sich jds/etw (gen) erinnern	sich an jdn/etw erinnern
	sich jds/etw (gen) erwehren	jdn/etw abwehren
	sich etw (gen) rühmen	auf etw stolz sein
	sich jds/etw (gen) schämen†	sich wegen jds/etw (gen) schämen

A few other verb constructions with the genitive are found in set phrases. These are mainly restricted to R3, eg:
der Gefahr nicht achten
jdn eines Besseren belehren
sich eines Besseren besinnen
jeder Grundlage entbehren
sich etw (gen) nicht enthalten können
der Ruhe pflegen
jeder Beschreibung spotten
jdn des Landes verweisen
eines Amtes walten
jdn keines Blickes würdigen

> † verb with which more than one construction is possible

4.1.4 Verbs governing a prepositional object

A great many verbs are followed by an object introduced by a preposition. These are quite different from usual prepositional phrases, as the preposition involved loses its full meaning, and the choice of preposition is totally dependent on the individual verb. The learner therefore has to treat each combination of verb and preposition separately and remember the verb and preposition as a whole.

NOTE: for the use of the prepositional adverb (*da(r)* + preposition) when these verbs are followed by an infinitive phrase or a *daß*-clause, see **4.1.5**.

AN (dat)

For prepositional objects the dative is commoner than the accusative, often with the idea of 'in respect of', 'in connection with':

an etw (dat) arbeiten	**an** etw (dat) mitwirken†
jdn/etw **an** etw (dat) erkennen	sich **an** etw (dat) orientieren
an etw (dat) erkranken	etw **an** jdm rächen
sich **an** jdm/etw (dat) freuen	**an** etw (dat) riechen†
an etw (dat) gewinnen†	etw **an** jdm sehen†
an jdm/etw (dat) hängen	**an** etw (dat) sterben
jdn **an** etw (dat) hindern	**an** etw (dat) teilnehmen
jdn **an** etw (dat) interessieren	**an** etw (dat) verlieren†
an etw (dat) leiden	**an** etw (dat) zweifeln
an jdm/etw (dat) liegen†	

NOTE: es fehlt jdm **an** etw (dat) (see **4.1.1**)

AN (acc)	A few verbs, mainly of mental processes:

an jdn/etw denken[†]   sich **an** jdn/etw gewöhnen
sich **an** jdn/etw entsinnen[†]   **an** jdn/etw glauben[†]
sich **an** jdn/etw erinnern[†]   sich **an** jdn/etw halten[†]

AUF (dat)	The dative is found with very few verbs, all of which express very clearly the idea of not moving:

auf etw (dat) basieren (R3)   **auf** etw (dat) bestehen[†]
auf etw (dat) beharren (R3)   **auf** etw (dat) fußen (R3)
auf etw (dat) beruhen

AUF (acc)	The most common preposition with verbs:

auf jdn/etw achten[†]   **auf** jdn/etw lauern
auf jdn/etw aufpassen   **auf** etw pfeifen[†] (R1)
auf etw aussein   **auf** etw pochen (R3)
sich **auf** jdn/etw berufen[†]   **auf** etw reagieren
auf jdn/etw beschränken   **auf** jdn/etw rechnen[†]
sich **auf** jdn/etw beziehen[†]   **auf** jdn/etw schimpfen[†] (R3)
es **auf** etw bringen[†]   **auf** jdn/etw schwören[†]
auf etw drängen   **auf** jdn/etw sehen[†]
auf etw eingehen[†]   sich **auf** etw spezialisieren
such **auf** jdn/etw erstrecken   sich **auf** jdn/etw stützen
auf jdn/etw folgen[†]   **auf** etw verfallen[†]
sich **auf** jdn/etw freuen[†]   sich **auf** jdn/etw verlassen
sich **auf** etw gründen   sich **auf** etw verstehen
auf jdn/etw halten[†]   **auf** etw verweisen
auf etw hinauslaufen   **auf** etw verzichten
jdn **auf** etw hinweisen   **auf** jdn/etw warten[†]
auf etw hoffen   **auf** jdn/etw zählen[†]
auf jdn/etw hören[†]   etw **auf** etw zurückführen[†]
sich **auf** etw konzentrieren   **auf** etw zurückkommen

NOTE: es kommt jdm **auf** etw an[†]

AUS	**aus** etw (dat) bestehen[†] etw **aus** etw (dat) ersehen (R3)

etw **aus** etw (dat) entnehmen[†] (R3)   etw **aus** etw (dat) folgern
sich **aus** etw (dat) ergeben[†]   etw **aus** etw (dat) schließen[†]

FÜR	sich **für** etw bedanken jdn/etw **für** jdn/etw halten

sich **für** etw begeistern   sich **für** jdn/etw interessieren[†]
jdm **für** etw danken   sich **für** jdn schämen
sich **für** etw eignen[†]   **für** jdn/etw sorgen
sich **für** etw entscheiden[†]

IN (dat)	**in** etw (dat) bestehen[†] sich **in** jdm/etw (dat) täuschen

IN (acc)	**in** etw ausbrechen sich **in** etw schicken[†] (R3)

jdn **in** etw einführen[†]   **in** etw verfallen[†]
in etw einwilligen   sich **in** jdn verlieben
sich **in** etw ergeben[†] (R3) sich **in** etw vertiefen
sich **in** etw fügen (R3)

MIT

sich **mit** etw (dat) abfinden
mit etw (dat) anfangen[†]
mit etw (dat) aufhören
sich **mit** jdm/etw (dat) befassen
mit etw (dat) beginnen[†]
sich **mit** etw (dat) begnügen
sich **mit** jdm/etw (dat) beschäftigen
jdm **mit** etw (dat) drohen
mit jdm/etw (dat) rechnen[†]
mit jdm sprechen[†]
mit jdm telefonieren
mit jdm/etw (dat) übereinstimmen
sich **mit** jdm unterhalten
jdn/etw **mit** jdm/etw (dat) vergleichen
sich **mit** jdm verheiraten
jdn/etw **mit** etw (dat) versehen
mit jdm/etw (dat) zusammenstoßen

NACH

Often = *for* with verbs of calling, longing, striving, etc:

sich **nach** jdm/etw (dat) erkundigen
nach etw (dat) fischen (R1)
jdn **nach** etw (dat) fragen
nach etw (dat) greifen
nach etw (dat) hungern (R3)
nach jdm/etw (dat) rufen[†]
nach jdm/etw (dat) schreien
nach jdm/etw (dat) sehen[†]
sich **nach** jdm/etw (dat) sehnen (R3)
nach etw (dat) streben
nach jdm/etw (dat) suchen
nach jdm/etw (dat) verlangen

Often = *of* with verbs of smelling, etc:

nach etw (dat) aussehen
nach etw (dat) duften
nach etw (dat) riechen[†]
nach etw (dat) schmecken[†]

ÜBER (acc)

Usually = *about* with verbs of saying, etc:

sich **über** jdn/etw ärgern
sich bei jdm **über** etw beklagen
über jdn/etw fluchen[†]
sich **über** jdn/etw freuen[†]
jdn **über** etw informieren
über etw jubeln
über jdn/etw klagen
über jdn/etw lachen
über jdn/etw nachdenken
über jdn/etw spotten
über jdn/etw sprechen[†]
sich **über** etw streiten[†]
über jdn/etw urteilen
sich **über** jdn/etw wundern

Other meanings:

sich **über** etw hinwegsetzen
über etw verfügen

UM		
jdn **um** etw angehen[†]	jdn **um** etw ersuchen (R3)
sich **um** jdn ängstigen	**um** jdn/etw kämpfen[†]
sich **um** jdn/etw (be)kümmern	**um** etw kommen[†]
sich **um** jdn/etw bemühen	sich **um** jdn/etw sorgen
jdn **um** etw beneiden	**um** etw spielen[†]
jdn **um** etw betrügen	sich **um** jdn/etw streiten[†]
jdn **um** etw bitten	**um** jdn/etw weinen[†]
jdn **um** etw bringen[†]	

NOTE: es geht (jdm) **um** jdn/etw
es handelt sich **um** jdn/etw

VON

jdn **von** etw (dat) abhalten
von jdm/etw (dat) abhängen
jdm **von** etw (dat) abraten
von etw (dat) absehen[†]
von etw (dat) ausgehen[†]
jdn **von** jdm/etw (dat) befreien
sich **von** jdm/etw (dat) distanzieren
sich **von** etw (dat) erholen
von jdm/etw (dat) herrühren
jdn **von** etw (dat) informieren[†]
von jdm/etw (dat) sprechen[†]
von jdm/etw (dat) träumen
jdn **von** etw (dat) überzeugen
jdn **von** etw (dat) verständigen
von etw (dat) wissen[†]
von etw (dat) zeugen

VOR (dat)

Commonly = *of* with verbs of fearing, etc:

sich **vor** jdm/etw (dat) ängstigen[†]
sich **vor** etw (dat) drücken (R1)
vor jdm/etw (dat) ekeln
vor jdm/etw (dat) erschrecken (R3)
sich **vor** jdm/etw (dat) fürchten
Angst **vor** jdm/etw (dat) haben[†]
sich **vor** jdm/etw (dat) hüten
sich **vor** jdm schämen[†]
sich **vor** etw (dat) scheuen
jdn **vor** jdm/etw (dat) warnen
vor jdm/etw (dat) zittern

Often = *from* with verbs of protecting, etc:

jdn **vor** jdm/etw (dat) (be)schirmen (R3)
jdn **vor** jdm/etw (dat) (be)schützen
jdn/etw **vor** etw (dat) bewahren
vor jdm/etw (dat) fliehen[†] (R3)
jdn **vor** etw (dat) retten
jdn/etw **vor** jdm verstecken

> [†] verb with which more than one construction is possible

ZU

Commonly = English *to* with verbs of empowering, leading, persuading, etc. All have the construction *jdn zu etw* (dat):

anhalten†	**drängen**†	**reizen**
antreiben	**einladen**	**treiben**
autorisieren	**ermächtigen**	**veranlassen**
befähigen	**ermutigen**	**verführen**
berechtigen	**herausfordern**	**verleiten**
bewegen	**nötigen**	**zwingen**
breitschlagen (R1)	**provozieren**	

Other meanings:

etw **zu** etw (dat) beitragen
jdn/etw **zu** etw (dat) bestimmen
jdn **zu** etw (dat) bringen†
zu etw (dat) dienen†
sich **zu** etw (dat) eignen†
sich **zu** etw (dat) entschließen
zu etw (dat) führen
zu etw (dat) gehören†
zu etw (dat) gelangen
jdn **zu** etw (dat) gratulieren
zu etw (dat) neigen
zu jdm/etw (dat) passen†
jdm **zu** etw (dat) raten
jdn/etw **zu** etw (dat) rechnen†
zu etw (dat) stehen
zu etw (dat) stimmen†
sich **zu** jdm/etw (dat) verhalten
jdm **zu** etw (dat) verhelfen
jdn/etw **zu** etw (dat) zählen†

> † verb with which more than one construction is possible

4.1.5   Infinitive phrases and *daß*-clauses with verbs governing a prepositional object

When verbs with a prepositional object are followed by an infinitive phrase or a *daß*-clause, this is normally anticipated in German by the prepositional adverb (ie *da(r)* + preposition), eg:

Wir bestanden **darauf**, daß er die Rechnung sofort bezahlte
Ich verlasse mich **darauf**, ihn morgen sprechen zu können

However, with some verbs, this is optional, eg:
> Sie hat sich nicht (**davor**) gescheut, ihm die Wahrheit zu sagen
> Sie haben sich (**darüber**) gefreut, daß er gekommen ist

The following lists give most of the common verbs with which the prepositional adverb may be omitted:

(a)   Verbs with which *da(r)* + preposition **may** be omitted before infinitive phrases **and** *daß*-clauses:

> **auf** jdn/etw aufpassen
> sich bei jdm **über** etw beklagen
> sich **um** jdn/etw bemühen
> jdn **um** etw bitten
> sich **für** etw entscheiden
> sich **zu** etw (dat) entschließen
> sich **an** jdn/etw erinnern
> jdn **nach** etw (dat) fragen
> sich **auf** jdn/etw freuen
> sich **über** jdn/etw freuen
> **an** jdn/etw glauben
> jdn **über** etw informieren
> jdn **von** etw (dat) informieren
> **über** jdn/etw klagen
> jdm **zu** etw (dat) raten
> sich **vor** etw (dat) scheuen
> **für** jdn/etw sorgen
> sich **um** jdn/etw sorgen
> sich **über** etw streiten
> **über** jdn/etw urteilen
> sich **über** jdn/etw wundern

In addition, the prepositional adverb may be omitted with all the verbs of empowering, leading, persuading, etc (ie *anhalten, antreiben,* etc) which have the construction *jdn zu etw* (dat) and are listed opposite.

(b)   Verbs with which *da(r)* + preposition **may** be omitted before infinitive phrases but **must** be used before *daß*-clauses:

> jdm **von** etw (dat) abraten
> **mit** etw (dat) anfangen
> **mit** etw (dat) beginnen
> **vor** jdm/etw (dat) ekeln
> jdn **an** etw (dat) hindern
> sich **vor** jdm/etw (dat) hüten

(c)   Verbs with which *da(r)* + preposition **may** be omitted before *daß*-clauses, but **must** be used before infinitive phrases:

> jdn **von** etw (dat) überzeugen
> **an** etw (dat) zweifeln

4.1.6   Verbs with varying constructions

A large number of verbs, some of which are included in sections
4.1.1–4.1.5 (where they are marked with †) are used in more than
one construction. Sometimes these are alternatives, more often there
is a clear difference in meaning, register or usage. Alternatives
involving a genitive are dealt with in **4.1.3**; some other common
instances are given below in sentences illustrating the different
constructions.

absehen
> Er hat mir diesen Kunstgriff abgesehen
> *He copied that trick from me*
> Ich sehe von etwas ab
> *I am refraining from sth*
> Sie hat es auf mich abgesehen (R1)
> *She's got it in for me*

achten
> Ich achte ihre Leistungen
> *I respect their achievements*
> Wir haben auf ihn geachtet
> *We paid attention to him*

angeben
> Sie müssen den Grund angeben
> *You must state the reason*
> Er hat gewaltig angegeben (R1)
> *He boasted dreadfully*

angehen
> Das Licht ging an
> *The light came on*
> Wie sollen wir diese Aufgabe angehen?
> *How are we to tackle this task?*
> Er ging mich um Unterstützung an
> *He asked me for support*
> Das geht dich nichts an (R1)
> *That's none of your business*

ankommen
> Wir kommen gleich in Münster an
> *We shall shortly be arriving in Münster*
> Mit so einer Bitte kommst du bei mir nicht an (R1)
> *You won't get anywhere with me with a request like that*
> Sie kommt mit dem Jungen nicht mehr an
> *She can't cope with the boy any more*
> Es kommt sehr auf das Wetter an
> *It depends a lot on the weather*

bestehen
> Das Schloß besteht nicht mehr
> *The castle doesn't exist any more*

Er muß die Prüfung bestehen
He has got to pass the examination
Der Teller bestand aus reinem Gold
The plate was made of pure gold
Das Problem besteht darin, daß wir es nicht beweisen können
The problem lies in the fact that we can't prove it
Sie besteht auf ihr Recht
She is insisting on her right
Wir können vor ihm kaum bestehen
We shall scarcely be able to stand up to him

bringen

Er hat mir die Äpfel gebracht
He brought me the apples
Sie hat mich auf diese Idee gebracht
She put this idea into my head
Er hat es auf 10 Punkte gebracht
He managed to get 10 points
Sie haben es im Leben zu nichts gebracht
They achieved nothing in their lifetime
Das hat mich heute um den Schlaf gebracht
That made me lose my sleep today
Das wird mich noch zur Verzweiflung bringen
That will drive me to despair

drängen

Die Polizei drängte sie vorwärts
The police pushed them forward
Sie drängen auf Zahlung
They are pressing for payment
Sie drängte ihn zu dieser Entscheidung
She urged him to (take) this decision

sich eignen

Der Film eignet sich nicht für Kinder
The film is not suitable for children
Er eignet sich nicht zum Lehrer
He is not suitable as a teacher

sich ergeben

Er hat sich mir ergeben
He gave in to me
Sie haben sich in ihr Schicksal ergeben (R3)
They submitted to their fate
Das eine ergibt sich aus dem anderen
The one follows from the other

folgen

Sie ist ihm heimlich gefolgt
She followed him secretly
Auf Karl II. folgte Jakob II.
James II followed Charles II
Aus diesem Brief folgt, daß . . .
It follows from this letter that . . .

sich freuen

Ich habe mich über seinen Erfolg gefreut
I was pleased about his success
Sie freut sich auf Ihren Besuch
She is looking forward to your visit
Er freut sich sehr an seinen Kindern
He gets a lot of pleasure from his children

gelten

Diese Fahrkarte gilt nicht mehr
This ticket is no longer valid
Es darf als sicher gelten, daß . . .
It may be regarded as certain that . . .
Diese Bemerkung galt mir
That comment was meant for me
Jetzt gilt es, einen Entschluß zu fassen (R3)
Now it is necessary to reach a decision

halten

Der Wagen hält nicht
The car is not stopping
Er hielt das Kind im Arm
He was holding the child in his arms
Ich halte sehr auf seine Meinung
I attach a lot of importance to his opinion
Ich halte viel von ihm
I think a lot of him
Du hast immer zu ihm gehalten
You've always stood by him
Ich halte sie für eine Freundin
I consider her a friend

kommen

Heute kommt sie nicht
She's not coming today
Wie bist du auf diese Idee gekommen?
How did you get that idea?
Ich bin hinter sein Geheimnis gekommen
I found out his secret
Er ist um ein Vermögen gekommen
He lost a fortune
Das kommt davon/daher, daß . . .
The reason for that is that . . .

liegen

Das Kind lag auf dem Boden
The child was lying on the floor
Es lag ihm viel an diesem Beruf
This job was very important to him
Diese Arbeit liegt mir nicht
I don't like this work
An mir soll es nicht liegen
It shouldn't be up to me

passen

Ich passe
I pass (at cards)
Das Kleid paßt dir gut
The dress fits/suits you
Er paßt nicht zum Lehrer
He's not suited to be a teacher

passieren

Wir passierten die deutsche Grenze
We passed over the German border
Was ist dir gestern passiert?
What happened to you yesterday?

rechnen

Ich rechne auf dich
I'm counting on you
Du mußt mit dem Schlimmsten rechnen
You have to reckon with the worst
Sie rechnet ihn zu ihren Freunden
She counts him as her friend

reichen

Die Felder reichen bis zum Wald
The fields extend to the forest
Sie hat mir den Teller gereicht
She handed me the plate
Das Geld reicht mir nicht (R1)
I haven't got enough money

sich schämen

Er schämte sich wegen seiner Feigheit
He was ashamed of his cowardice
Du sollst dich nicht vor ihm schämen
You don't need to feel ashamed in front of him
Sie schämte sich für ihn
She was ashamed for him

schließen

Ich habe die Tür geschlossen
I have shut the door
Aus seinem Verhalten kann man auf seinen Charakter schließen
You can deduce his character from his behaviour

stimmen

Stimmt das, was er sagt?
Is what he says correct?
Für diese Partei habe ich nicht gestimmt
I didn't vote for that party
Ich muß die Gitarre stimmen
I've got to tune the guitar

4.2   Cases: dative and genitive

4.2.1   Possessive dative

- To indicate possession with parts of the body, clothing, etc, German will most often use a dative of the person(s) concerned. The body-part, etc, will then have a definite article and must come after this dative, eg:

Sie fuhr *dem Jungen* über das Haar	She ran her fingers through *the boy's* hair
Er sah *ihr* in die Augen	He looked into *her* eyes
***Dem Kranken* wurde der Blinddarm operiert**	*The patient's* appendix was operated on

- Especially in R3 such a dative may appear a long way from the noun it refers to in the sentence, eg:

Dem in seiner Zelle Eingeschlossenen* drang sich das Bild des Vaters in *die Erinnerung	The image of his father pressed itself into *the memory of the man shut up in his cell*

- When more than one person is involved, the singular of the noun will be used if each person has one of each (see **3.1.6**), eg:

Ihnen klopfte *das Herz*	*Their hearts* were beating
Er hat uns *das Leben* gerettet	He saved *our lives*

- In most cases a construction with the genitive (at least in R3) or with a possessive is quite possible, eg:

Ich verband *dem Kind die Hand* OR **Ich verband *die Hand des Kindes***	I bandaged *the child's hand*
Ich verband *ihm die Hand* OR **Ich verband *seine Hand***	I bandaged *his hand*

However, the dative construction stresses that the whole person is immediately affected as well as the body-part specifically mentioned and is usually preferred. Occasionally there may be a difference in meaning. Compare the following pairs of examples:

Regen tropfte ihm auf den Hut	(ie he was getting wet)
Regen tropfte auf seinen Hut	(here it is not clear whether he was actually wearing it at the time)
Rehe liefen mir über den Weg	(ie they startled me)
Rehe liefen über meinen Weg	(ie across *my* – not someone else's – path)

R1* = vulgar
R1 = informal
     colloquial
R2 = neutral
R3 = formal
R3a = literary
R3b = non-literary
(see 1.1.5)

- With some verbs an accusative of the person involved may be used rather than a dative, eg:

Er hat *mich/mir* auf die Schulter geklopft	He tapped *me* on the shoulder
Die Biene hat *ihn/ihm* in den Finger gestochen	The bee stung *his* finger
Sie hat *ihn/ihm* ins Gesicht gelacht	She laughed in *his* face

It has been claimed that there is a distinction between the accusative and the dative in such cases, with the accusative emphasizing more strongly that the person is directly affected. This is rarely adhered to and in practice the two cases are used interchangeably with these verbs, although the dative is usual in R1. In R2 and R3 the accusative is common with the following verbs:

beißen, küssen, stechen, stoßen

With the following verbs the accusative is sometimes found in R2 and R3 but the dative is more frequent:

hauen, klopfen, schießen, schlagen, schneiden, treten

4.2.2 Genitive or *von*?

This section deals only with the use of the genitive to link nouns; its use with prepositions is covered in **2.5.4**, with verbs in **4.1.3**.

The use of the genitive case is very much dependent on register: the more formal the register, the more it occurs. It is widely used in R3 and is particularly frequent in R3b, but it is avoided entirely in R1, except with names, eg:

Alfreds Tasche, Monikas Schwester, Angelikas Handschuhe, Vatis Schuhe, Frau Mayers Bluse

The common alternative to the genitive is a phrase with the preposition *von*, eg:

R1: das Dach **vom Haus**
R2/R3: das Dach **des Hauses**

Although the genitive is used regularly in R3 and commonly in R2, there are constructions where *von* must be used even in these more formal registers, and others where it is quite frequent.

(a) **von** *must* be used, even in R3:

- if a noun stands by itself, without any article or adjective which declines

  der Geruch *von* Benzin
  die Wirkung *von* wenig Wein
  eine Mutter *von* sechs Kindern
  der Tod *von* Tausenden
  der Vater *von* zwei Töchtern
  (*zweier* is older R3a)

- with personal pronouns

  jeder *von* uns
  eine Tante *von* mir

- after *viel, wenig*

  viel *von* dem, was sie sagte
  wenig *von* dem guten Wein

N = North
C = Central
S = South
SW = South West
SE = South East
AU = Austria
CH = Switzerland
(see 1.2.3)

(b) **von** is *more usual* than the genitive, even in R3:

- to avoid consecutive genitives in *-s*, especially with names

  die Tür *von* dem Haus meines Bruders
  die Übersetzung *von* Goethes *Faust*
  die Antwort *von* Martins Freund

- if a noun has an adjective, but no article

  der Bau *von* modernen Kraftwerken
  ein Erzeugnis *von* höchster Qualität
  die Produktion *von* reinem Stahl
  der Preis *von* sechs neuen Fahrrädern

- with indefinite pronouns

  eine Dauer *von* mehreren Jahren
  in der Gesellschaft *von* einigen Freunden
  die Ansicht *von* vielen Wissenschaftlern

(c) **von** is *often found* in R2 and R3, although the more formal registers prefer the genitive:

- with words of quantity in partitive constructions

  die Hälfte *von* diesem Buch
  eines *von* diesen neuen Häusern
  drei *von* unseren Nachbarn
  ein Teil *von* den Zuschauern
  viele *von* den Maßnahmen

- with geographical names

  die Zerstörung *von* Dresden
  die Hauptstadt *von* Deutschland
  das Alpengebiet *von* Kärnten
  die Straßen *von* Frankfurt

- In all other cases R3 always has, and R2 usually has, a genitive, but in R1 *von* is normally used, eg:

R1	R2 + R3
die Adresse **von meiner Tante**	die Adresse **meiner Tante**
in der Nähe **vom Rathaus**	in der Nähe **des Rathauses**
das Dach **von der alten Kirche**	das Dach **der alten Kirche**
das Benehmen **von den Kindern**	das Benehmen **der Kinder**
die Abfahrt **vom D-Zug**	die Abfahrt **des D-Zuges**

- *von* is not infrequent in R1 even with names, eg:
  das Buch **von** (der) Petra
  das Haus **von** (der) Frau Müller

- To express possession with persons, the most casual R1 often uses a paraphrase with the dative, eg:

  dem Jürgen seine Tasche
  der Mutter ihr Schlüssel
  meinen Freunden ihre Fahrräder

  This construction is *never* used in higher registers.

- The genitive occurs in a number of set phrases, some of which are not found in less formal registers, eg:

letzten Endes (R2)	*when all is said and done*
allen Ernstes (R3)	*in all seriousness*
meines Erachtens (R3)	*in my view*
stehenden Fußes (R3)	*immediately*
erhobenen Hauptes (R3)	*with his head held high*
erster Klasse fahren (R2)	*to travel first class*
ich bin deiner Meinung (R2)	*I agree with you*
frohen Mutes (R3)	*in good spirits*
er ging seines Weges (R3)	*he went his way*
meines Wissens (R2)	*to my knowledge*

- The genitive also occurs in some time expressions which are used in all registers:

eines Tages, Abends, Nachts, etc	*one day, evening, night,* etc
eines schönen Sommers	*one fine summer*

4.2.3   The position of genitive phrases

In modern German, the genitive follows the noun it qualifies, eg:

die Gefahr **eines Erdbebens**
die Hälfte **meines Vermögens**
die Kultur **des Ostens**
die Auswirkungen **dieser schweren Krise**

The only exception is with names, eg:

Manfreds Steroanlage
Antjes neue Bluse   } normal in all registers

Frau Müllers Sohn   R1 also: der Sohn von (der) Frau Müller
                        R2–R3 also: der Sohn der Frau Müller

Goethes Werke   R3 also: die Werke Goethes
                    R1–R3 also: die Werke von Goethe

Frankfurts Straßen   R3 also: die Straßen Frankfurts
                         R1–R3 also: die Straßen von Frankfurt

In R3a other genitives may come first. However, this construction is rare and usually sounds archaic (or facetious), eg:

des Mannes Ehre
des kühnen Helden blankes Schwert
des Postministers Kabelpläne

4.2.4   Measurement phrases

(a)   Normal usage in all registers is for the nouns to be in the same case, eg:

> **eine Menge Fehler**
> **ein Glas badischer Wein**
> **ein Kilo italienische Tomaten**
> Er trank **eine Tasse schwarzen Tee**
> mit **einem Zentner polnischer Kohle**

(b)   R3a may have the genitive. With an adjective this has a rather archaic flavour, especially in the singular, eg:

> **ein Glas badischen Weines**
> **ein Becher frischer Milch**
> **ein Dutzend erbaulicher Bücher**

(c)   *von* is often used with vague quantity words such as *Anzahl*, *Haufen*, *Menge*, especially if they are plural, eg:

> **eine Menge von Fehlern**
> **eine Anzahl von Touristen**
> **zwei Gruppen von Schulkindern**
> **vier Kategorien von Ausnahmen**
> **eine ganze Reihe von Beispielen**

(d)   With these vague words, the genitive is quite frequent in R3 if an adjective follows, eg:

> **ein Haufen alter Zeitschriften**
> **eine Anzahl deutscher Touristen**
> **Millionen hungernder Menschen**

4.3   Tenses

4.3.1   Present and future

The future tense is used much less in German than in English, particularly in R1.

As long as the future meaning is clear from the context, German can use the present tense where English must have a future, eg:

In zwei Stunden bin ich wieder da	*I'll be back . . .*
Weitere Einzelheiten erteilt Ihnen unser Fachpersonal	*Our specialist staff will give you . . .*
Ich erwarte, daß sie kommt	*. . . that she'll come*
Sie findet es nie	*She'll never find it*
Wir sagen es ihm morgen	*We're going to tell him . . .*

Only if the future meaning is not clear does German have to use the future tense, eg:

> Er **wird** wieder als Ingenieur **arbeiten**
> (*arbeitet* would mean 'is working')

R1* = vulgar
R1 = informal colloquial
R2 = neutral
R3 = formal
R3a = literary
R3b = non-literary
(see 1.1.5)

N = North
C = Central
S = South
SW = South West
SE = South East
AU = Austria
CH = Switzerland
(see 1.2.3)

If the future is used, it can stress determination, eg:
> Ich **werde** es heute abend noch **erledigen**
> Wir **werden** es schon **schaffen**

It also often expresses a prediction or probability, and this is frequently strengthened by *wohl* (see **2.6**), eg:
> Er **wird** den Zug (**wohl**) noch **erreichen**
> Dagmar **wird** (**wohl**) auch **kommen wollen**
> Die Vorstellung **wird** (**wohl**) gegen 11 Uhr **zu Ende sein**
> Schalke **wird** (**wohl**) auch in München **verlieren**

The future perfect is uncommon in any register, and the perfect is a frequent alternative, eg:

Bald **wird** er es **geschafft haben**	= Bald **hat** er es **geschafft**
Er **wird** (**wohl**) nicht ohne Absicht **gekommen sein**	= Er **ist** wohl nicht ohne Absicht **gekommen**
Er **wird** (**wohl**) den Schlüssel **verloren haben**	= Er **hat** wohl den Schlüssel **verloren**

4.3.2 Past and perfect

NOTE: the term 'imperfect', which is sometimes used to refer to the past tense, is better avoided as it is misleading. Neither in German nor English does the past tense express any idea of uncompleted action.

In modern German there is little essential difference in meaning between the past and perfect tenses. Both *ich kam* and *ich bin gekommen* express much the same idea and both can be used to translate *I came* or *I have come*. Which one is used depends largely on register: broadly speaking, written registers (R2 and R3) prefer the past tense, spoken registers (R1 and R2, especially in S) prefer the perfect, eg:

Speech	**Writing**
Sein Bruder Robert **ist** gestern mit ein paar Freunden nach Hamm **gefahren**, wo sie den Uwe Fuhrmann **besucht haben**	Sein Bruder Robert **fuhr** gestern mit ein paar Freunden nach Hamm, wo sie Uwe Fuhrmann **besuchten**

(a) The past is not used at all in speech in S. In N + C, however, it does occur, in particular if not exclusively:

- almost always in *als*- and *wie*-clauses

  Als ich sie **sah**, hat sie mich nicht erkannt
  Ich habe gehört, wie er die Treppe herunter**kam**

⟫→

• as often as not in the passive, with the modals, with verbs of saying, hearing and feeling and many common verbs, such as *sein, haben, bleiben, gehen, kommen, stehen*, etc	Da **blieb** ich stehen und **sagte** nichts Ich **konnte** auch nichts sagen Ich **war** vor ihm dran Sie **hatte** nichts dagegen Er **wurde** schlecht behandelt

(b)   The perfect is normally used in writing to stress a result, to express the immediate past or actions which have continued up to now. In all these instances English typically also uses a perfect, eg:

• stressing result	Es hat **geschneit** (ie I can see the snow) Wir **sind gelandet** (ie we're on the ground) Man sieht, daß er schwer **gearbeitet hat**
• immediate past	Jetzt **hat** Breitner den Ball **eingeworfen** Damit **haben** wir unsere kurze Einleitung **beendet** In diesem Augenblick **ist** der Zug **abgefahren**
• events continuing up to now	Seit dem Sommer **hat** sie zwanzig Bücher **gelesen** Bis jetzt **hat** alles **geklappt** Das **habe** ich wiederholt **gesagt**

(c)   However, this is not universally so, and even in the instances in (b) the past may be found, especially in R3b (newspaper headlines, etc), though it is less frequent than the perfect:

• stressing result	Das ist der erste solche Bericht, der uns **erreichte**
• immediate past	Sie **hörten** soeben eine Sendung des österreichischen Rundfunks
• events continuing up to now	Noch nie **wurde** ein Auto so oft gebaut

4.3.3 *haben* or *sein* in the perfect?

In most instances the choice is quite straightforward.

(a) The following verbs form the perfect with *sein*:
  (i) intransitive verbs which express a change of place, eg:
   Sie *ist* geflogen/geflohen/gegangen/gelaufen, etc
  (ii) intransitive verbs expressing a change of state, eg:
   Es *ist* geworden/gestorben/verblüht, etc
  (iii) verbs meaning 'happen', 'fail', 'succeed', eg:
   Es *ist* geschehen/passiert/vorgekommen/zugestoßen, etc
   Es *ist* gelungen/mißlungen/geglückt, etc
   NOTE: **es *hat* geklappt** (R1)
  (iv) the verbs *sein* and *bleiben*, eg:
   Er *ist* gewesen/geblieben
  (v) some other verbs in certain regions only, eg:
   N: **anfangen/beginnen**
   S: **liegen/sitzen/stehen**
   (In standard German these always have *haben*.)

(b) The following verbs form the perfect with *haben*:
  (i) verbs which have an accusative object, eg:
   Sie *hat* ihn geschlagen/gesehen/getragen/gewaschen, etc
   There are very few exceptions to this, but cf:
   Das *ist* ihn nichts angegangen
   Wir *sind* die Rechnung durchgegangen
   Er *ist* diese Wette eingegangen
   Sie *ist* ihn endlich losgeworden
  (ii) reflexive verbs, eg:
   Er *hat* sich beeilt/gefreut/verabschiedet, etc
   Occasional exceptions involve verbs with a dative reflexive, eg:
   Sie *sind* sich gestern begegnet
  (iii) intransitive verbs which express a continuous action, eg:
   Wir *haben* gewartet/gearbeitet/geholfen, etc
  (iv) impersonal verbs, eg:
   Es *hat* geregnet/geschneit/gedämmert, etc
   Exceptions to this are the verbs meaning 'happen', 'fail',
   'succeed' listed under (a.iii) above.

It is important to realize that the choice of auxiliary is not absolutely bound up with a particular verb, but depends only on meaning. A fair number of verbs can fall into more than one of the above categories if their meaning varies or if they can be transitive or intransitive, and they will then sometimes take *haben* and sometimes take *sein*. The following examples show the effect of this with some common verbs:

Die Katze **hat** ihn angesprungen	. . . *jumped up at him*
Der Motor **ist** angesprungen	. . . *started*
Ich **habe** das Geschenk bekommen	. . . *received* . . .
Die Muscheln **sind** ihr nicht bekommen	. . . *didn't agree with her*

≫→

201

Er **hat** die Röhre gebogen	*. . . bent the tube*
Wir **sind** um die Ecke gebogen	*. . . turned round the corner*
Er **hat** das Brot gebrochen	*. . . broke the bread* (tr)
das Rohr **ist** gebrochen	*. . . broke* (itr)
Sie **hat** auf Zahlung gedrungen	*. . . pressed for payment*
Wasser **ist** in das Haus gedrungen	*. . . penetrated . . .*
Er **hat** einen Audi gefahren	*. . . drove an Audi* (tr)
Er **ist** nach Gießen gefahren	*. . . went/drove to Gießen* (itr)
Sie **hat** ihm gefolgt	*. . . obeyed him*
Sie **ist** ihm gefolgt	*. . . followed him*
Es **hat** in der Nacht gefroren	*It froze/There was a frost*
Der See **ist** gefroren	*. . . has frozen*
Da **haben** Sie sich geirrt	*. . . were mistaken*
Da **sind** wir durch den Wald geirrt	*. . . wandered . . .*
Er **ist** in die Stadt gelaufen	*. . . ran into town*
Er **hat sich** die Füße wund gelaufen	*. . . got sore feet from running*
Sie **hat sich** ein Loch ins Kleid gerissen	*. . . tore a hole . . .*
Der Strick **ist** gerissen	*. . . snapped*
Er **hat** ihn in den Kopf geschossen	*. . . shot him in the head*
Das Unkraut **ist** aus dem Boden geschossen	*. . . shot out of the ground*
Sie **hat** ihn zur Seite gestoßen	*. . . pushed him to one side*
Ich **bin** an den Schrank gestoßen	*. . . bumped into the cupboard*
Er **hat** es aus Versehen getreten	*. . . kicked it by accident*
Er **ist** in das Wasser getreten	*. . . stepped into the water*
Sie **hat** am Strick gezogen	*. . . pulled on the string*
Sie **ist** nach Emden gezogen	*. . . moved to Emden*

A rather special case concerns some verbs of motion which can take *sein* if they express movement from one spot to another, but *haben* if they just refer to the activity as such, eg:

> Er *hat* den ganzen Tag gebummelt/gefahren/geflogen, geritten/gerudert/geschwommen/gesegelt/getanzt
> Er *ist* durch Husum gebummelt/gefahren/geflogen/ geritten/gerudert/geschwommen/gesegelt/getanzt

The tendency in R1 is to use *sein* with all these verbs in both meanings, and this usage is also well established in R2 and R3. Only with *rudern*, *segeln* and *tanzen* is the distinction kept at all consistently.

4.4 The passive

4.4.1 *werden-* or *sein-*passive?

The real passive in German is formed from the appropriate tense of the verb *werden* with the past participle:

Present	Die Ausstellung **wird eröffnet**
Past	Die Ausstellung **wurde eröffnet**
Perfect	Die Austellung **ist eröffnet worden**
	(Note the form *worden* as the past participle of *werden* in passives.)
Future	Die Ausstellung **wird eröffnet werden**

These forms with *werden* are four times more frequent than the forms with *sein*, eg:

Die Tür **ist geschlossen**	= Die Tür **ist zu** (ie somebody has shut it)
Der Brief **ist geschrieben**	= Der Brief **ist fertig** (ie somebody has written it)
Die Stadt **war zerstört**	= Die Stadt **war kaputt** (ie somebody had destroyed it)

The past participle here is descriptive, like an adjective. It describes the state the subject is in as a result of some previous action.

Compare the meaning when *werden* is used:

Die Tür **wird geschlossen**	ie somebody is shutting it
Der Brief **wird geschrieben**	ie somebody is writing it
Die Stadt **wurde zerstört**	ie somebody destroyed it

Note that for this reason the *sein-*passive is often the equivalent of an English perfect or pluperfect, eg:

*The letter **has been written***	Der Brief **ist geschrieben**
*The town **had been destroyed***	Die Stadt **war zerstört**

In practice, the difference in meaning may be very slight, as in the following pairs of examples:

Der Brief **ist geschrieben/**	Der Brief **ist geschrieben worden**
Die Stadt **war zerstört/**	Die Stadt **war zerstört worden**

On the other hand, the *werden-*passive, especially in the present, often corresponds to an English progressive, eg:

Der Brief **wird geschrieben**	*The letter **is being written***
Der Antrag **wird bearbeitet**	*The application **is being dealt with***

As the *sein-*passive expresses a state resulting from a previous action, it is only ever used with verbs which have some tangible result, like *verletzen*, eg:

Meine Hand **ist verletzt**	ie you can see the resulting injury
Der Wagen **ist beschädigt**	ie you can see the resulting damage

R1* = vulgar
R1 = informal
    colloquial
R2 = neutral
R3 = formal
R3a = literary
R3b = non-literary
(see 1.1.5)

N = North
C = Central
S = South
SW = South West
SE = South East
AU = Austria
CH = Switzerland
(see 1.2.3)

Verbs which do not express a clear result cannot be used in the *sein*-passive at all, eg:

Das Mädchen **wurde**   *The girl was admired*
   bewundert

war bewundert is quite impossible, as admiring does not produce a result which can be seen.

Other common verbs which similarly cannot be used in the *sein*-passive are:

anbieten	**erblicken**	**schmeicheln**
befragen	**erinnern**	**schulden**
begrüßen	**erwarten**	**senden**
bemerken	**hindern**	**zeigen**
brauchen	**loben**	

In N and CH the *sein*-passive may be more widely used to refer to an action, eg:

Die Anwesenden **sind aufgefordert**, ihre Plätze einzunehmen
In standard German, only *werden* is acceptable here.

Only in a very few cases is the distinction between *werden* and *sein* unimportant in standard German, most commonly when we are dealing with a general truth or a permanent state of some kind, usually referring to things, eg:

Die Stadt **wird/ist** von etwa eine Million Menschen **bewohnt**
Das Zentrum **wird/ist** durch die Ringstraße von den
   Außenbezirken **getrennt**

4.4.2 The impersonal passive

A characteristic and frequent use of the passive in German is in an impersonal construction to refer, in general terms, to an action or activity going on. It is particularly common in written German (especially R3b), but it is by no means restricted to that register. The following examples illustrate this construction.

Es **wird** wieder **getanzt**
The dancing is starting up again
Es **wurde abgestimmt**
A vote was taken
Es **wurde** noch lange **diskutiert**
The discussion still continued for a long time

If another part of speech is in initial position in a main clause statement, or in questions and subordinate clauses, the *es* is dropped (though the verb still agrees with it), giving the so–called 'subjectless' passive, eg:

Jetzt **wird** wieder **getanzt**
The dancing is starting up again now
Nachmittags **wurde** Karten **gespielt**
People played cards in the afternoons
Wurde noch lange **diskutiert**?
Did the discussion still continue for a long time?
Er langweilte sich, weil noch lange **diskutiert wurde**
He was bored because the discussion still continued for a long time

4.4.3 Passive with dative objects

In German, *only* the accusative object of a transitive verb can become the subject of the passive, eg:

> Herr Altmann baut **das Haus** → **Das Haus** wird von Herrn Altmann gebaut
> Der Feind zerstörte **die Stadt** → **Die Stadt** wurde vom Feind zerstört

This means that dative objects and prepositional objects can never become the subject of a passive sentence; they remain as datives or prepositional phrases in the passive, eg:

> **Dem Mädchen** wurde eine Puppe geschenkt   *The girl was given a doll*
> **Dem König** wurde nicht geantwortet   *The king was not answered*
> **Für die Kinder** wurde gesorgt   *The children were looked after*

4.4.4 *von* or *durch*?

The equivalent of English *by* may be *von* or *durch* in German. *von* is much more frequent and is used for the 'doer' or the cause of an action, which is most often a person but may sometimes be some natural agency, eg:

> Holger wurde **von** seiner Schwester informiert
> Die Zeitschrift wird eher **von** anspruchsvollen Menschen gelesen
> Sie wurden **von** einer Lawine mitgerissen

durch refers to the means of doing an action, which is commonly a thing, or to an intermediary, eg:

> Die Stadt wurde **durch** Bomben verwüstet
> Die Fähigkeit des Fahrers wurde **durch** Alkohol erheblich gemindert
> Die Katastrophe wurde **durch** die ungewöhnliche Kälte herbeigeführt

However, in modern usage this distinction between *von* and *durch* is not always strictly adhered to, especially in R1 and R2. In particular, there are many instances where it is not clear whether one is dealing with a 'doer' or the means of doing an action, and *von* or *durch* are used interchangeably, eg:

> Die Stadt wurde **durch/von** Bomben verwüstet
> Alle unsere Erzeugnisse werden **durch/von** Fachexperten geprüft

NOTE: by and large a *von/durch* phrase can only be used with the *werden*-passive, not with the *sein*-passive.

4.4.5 Alternative passive constructions

In general, it is misleading to say that the passive is used less in German than in English. If it is true to any extent it is because German can use an active construction with something other than the subject in initial position in a way not possible in English (see **5.1.4**). However, the German passive is widely used, if rather more in R3 than R1, and it is certainly not to be 'avoided' almost as a matter of course.

Nevertheless, German is rich in alternative means of expressing passives, and it is worth while being aware of these constructions, which are very frequent, as they can provide useful variation and differences in emphasis.

(a) *man* can be used if the subject is truly indefinite, eg:

Man sagt	= Es wird gesagt
Das tut **man** nicht	= Das wird nicht getan
Man schloß die Sitzung	= Die Sitzung wurde geschlossen

(b) *bekommen, erhalten* (R3), *kriegen* (R1) can be used to emphasize the receiver, eg:

Ich **bekam** den Weg von einem Passanten beschrieben	= Mir wurde der Weg von einem Passanten beschrieben
Er **erhielt** das Geld ausgezahlt (R3)	= Ihm wurde das Geld ausgezahlt
Die Kleine **hat** eine Puppe geschenkt **gekriegt** (R1)	= Der Kleinen wurde eine Puppe geschenkt

(c) *gehören* (S) has the force of *müssen* or *sollen*, eg:

Das **gehört** doch bestraft (S)	= Das **muß/soll** doch bestraft werden
Dem **gehört** das deutlich gesagt (S)	= Ihm **muß/soll** das deutlich gesagt werden

(d) Phrasal verbs, especially those with *kommen,* are frequent in R3b, eg:

Es **kommt** demnächst **zur Entschiedung** (R3b)	= Darüber wird demnächst entschieden
Die Verhandlungen **kommen zum Abschluß** (R3b)	= Die Verhandlungen werden heute abgeschlossen
Die Angelegenheit soll **einer gründlichen Überprüfung unterliegen**	= Die Angelegenheit soll gründlich überprüft werden

(e) Reflexive verbs are frequently found instead of passives in all registers, eg:

Sie **nennt sich** Hildegard	= Sie **wird** Hildegard **genannt**
Der Schlüssel **wird sich** sicher noch **finden**	= Der Schlüssel **wird** sicher noch **gefunden werden**
Das Buch **liest sich** schnell	= Das Buch **kann** schnell **gelesen werden**

Note that the natural German equivalent of many English passive constructions is a reflexive verb, eg:

sich ärgern	*to be annoyed*	sich schämen	*to be ashamed*
sich freuen	*to be pleased*	sich verbinden	*to be associated*

(f) *sich lassen*, with an impersonal subject, has the force of *können*, eg:

Das **läßt sich** noch **machen** = Das **kann** noch **gemacht werden**

Der Apparat **läßt sich** nicht mehr **reparieren** = Der Apparat **kann** nicht mehr **repariert werden**

Dieser Satz **läßt sich** nur schwer **übersetzen** = Dieser Satz **kann** nur schwer **übersetzt werden**

(g) *sein* with an infinitive phrase has the force of *können* or *müssen* (and may then be ambiguous), eg:

Die Arbeit **ist** bis morgen **zu erledigen** = Die Arbeit **muß** bis morgen **erledigt werden**

Diese Säulen **sind** an jeder Straßenecke **zu finden** = Diese Säulen **können** an jeder Straßenecke **gefunden werden**

Diese Ausdrücke **sind** tunlichst **zu vermeiden** = Diese Ausdrücke **müssen** tunlichst **vermieden werden**

This construction can be converted into an extended adjective (used especially in R3b) using the present participle rather than the infinitive, eg:

Diese **tunlichst zu vermeidenden** Ausdrücke . . .

(h) *bleiben* and *gehen* (R1) can also occur with infinitive phrases, eg:

Das Ergebnis **bleibt abzuwarten** = Das Ergebnis **muß abgewartet werden**

Das Radio **geht** noch **zu reparieren** (R1) = Das Radio **kann** noch **repariert werden**

(i) Adjectives in -*bar* (and some in -*lich*) have the force of passives with *können*, eg:

Die Pfirsiche sind kaum **eßbar** = Die Pfirsiche **können** kaum **gegessen werden**

Solche Wörter sind jederzeit **bildbar** = Solche Wörter **können** jederzeit **gebildet werden**

Seine Antwort war **unverständlich** = Seine Antwort **konnte** nicht **verstanden werden**

4.5   The subjunctive

The use of the subjunctive in German is subject to considerable variation dependent on register. 'Rules' which are given in most grammar books hold for R3 only, and everyday R1 usage can be very different, particularly in the area of indirect speech.

4.5.1   Forms of the subjunctive

In English, we usually speak of the major forms of the German subjunctive as *present* and *past*. However, as the difference in meaning between these has very little to do with tense, it is common practice in books on German nowadays to refer to them as *Konjunktiv I* and *Konjunktiv II*, as follows:

Konjunktiv I	present subjunctive	**er schlafe**
	perfect subjunctive	**er habe geschlafen**
	future subjunctive	**er werde schlafen**
Konjunktiv II	past subjunctive	**er schliefe**
	pluperfect subjunctive	**er hätte geschlafen**
	conditional	**er würde schlafen**

The terms *Konjunktiv I* and *Konjunktiv II* are used in this section as they are less misleading and make it simpler to explain the use of the subjunctive in modern German.

The forms of Konjunktiv I

Konjunktiv I only has a distinct form in the third person singular, except for the verb *sein*. There are no irregularities such as there are in the present indicative of strong verbs such as *nehmen* and *werden*:

er mache   er nehme   er solle   er werde   er habe

Other forms sometimes found in grammar books, eg *du machest, ihr machet*, are wholly artificial and never used, even in R3.

The verb *sein* has distinct forms for all persons:

ich sei	**wir seien**
du sei(e)st	**ihr seiet**
er sei	**sie seien**

However, in practice only the third person singular and plural are at all frequently used.

The forms of Konjunktiv II

(a) *Konjunktiv II* has alternative forms, as follows:

A one–word form. For weak verbs this is identical with the past tense; for strong (and some irregular) verbs this is formed by umlauting the vowel of the past tense, if possible, and adding -*e*- if possible (this -*e*- is often dropped in R1 or spoken R2), eg:

ich machte	ich gäbe	ich ginge	ich könnte
du machtest	du gäbest	du gingest	du könntest
er machte	er gäbe	er ginge	er könnte
wir machten	wir gäben	wir gingen	wir könnten
ihr machtet	ihr gäbet	ihr ginget	ihr könntet
sie machten	sie gäben	sie gingen	sie könnten

R1* = vulgar
R1 = informal
        colloquial
R2 = neutral
R3 = formal
R3a = literary
R3b = non-literary
(see 1.1.5)

A few strong verbs have an irregular form with a different vowel, sometimes as an alternative. Only the following are used nowadays:

helfen   **hülfe** (less common: **hälfe**)
stehen   **stünde** (less common: **stände**)
sterben   **stürbe**

(b)   The so-called 'conditional' forms with *würde*, eg:
ich **würde** machen
ich **würde** geben
ich **würde** gehen

There is no difference at all in meaning between one-word forms and the *würde*-form. In principle, forms such as
ich käm**e**   ich **würde** kommen
ich wüßt**e**   ich **würde** wissen
could replace each other in any context, as they are completely interchangeable in meaning. In practice, whether a one-word form or a *würde*-form is used depends on the individual verb involved and on register. Note that the 'rule' that two *würde*-forms in one sentence should be avoided is totally ignored in R1 and it is not always followed even in R3.

● The use of the one-word form of *Konjunktiv II* and the *würde*-form

(a)   *With weak verbs* the one-word form is sometimes used in R3 and, less often, in R2, *if* the meaning is otherwise clear from the context, ie from a distinct subjunctive form in the other half of a conditional sentence, eg:
Wenn er noch **lebte**, würde ich diese Frage nicht beantworten
Wenn wir das Fenster **aufmachten**, hätten wir ein bißchen frische Luft hier im Zimmer

In R1 always, in R2 commonly, and sometimes in R3, the *würde*-form is preferred, eg:
Wenn er noch **leben würde**, würde ich diese Frage nicht beantworten
Wenn wir das Fenster **aufmachen würden**, hätten wir ein bißchen frische Luft hier im Zimmer

(b)   *With some very common irregular verbs* the *würde*-form is infrequent or unknown, ie with *sein, werden, haben* and the modals:

wäre	**dürfte**	**müßte**
würde	**könnte**	**sollte**
hätte	**möchte**	**wollte**

NOTE: this also means that the forms of the pluperfect subjunctive almost always have *hätte* and *wäre*, eg:
Ich **hätte** es getan
Wir **wären** gefahren

The forms *würde haben, würde sein* and *würde werden*, if not unknown, are uncommon in any register.

N = North
C = Central
S = South
SW = South West
SE = South East
AU = Austria
CH = Switzerland
(see 1.2.3)

(c) *With a few other common strong or irregular verbs* the one–word forms are about as frequent as *würde*-forms in the registers indicated:

R1, R2 & R3: **käme**, **täte**, **wüßte** (S also: **bräuchte**)
R2 & R3:   **fände**, **gäbe**, **ginge**, **hielte**, **hieße**, **ließe**, **stünde**

(d) *With a limited number of other strong or irregular verbs* the one–word forms are found in R3 only, and even there they are far less frequent than *würde*-forms. The following are still not unusual in R3:

bliebe	**hülfe**	**schlüge**
brächte	**kennte**	**schriebe**
dächte	**läge**	**stürbe**
fiele	**liefe**	**träfe**
führe	**nähme**	**trüge**
gelänge	**sähe**	**verschwände**
geschähe	**schiene**	**würfe**
hinge	**schliefe**	**zöge**

(e) *With the remaining strong and irregular verbs*, the one–word forms may still very occasionally be encountered in R3a, but the *würde*-forms are far more usual. These one–word forms, especially those in -ö- and -ü- (eg *begönne, flöge, hübe, würbe,* etc) sound pompous and comical nowadays and are best avoided entirely.

4.5.2 Indirect speech

Problems for the foreign learner arise largely from the fact that usage is highly variable and determined mainly by register. Grammatical 'rules' are widely ignored and in any case those given in a number of reference works are misleading, inaccurate or unrepresentative of actual usage.

A basic starting point would be that whereas the most formal R3 uses *Konjunktiv I* wherever possible, informal R1 avoids it almost entirely.

Typical R3 usage

Konjunktiv I is used where there is a clear form, retaining the tense of the original direct speech (though if this was past, the perfect subjunctive is used), eg:

Sie sagte, sie **wisse** es schon
Sie sagte, sie **habe** es verstanden
Sie sagte, sie **werde** es versuchen

BUT if there is no clear *Konjunktiv I* form, then the corresponding *Konjunktiv II* forms are used, eg:

Sie sagten, sie **wüßten** es schon
Sie sagten, sie **hätten** es verstanden
Sie sagten, sie **würden** es versuchen

BUT if the one–word *Konjunktiv II* form is unusual (see **4.5.1**) then the *würde*-form is used.

Sie sagte, diese Bäche **würden** alle in den Neckar **fließen**
    (*flössen* is no longer used)

The pattern given above is most closely adhered to in the R3b of newspaper reports, where the subjunctive provides a handy means of indicating reported speech, eg:

> Der iranische Parlamentspräsident Rafsanjani ist mit dem äußeren Erscheinungsbild der schiitischen Revolutionäre unzufrieden. Die fundamentalistischen Moslems **würden** immer mehr mit Begriffen wie „ungewaschen, unrasiert und unordentlich gekleidet" **gleichgesetzt**. Außerdem **sei** es an der Zeit, den revolutionären Eifer etwas zu zügeln ... Im übrigen **solle** man den Personenkult um den Ajatollah Chomeini nicht übertreiben. Etwas weniger Porträts des Imam **täten** es auch.
>
> *Die Zeit*

Note the alternation of *Konjunktiv I* and *Konjunktiv II* forms and the lack of any explicit verb of saying; only the subjunctive shows us that this is reported speech.

There are one or two common deviations from this pattern in R3, as follows:

(a) If *daß* is used, the indicative is as frequent as *Konjunktiv I* (*but* still in the tense of the original direct speech), eg:
Er sagte, daß er schon länger hier **wohnt**

BUT if *daß* is omitted, then *Konjunktiv I* is essential, eg:
Er sagte, er **wohne** schon länger hier

(b) The indicative is often used if there is no clear *Konjunktiv I* form, eg:
Sie sagten, sie **arbeiten** schon in der Schweiz

If the indicative is used in indirect speech, there is *no* difference in meaning to the subjunctive, ie it does *not* represent 'fact' as opposed to 'mere report'.

(c) *Konjunktiv II* is common even when a clear *Konjunktiv I* form is available, eg:
Er hat gefragt, ob sie schon lange in Göttingen **wäre**
Er behauptete, er **hätte** ihn nicht geschlagen

Note that if *Konjunktiv II* is used, there is *no* difference in meaning to *Konjunktiv I*, ie it does *not* imply 'doubt' as opposed to 'mere report'.

R2 usage

R2 usage differs from R3 mainly in that *Konjunktiv I* forms are less frequent:

(a) *Konjunktiv II* forms are used rather than *Konjunktiv I*, with the exception of *sein* and *haben*.
Sie sagte, sie **wüßte** es schon
Sie sagte, sie **habe** es verstanden
Sie sagte, sie **würde** es versuchen

(b) The one-word *Konjunktiv II* forms are used only with a few common verbs (see **4.5.1**), eg:
Er sagte, er **käme** heute nicht
Sie meinte, sie **könnte** es schon machen

⧽⧽⧽→

[R2 USAGE] (c) In other cases, *würde*-forms or the indicative are used, eg:
Der Schaffner sagte, daß unsere Rückfahrkarten nicht mehr
gelten/gelten würden
Viele behaupten, sie **lesen** keine Tageszeitung mehr/ . . . sie
würden keine Tageszeitung mehr **lesen**

R1 usage

In R1, *Konjunktiv I* is not used at all (except in SW). The indicative
and *Konjunktiv II* are used interchangeably, with the indicative
predominating, eg:

Sie hat gesagt, sie { **weiß** es schon
{ **wüßte** es schon

Sie hat gesagt, sie { **hat** es verstanden
{ **hätte** es verstanden

Sie hat gesagt, sie { **wird** es versuchen
{ **würde** es versuchen

When *Konjunktiv II* is used, it is in the *würde*-form except with a few
common verbs (see **4.5.1**), eg:
Er hat gesagt, er **käme** heute nicht
Sie sagt, sie **würde** auf dem Land **leben**

Konjunktiv II is used mainly if there is a longer stretch of reported
speech covering more than one sentence, eg:
Der sagt, daß er 'nen neuen Wagen gekauft **hat**. Der **hätte** über
50 000 Mark gekostet und **hätte** eine Klimaanlage

4.5.3 Conditional sentences

Konjunktiv II is used in all types of 'unreal' conditional sentences in
all registers, eg:
Wenn wir Zeit **hätten**, **könnten** wir einen Ausflug machen
Die Europäer **wären** erleichtert, wenn England wieder **austreten**
würde
Wir **würden** es **begrüßen**, wenn du uns besuchen **könntest**
Ich **würde** mich **freuen**, wenn sie es **schaffen würde** (R3:
schaffte)
Wenn sie auf der Autobahn **gefahren wären**, **hätten** sie die
Fähre auch rechtzeitig **erreicht**
Bei dem Wetter **wäre** ich nicht in Urlaub gefahren
Ich **würde** sonst das Fenster **aufmachen**
Ich **hätte** schon an sie **geschrieben**, nur habe ich ihre Adresse
nicht gewußt

The choice of one-word form or *würde*-form depends on the
individual verb or on register, see **4.5.1**.

A common variant in conditional sentences in all registers, but very
frequent in R1, is the combination of *sollte* in the *wenn*-clause and a
future (or present, see **4.3.1**) in the main clause. This is similar to the
use of *should* or *were to* in English, eg:
Wenn er sich dazu entschließen **sollte**, werden wir
zusammenarbeiten können
Wenn sich die Umstände nun ändern **sollten**, wird die Situation
wohl etwas besser aussehen
Sollte ich es fallen lassen, zerbricht es sicher

wollte is also a frequent alternative, especially (though not only) in R3 with *wenn* omitted, eg:

Es würde uns zu lange aufhalten, **wollten wir** alle diese Probleme ausführlich behandeln

For 'real' or 'open' conditions, where the present and future tenses are used in English, German uses the indicative, eg:

Wenn ich Zeit habe, komme ich mit
If I have time, I'll come with you

Contrast:

Wenn ich Zeit hätte, käme ich mit
If I had time, I'd come with you

4.5.4 Other uses of the subjunctive

(a) Comparative clauses with *als ob* and other conjunctions with the meaning 'as if'

Konjunktiv II is the most usual form, and is found in all registers, eg:
als ob sie sich **amüsierte**
als ob er nicht einverstanden **wäre**
als ob sie nicht **kämen**
als ob sie nicht **bezahlt hätten**

In R3, *Konjunktiv I* is sometimes found, *if* there is a distinct form. However, it is less frequent than *Konjunktiv II*. There is no difference in meaning whatsoever, eg:
als ob sie sich **amüsiere**
als ob er nicht einverstanden **sei**

In R2 and R1, *würde*-forms are frequent in appropriate cases (see **4.5.1**), eg:
als ob sie sich **amüsieren würde**

In R1, the indicative is equally common, without any distinction in meaning, eg:
als ob sie sich **amüsiert**
als ob er nicht einverstanden **ist**
als ob sie nicht **kommen**
als ob sie nicht **bezahlt haben**

For English 'as if', *als ob* is possible in all registers. In written R3 and R2, though, *als* + verb is the commonest alternative, eg:
als amüsierte sie sich
als wäre er nicht einverstanden

als wenn is used only in R3, where it is the least common alternative, eg:
als wenn sie nicht kämen

wie wenn, usually with the indicative, is frequent in R1, eg:
wie wenn sich nicht kommen

(b)   Consecutive clauses with *als daß, ohne daß*

Konjunktiv II is fairly regular with these in R3, eg:
  Diese Hi-Fi-Anlage ist viel zu teuer, als daß ich sie mir leisten
  könnte
  Diese Mannschaft ist seit Jahren in der Bundesliga, ohne daß sie je
  deutscher Meister **geworden wäre**

The indicative is used in other registers (and, in practice, main clause
constructions are often preferred in R1, see **5.2**) and is not unknown
in R3, eg:
  Diese Hi-Fi-Anlage ist zu teuer, als daß ich es mir leisten **kann**
  Diese Mannschaft ist seit Jahren in der Bundesliga, ohne daß sie je
  deutscher Meister **geworden ist**

(c)   Purpose clauses with *damit*

Konjunktiv II (or *Konjunktiv I*, *if* there is a clear form) is occasionally
found in rather old-fashioned R3, eg:
  Er zog sich zurück, damit wir ihn nicht **sähen**
  Er gab ihr Geld, damit sie einen neuen Mantel **kaufe**
  Ich will ihm die Uhr bringen, damit er sie **repariere**

However, even in R3, the indicative is now more usual, ie:
  Ich will ihm die Uhr bringen, damit er sie **repariert**

Nevertheless, the most natural construction in these sentences is to
use **können** or **sollen**, ie:
  Er zog sich zurück, damit wir ihn nicht sehen **konnten/sollten**
  Er gab ihr Geld, damit sie einen neuen Mantel kaufen
  konnte/sollte
  Ich will ihm die Uhr bringen damit er sie reparieren **kann/soll**

(d)   Idiomatic uses

Konjunktiv II is very common, especially in spoken R1 and R2, and
particularly in C + S, to moderate the tone of an assertion, a
statement, a request or a question and make it sound more polite, eg:
  Das **wäre** eigentlich alles, was ich dazu zu sagen **hätte**
  Ich **würde** auch **meinen**, daß es jetzt viel zu spät ist
  Das **dürfte** Peter gewesen sein
  Das **wäre** nun das letzte
  Somit **hätten** wir es geschafft
  Könnten Sie mir bitte sagen, wo hier die Pauluskirche ist?
  Würden Sie mir bitte das Salz **reichen**?

Konjunktiv I, in particular of the *sein*-passive, is frequent in technical
R3b to express a proposition, eg:
  In diesem Zusammenhang **sei** nur darauf verwiesen, daß diese
  Hypothese auf Humboldt zurückgeht
  Hier **sei** nur vermerkt, daß ihm dieses Experiment nie einwandfrei
  gelungen ist

4.6 The modal auxiliaries

The six modal auxiliary verbs, *dürfen, können, mögen, müssen, sollen* and *wollen*, are used typically to show the attitude of the speaker to the content of the sentence, expressing volition, possibility, necessity, permission, etc. They tend to be difficult for the English learner because they each have a wide range of meanings which shade into one another, because they have a number of idiomatic uses, and because the English verbs to which they are deceptively similar are themselves irregular and elusive in meaning. Given these problems it is good practice to treat each possible combination of modal auxiliary and main verb, in the various tenses and moods, separately and to know the possible equivalent(s) for each in the other language. In this section these major correspondences are illustrated as fully as possible.

A significant initial difference between these verbs in English and German is that, whereas the English modals have at most only a present tense and a past tense (often with conditional meaning), the German modals have a full range of moods and tenses. The following forms are the most common and will need to be learned for all the verbs:

Tense	Construction	Example
present	+ infinitive	er **kann es machen**
present	+ past infinitive	er **kann es gemacht haben**
future	+ infinitive	er **wird es machen können**
past	+ infinitive	er **konnte es machen**
perfect	+ infinitive	er **hat es machen können**
past subj	+ infinitive	er **könnte es machen**
past subj	+ past infinitive	er **könnte es gemacht haben**
pluperf subj	+ infinitive	er **hätte es machen können**

NOTE: there is no real difference in meaning between the past and perfect forms (see **4.3.2**). In general usage, the past is commoner with most of these verbs, even in R1 (except in S). Only with *können* and *müssen* is the perfect equally frequent.

4.6.1 The German modals

DÜRFEN

dürfen expresses permission or, in *Konjunktiv II*, probability, eg:

Sie **dürfen** hereinkommen	{ *They **may/can** come in* { *They **are allowed to** come in*
Sie **dürfen nicht** hereinkommen	{ *They **mustn't** come in* { *They're not **allowed to** come in*
Das **darf** als Vorteil betrachtet werden	*That **can/may** be seen as an advantage*
Das **darf** doch **nicht** wahr sein	*But that **can't** be true*
Wir freuen uns, Ihnen mitteilen zu **dürfen** . . . (R3b)	*We are pleased **to be able to** inform you . . .*
Sie werden spielen **dürfen**	*You will **be allowed to** play* ⟫→

[DÜRFEN]	Er **durfte** diese Reise machen	He *was allowed to* go on that journey
	Endlich **durfte** er die Augen aufmachen	At last he *could* open his eyes again
	Dürfte ich das Fenster aufmachen?	*Would you mind if* I opened the window?
	Das **dürfte** sie doch gar nicht wissen	She *ought not to know that* (ie it shouldn't be allowed)
	Sie **dürfte** krank sein	{ She *will* be ill { She is *probably* ill
	Sie **dürfte** krank gewesen sein	{ She *will* have been ill { She was *probably* ill
	Das **hätten** Sie **nicht** unterschreiben **dürfen**	You *ought not to have* signed that (ie it shouldn't have been allowed)

KÖNNEN

NOTE: the use of *kann* to express possibility (= English *may*, see **4.6.2**) is limited to cases where it is not ambiguous (ie where it could not be interpreted as expressing ability = English *be able to*). It is thus most frequent with a past infinitive, but even then, especially in the negative, *auch* is usually added to resolve the possible ambiguity.

können expresses possibility or ability and, in R1, permission, eg:

Er **kann** gut schwimmen	He *can swim well*
Sie **kann** es **nicht** machen	{ She *can't do it* { She *isn't able to do it*
Du **kannst** Fußball spielen (R1)	{ You *can/may play football* { *I'll let* you play football
Er **kann** jeden Augenblick kommen	He *may* come at any moment
Sie **kann** es (auch) verloren haben	She *may* (well) have lost it
Er **kann** es (auch) gesehen haben	He *may* have seen it
Er **kann** es **nicht** 'gesehen haben	He *can't* have seen it
Er **kann** es auch 'nicht gesehen haben	He *may not* have seen it
Er **kann** Spanisch	He *can* speak Spanish
Du **wirst** es schon finden **können**	You'll *be able to* find it
Ich **konnte** ihm **nicht** helfen Ich **habe** ihm **nicht** helfen **können**	{ I *couldn't* help him { I *wasn't able to* help him
Ich **könnte** genau so schnell laufen	{ I *could* run just as fast { I *would be able to* run just as fast
Das **könnte** schwierig sein	That *could/might* be difficult
Er **könnte** (wenigstens) seine Schulden bezahlen	He *could/might* (at least) pay his debts
Könnten Sie ihn darum bitten?	*Could* you ask him for it?

' stressed syllables are preceded by a stress mark

Er **könnte** uns belauscht **haben**	He *could have* eavesdropped on us (ie it is possible that he did)
Er **hätte** uns belauschen **können**	He *could have* eavesdropped on us (ie he would have been able to, but he didn't)
Sie **könnte** den Brief **nicht** geschrieben **haben**	She *couldn't have* written the letter (ie it wasn't possible that she did)
Sie **hätte** den Brief **nicht** schreiben **können**	She *couldn't have* written the letter (ie she wouldn't have been able to)
Sie **hätten** etwas höflicher sein **können**	You *might have* been rather more polite

MÖGEN

mögen expresses liking or desire, normally in the present or *Konjunktiv II*. In R3, and a few more generally used set phrases, it can express possibility (like English 'may'). In this case, it often has a concessive sense, with the force of 'although'.

Sie **mag keinen** Kaffee	She *doesn't like* coffee
Wir **mögen** den Lehrer **nicht**	We *don't like* the teacher
Das **mag** (wohl) sein	That *may well* be
Wie dem auch sein **mag**	However that *may* be
Er **mag** etwa dreißig (gewesen) sein (R3)	He is (was) *perhaps* about thirty
Wie schwierig es auch sein **mag/möge** (R3)	However difficult it *may* be
Das **mag** deutschen Ohren etwas fremd klingen, aber . . . (R3)	That *may* sound rather strange to German ears, but . . .
Das **mag** vielen **nicht** einleuchten, aber . . . (R3)	That *may not* be clear to many, but . . .
Er sagte ihr, sie **möge** unten warten (R3)	He asked her to kindly wait downstairs (indirect command)
Das Zeichen x **möge** ein Winkel von 30° bezeichnen (R3b)	*Let* x be an angle of 30°
Die Herren **mögen** sich beim Direktor melden (R3)	Would the gentlemen *be good enough to* go and see the principal
Er **mochte** etwa dreißig sein (R3)	He was *probably* about thirty
Er **hat** sie auch **nicht gemocht**	He *didn't like* her, either
Er **möchte** nach Wien fahren	He *would like to* go to Vienna
Möchten Sie noch Wein?	*Would you like* some more wine?
Ich **möchte** Sie **nicht** länger aufhalten	I *wouldn't want to* keep you any longer
Sagen Sie ihr, sie **möchte** (R3 **möge**) zu mir kommen	Ask her to be kind enough to come and see me (indirect command)
Ich **möchte**, daß sie sofort weggeht	I *want* her to leave immediately
Ich **möchte** dein Gesicht gesehen haben	I *would like to* have seen your face

217

MÜSSEN

müssen expresses necessity, compulsion or certainty, eg:

Wir **müssen** jetzt gehen	{ *We **must** go now* { *We **have (got) to** go now*
Wir **müssen** noch **nicht** gehen	{ *We **needn't** go yet* { *We **don't have to** go yet*
Das **muß** das Richtige sein	*That **must** be the right one*
Das **muß nicht** das Richtige sein	*That **isn't necessarily** the right one*
Etwas **muß** passiert sein	*Something **must** have happened (ie just now)*
Sie **wird** sich beeilen **müssen**	*She'**ll have to** hurry*
Ich **mußte** zu Hause arbeiten Ich **habe** zu Hause arbeiten **müssen**	*I **had to** work at home*
Ich **mußte** einfach lachen	*I **couldn't help** laughing*
Etwas **mußte** passiert sein	*Something **must** have happened (ie a long time ago)*
Du **müßtest** den Chef fragen	*You **would have to** ask the boss*
Ich **müßte** den Brief **nicht** schreiben	*I **wouldn't need to** write the letter*
Er **müßte** es eigentlich besser wissen	*He really **ought to/should** know better*
Er **müßte** schon dort sein	*He **should/ought to** be there by now*
Er **müßte** längst angekommen sein	*He **should/ought to** have arrived long ago (ie we can fairly assume that he has arrived)*
Er **hätte** heute ankommen **müssen**	*He **should/ought to** have arrived today (ie he ought to have done, but he hasn't)*

SOLLEN

sollen most commonly expresses an obligation, occasionally an assertion, a supposition or a condition, eg:

Ich **soll** hier bleiben	{ *I'm **supposed/meant to** stay here* { *I've **got to** stay here*
Du **sollst** die Tür zumachen	*I want you to shut the door*
Er **soll** sofort kommen	{ *He **is to/has got to** come at once* { *Tell him to come at once*
Ich **soll nicht** hier bleiben	{ *I'm **not supposed to** stay here* { *I **mustn't** stay here*
Er hat gesagt, ich **soll** unten warten	*He told me to wait downstairs (indirect command)*
Hier **soll** das neue Rathaus gebaut werden	*The new town hall **is to be** built here*
Sollen wir uns die Stadt ansehen?	***Shall** we look round the town?*
Sie **soll** sehr ehrgeizig sein	*She's **supposed/said to be** very ambitious*
Sie **soll** sehr ehrgeizig gewesen sein	*She's **supposed/said to** have been very ambitious*
Wir **sollten** uns dort treffen	*It **was agreed that we should** meet there*

Es **sollte** eine Überraschung sein	It **was meant** to be a surprise
Jeder **sollte** das Buch lesen	Everyone **should/ought to** read the book
Das **solltest** du mal probieren	You **should/ought to** try that
Sollte das wahr sein?	**Could** that be true?
Er **sollte** den Freund nie wiedersehen	He **was (destined)** never **to** see his friend again
Wenn/Falls es morgen regnen **sollte**, ...	If it **should/were to** rain tomorrow ...
Ich trat zurück, damit sie mich **nicht** sehen **sollten**	I stepped back, so that they **shouldn't** see me
Jeder **sollte** das Buch bis Freitag gelesen haben	Everyone **should/ought to** have read the book by Friday (ie I would expect it of everyone)
Jeder **hätte** das Buch voriges Jahr lesen **sollen**	Everyone **should/ought to have** read the book last year (ie it was expected of everyone, but they didn't)
Das **sollte** ihr inzwischen klar geworden sein	She **should/ought to have** realized that by now (ie I would expect she has)
Er **hätte** es mir doch gleich sagen **sollen**	He **should/ought to have** told me right away (ie I would have expected it, but he didn't)

NOTE: the form *sollte* is potentially ambiguous, as there is nothing to show the difference between indicative and subjunctive. *Er sollte mitkommen* could mean 'He was supposed to come with us' or 'He ought to come with us', depending on the context.

WOLLEN

wollen most often expresses desire or intention, occasionally a claim or necessity, eg:

Ich **will** das Klavier verkaufen	{ I **want to/will** sell the piano { I'm **going to** sell the piano
Willst du uns **nicht** helfen?	**Won't** you help us?
Der Regen **will nicht** aufhören	The rain **isn't going to** stop
Er **will**, daß du es liest	He **wants** you to read it
Wollen wir uns die Stadt ansehen?	**Let's** look round the town
Das **will** geübt sein	That **needs to be** practised
Ein solcher Wagen **will** gut gepflegt werden	A car like that **needs** looking after well
Er **will** krank sein	He **claims/says** he is ill
Er **will** krank gewesen sein	He **claims/says** he was ill
Sie **wird** dort **nicht** arbeiten **wollen**	She **won't want to** work there
Sie **wollte** ihn darum bitten	She **wanted to** ask him for it
Sie **hat** ihm darum bitten **wollen** (R1)	She **was going to** ask him for it

NOTE: the perfect of *wollen* is quite frequent in R1, although the past is commoner.

[WOLLEN]	Das Fenster **wollte nicht** zugehen	{ *The window **wouldn't** shut* { *The window **refused to** shut*
	Ich **wollte**, ich müßte es nicht tun	*I **wish** I didn't have to do it*
	Wenn er es nur zugeben **wollte**, . . .	*If he **would** only admit it . . .*
	Wenn wir ihn fragen **wollten**, würde er es bestreiten	*If we **were to** ask him, he would deny it*
	Es sah aus, als **wollte** er jeden Augenblick einschlafen	*It looked as if he **was going** to fall asleep at any minute*
	Ich **hätte** es auch **nicht** machen **wollen**	*I **wouldn't have wanted to** do it either*

4.6.2 The English modals

CAN

- *can* most often expresses ability or possibility and *können* is the usual German equivalent, although *vielleicht* or a paraphrase is sometimes needed in the sense of possibility in order to avoid ambiguity.

She **can** play tennis	**Sie *kann* Tennis spielen**
Pigs **can't** fly	**Schweine *können nicht* fliegen**
I **can't** come tomorrow	**Ich *kann* morgen *nicht* kommen**
He **can 'not** come	**Er *kann* auch '*nicht* kommen**
Can he be mending the car?	{ **Repariert er den Wagen *vielleicht*?** { ***Kann es sein*, daß er den Wagen repariert?**

> ' stressed syllables are preceded by a stress mark

NOTE: **Kann er den Wagen reparieren?** = *Can he mend the car?*

| He **can't** be mending the car | ***Es ist unmöglich*, daß er den Wagen repariert** |

NOTE: **Er *kann* den Wagen *nicht* reparieren** = *He can't mend the car.*

| Can they have missed the connection? | { ***Können* sie den Anschluß verpaßt haben?**
 { **Haben sie *vielleicht* den Anschluß verpaßt?** |
| The road **can** be blocked | **Die Straße *kann* gesperrt werden** |

- In all but the most formal English, *can* also expresses permission. This is normally *dürfen* in German, though *können* is quite common in R1 or where the sense of possibility is close, eg:

| Can I go to the cinema? | ***Darf*** (R1: **Kann**) **ich ins Kino gehen?** |
| This **can** be regarded as a valid objection | **Das *darf/kann* als berechtigter Einwand angesehen werden** |

- With verbs of sensation (eg *see, hear, smell, feel*) *can* is often used in English with no real idea of ability. In these cases *können* is not used in German, eg:

We **can** hear the music	**Wir hören die Musik**
I **can** see him quite well	**Ich sehe ihn ganz gut**

COULD

- *could* may be used as the past tense of *can* in the senses given above (ie = *was able to*). In such cases appropriate past or perfect tense forms will be found in German, eg:

I **could** swim well when I was a child	**Ich *konnte* gut schwimmen, als . . .** **Ich *habe* gut schwimmen *können*, als...**
I **could**n't come yesterday	**Ich *konnte* gestern nicht kommen** **Ich *habe* gestern nicht kommen *können***
She **could** go out whenever she liked	**Sie *durfte*** (R1: ***konnte***) **ausgehen, wenn sie wollte**
They **could** see the church	**Sie sahen die Kirche** **Sie haben die Kirche gesehen**

- However, *could* frequently has a conditional sense, often expressing *would be able to*, and the German equivalent is then *könnte* (OR *dürfte*, if permission is involved). As with *can*, it may be preferable at times to use *vielleicht* or a paraphrase with *es ist möglich* to avoid ambiguity.

I should be pleased if you **could** come	**Ich würde mich freuen, wenn Sie kommen *könnten***
Could I open the window?	***Dürfte/Könnte* ich das Fenster aufmachen?**
You **could** be right	**Sie *könnten* recht haben**
That **could** be difficult	**Das *könnte* schwierig sein**
Could that be the gentleman?	***Könnte* das der Herr sein?**
Could the train be late?	***Könnte* der Zug Verspätung haben?** **Hat der Zug *vielleicht* Verspätung?** ***Wäre* es *möglich*, daß der Zug Verspätung hat?**
Could he be mending the car?	**Repariert er den Wagen *vielleicht*?** ***Wäre* es *möglich*, daß er den Wagen repariert?**

  NOTE: **Könnte er den Wagen reparieren?** could mean *Would he be able to . . . ?*

⟫⟫→

[COULD]

- Note that *could have* is ambiguous and has two possible equivalents in German depending on the sense of the English:

He **could have** done it (ie it is possible that he did it)	Er *könnte* es getan haben
He **could have** done it (ie he would have been able to, but he didn't)	Er *hätte* es tun *können*

- There are a number of German equivalents for *couldn't help*:

She **couldn't help** laughing	Sie *mußte einfach* lachen Sie *konnte nicht anders*, als zu lachen Sie *konnte nicht umhin* zu lachen (R3) Sie *konnte nichts dafür*, sie mußte lachen (R1)

MAY

- *may* expresses permission in rather formal English (for more usual *can*). The equivalents are *dürfen* or *können* (see **can** above).

You **may** go now	Sie *dürfen* (R1: *können*) jetzt gehen
We **may** take it as our starting point that . . .	Wir *dürfen/können* davon ausgehen, daß...

- The commonest sense of *may* is to express possibility. The most frequent German equivalent for this is *vielleicht* or a phrase with *möglich* (see **can** above). *können* can be used, often in the past subjunctive form *könnte*, but only if it cannot possibly be misunderstood in another sense (eg *be able to*). *mögen* is restricted to R3 or S, apart from a few set phrases, and most often expects or implies a concessive qualification, eg: *that may well be(, but . . .)*.

This survey **may** be correct	*Vielleicht* stimmt diese Umfrage *Es ist möglich*, daß diese Umfrage stimmt Diese Umfrage *kann/könnte* stimmen Diese Umfrage *mag* stimmen(, aber . . .) (R3)
This survey **may** not be correct	*Vielleicht* stimmt diese Umfrage nicht *Es ist möglich*, daß diese Umfrage nicht stimmt Diese Umfrage *kann* auch nicht stimmen

NOTE: **kann nicht stimmen** would mean *cannot be correct*.

He **may** be working in the garden	*Es kann sein*, **daß er im Garten arbeitet** *Vielleicht* **arbeitet er im Garten** *Es ist möglich*, **daß er im Garten arbeitet**

NOTE: **Er kann** . . . would mean *He is able to* . . .; **Er könnte** . . . would mean *He would be able to* . . .

The road **may** be blocked	**Die Straße ist** *vielleicht* **gesperrt** **Die Straße** *kann/könnte* **gesperrt sein**
He **may** have seen the bear	**Er** *kann/könnte* **den Bären gesehen haben** *Vielleicht* **hat er den Bären gesehen**
He **may** not have seen the bear	**Er** *kann* **den Bären auch nicht gesehen haben** *Vielleicht* **hat er den Bären nicht gesehen**

- *may* after verbs of hoping, fearing, wishing, etc, and after *so that*, has no equivalent in German.

I hope that he **may** recover	**Ich hoffe, daß er sich bald erholt**
I am telling you this so that you **may** know exactly what I am going to do	**Ich sage Ihnen das, damit Sie genau wissen, was ich vorhabe**

MIGHT

- *might* is sometimes used to ask permission (= *dürfte*), eg:

Might I ask you a favour?	*Dürfte* **ich Sie um einen Gefallen bitten?**

- However, the commonest sense of *might* is to express possibility. This is close to *could* (see under **could** above) and the usual German equivalent is *könnte*, *unless* this is ambiguous, as explained above under **can** and **may**.

She **might** be in Berlin now	**Sie** *könnte* **jetzt in Berlin sein**
The road **might** be blocked	**Die Straße** *könnte* **gesperrt sein**
You **might** shut the door (reproachful)	**Du** *könntest* **die Tür zumachen**
He **might** not come	**Er kommt** *möglicherweise* **nicht** **Er kommt** *vielleicht* **nicht** *Es wäre möglich*, **daß er nicht kommt**

NOTE: **Er könnte nicht kommen** = *He wouldn't be able to come.*

[MIGHT]

- *might have*, like *could have*, is ambiguous in English and the two senses have different German equivalents:

He **might** have been killed (ie it is possible that he was)	{	**Er *könnte* umgekommen sein** **Er ist *vielleicht* umgekommen**
He **might** have been killed (ie possible, but he wasn't)		**Er *hätte* umkommen *können***
He **might** have told Ursula (ie it is possible that he did)	{	**Er *könnte* es Ursula gesagt haben** ***Vielleicht* hat er es Ursula gesagt**
He **might** have told Ursula (ie possible, but he didn't)		**Er *hätte* es (doch) Ursula sagen *können***
He **might** not have received it	{	**Er hat es *vielleicht* nicht bekommen** **Er hat es *möglicherweise* nicht bekommen** ***Es wäre möglich*, daß er es nicht bekommen hat**

MUST

- *must* expresses necessity or compulsion; *müssen* is the usual German equivalent, eg:

I **must** talk to him today	**Ich *muß* ihn heute sprechen**
They **must** leave at seven	**Sie *müssen* um sieben abfahren**
Sabine **must** be mad	**Sabine *muß* verrückt sein**
They **must** have left at seven	**Sie *müssen* um sieben abgefahren sein**
I **must** have lost it	**Ich *muß* es verloren haben**

- However, *mustn't* is in standard German normally *nicht dürfen*. *nicht müssen* (see under **müssen** above) = English *don't have to* or *needn't* (although it is sometimes heard for *mustn't* in N).

You **mustn't** play football here	**Ihr *dürft* hier *keinen* Fußball spielen**
I **mustn't** forget that	**Das *darf* ich *nicht* vergessen**
She **mustn't** have seen the letter	{ **Sie hat den Brief *wohl nicht* gesehen** **Sie *kann* den Brief *nicht* gesehen haben**

SHALL

- *shall* is usually *sollen* in German, aside from its use for the future tense (see under **will** below), eg:

Shall I bring you the flowers?	***Soll* ich dir die Blumen bringen?**
He **shall** pay for this	**Er *soll* mir dafür büßen**
Thou **shalt** not steal	**Du *sollst* nicht stehlen**

- *Shall we . . .?* often corresponds to *Wollen wir . . .?* rather than *Sollen wir. . . ?*, which has more the sense 'do you want us to . . .?', eg:

Now what **shall we** do?	**Nun, was *wollen wir* machen?**
Shall we have lunch here?	***Wollen wir* hier zu Mittag essen?**

SHOULD/ OUGHT TO

- *should* is interchangeable with *ought to* in its commonest sense of expressing obligation or probability. The German equivalents are *sollte* or *müßte*, which are very close in meaning but not always interchangeable. *sollte* carries more the sense of being obliged, whereas *müßte* has rather the idea of probability or necessity.

We **should/ought to** try that	**Das** *sollten/müßten* **wir mal probieren**
He **should/ought to** drink less	**Er** *sollte/müßte* **weniger trinken**
She **should/ought to** be in the office today (ie it is her duty)	**Sie** *sollte* **heute im Büro sein**
She **should/ought to** be in the office today (ie it is most likely)	**Sie** *müßte* **heute im Büro sein**
We **ought to** hurry (ie we are obliged to)	**Wir** *sollten* **uns beeilen**
The letters **ought to** be on my desk (ie it is probable)	**Die Briefe** *müßten* **auf meinem Schreibtisch liegen**

- For the negative *shouldn't* or *ought not to*, *sollte nicht* is the usual equivalent, but *dürfte nicht* can be used to emphasize the idea that something ought not to be or have been allowed, eg:

She **ought not to** know that	**Das** *dürfte/sollte* **sie eigentlich** *nicht* **wissen**
Sales **shouldn't/ought not to** have fallen off so much	**So viel** *dürfte/sollte* **der Absatz** *nicht* **nachgelassen haben**

- Simple *dürfte* can also express the idea of probability, eg:

That **should/ought to** be enough	**Das** *dürfte/müßte* **reichen**
That **should/ought to** be right	**Das** *dürfte/müßte* **stimmen**

- *should have/ought to have* is ambiguous in English, but the ambiguity is resolved in German by using *sollte/müßte* or *hätte . . . sollen/müssen*, eg:

He **should/ought to have** grasped that now (ie it is an obligation on him)	**Das** *sollte* **er nun begriffen haben**
You **should/ought to** have told me that yesterday (ie it was an obligation on you, but you didn't)	**Das** *hätten* **Sie mir gestern sagen** *sollen*
He **should/ought to have** written the letter by now (ie it is probable that he has)	**Er** *müßte* **den Brief schon geschrieben haben**
He **should/ought to have** written the letter yesterday (ie it was most likely, but he seems not to have done)	**Er** *hätte* **den Brief schon gestern schreiben** *müssen*

[SHOULD/ OUGHT TO]

- *should* is used in some subordinate clauses in English as a kind of subjunctive substitute. In most cases this has no equivalent in German, although *sollte* is found in *damit*-clauses in R2 and increasingly in R3 (see **4.5.4**).

I am pleased that she **should** have come	**Ich freue mich, daß sie gekommen ist**
It is surprising that he **should** have failed	**Es ist erstaunlich, daß er durchgefallen ist**

- *should* is sometimes used rather than *would* (see under **would** below) in the first person conditional, but it is frequent, alongside *were to*, in other conditional sentences, where German uses *sollte* (see **4.5.3**), eg:

If you **should/were to** change your mind, please let me know	*Sollten* **Sie es sich anders überlegen, dann geben Sie mir bitte Bescheid**
If he **should/were to** arrive in the morning, I can pick him up from the station	**Wenn er schon am Vormittag ankommen** *sollte*, **dann kann ich ihm am Bahnhof abholen**

WILL

- *will* (or in the first person *shall* – and most often simply *'ll*) is in its most familiar sense the auxiliary for the future tense, which may correspond to a present or a future in German (see **4.3.1**). However, if *will* can be seen as having a sense of desire or intention, then *wollen* is quite possible in German, eg:

He **will** do everything in his power	**Er** *will* **alles tun, was in seiner Macht steht**
The door **won't** close	**Die Tür** *will nicht* **zugehen**
Will you come with us tonight?	*Wollt* **ihr heute abend mitkommen?**
He **won't** listen	**Er** *will nicht* **hören**

- Where the future expresses probability, German, too, can use a future, often strengthened by *wohl*. Common alternatives are *dürfte* or, especially in R1, simply *wohl*.

That'll be the postman	**Das** *wird* (*wohl*) **der Briefträger sein** **Das** *dürfte* **der Briefträger sein** **Das ist wohl der Briefträger**
He'll have left from Hamburg yesterday	**Er** *wird* (*wohl*) **gestern von Hamburg abgefahren sein** **Er** *dürfte* **gestern von Hamburg abgefahren sein** **Er ist** *wohl* **gestern von Hamburg abgefahren**

- *will* can also express a characteristic or habitual activity. This has no direct equivalent in German.

Pigs **will** eat anything	**Schweine fressen nun einmal alles**
Boys **will** be boys	**Jungen sind nun einmal so**
She **will** sit there for hours doing nothing	{ **Oft sitzt sie stundenlang da und macht nichts** **Sie pflegt stundenlang da zu sitzen...** (R3) }

WOULD

- *would* (or in the first person sometimes *should* – often simply '*d*) is most characteristically used for the conditional (= *Konjunktiv II*, see **4.5.3**). However, it can occur for the past tense of *will* in the other senses given above.

She **wouldn't** come when I called her	**Sie *wollte nicht* kommen, als ich sie rief**
The lift **wouldn't** come	**Der Aufzug *wollte nicht* kommen**
Every evening he **would** go for a walk by the river	**Jeden Abend ging er am Fluß spazieren**
She **would** get up early in the morning	{ **Sie stand gewöhnlich morgens früh auf** **Sie pflegte morgens früh aufzustehen** (R3) }
It '**would** rain today	**Ausgerechnet heute *mußte* es regnen**
He '**would** say that	{ **Natürlich hat er das gesagt** **Von ihm war nichts anders zu erwarten** }

> ' stressed syllables are preceded by a stress mark

5 Syntax and word order

5.1 Word order

German word order is much more flexible than English word order. Apart from the basic framework, it is rarely a matter of 'rules' and 'exceptions' because the order can often be varied for emphasis. This section gives some simple basic guidelines.

5.1.1 The verbal bracket

The basic framework for any German sentence (or clause – the traditional distinction is unhelpful and both are termed *Satz* in German) can be seen as a pair of 'brackets' made up of the verb and certain other elements linked to the verb. The position of these is fixed and most of the rest of the sentence is contained between these brackets. There are three main types of bracket construction:

		Initial element	Opening bracket [	Central elements	Closing bracket]
Type 1	a	Gestern	hat	er wohl damit	aufgehört
	b	Warum	hat	er gestern damit	aufgehört?
Type 2	a		Hat	er schon damit	aufgehört?
	b		Hören	Sie sofort damit	auf!
Type 3	a	...,	weil	er gestern damit	aufgehört hat
	b	...,	statt	sofort damit	aufzuhören

We see from this table that there are the following types of bracket construction in German:

Type 1:
finite verb second

The opening bracket is formed by the finite verb, which is always in second place after a single initial element. The closing bracket is usually another part of the verb, ie a separable prefix, an infinitive or a past participle, although this may be lacking, eg in the simple tenses of simple verbs. This type is found:

(1a) in statements, including those where clauses are joined by *und*, *aber*, *denn*, *oder* and *sondern*;

(1b) in wh-questions: the initial element is always a question word such as *was*, *wer*, *warum*, *welcher*, etc.

Type 2: **finite verb first**	The opening and closing brackets are formed by the same elements as in type 1, but nothing precedes the finite verb. This type is found:

(2a) in yes/no questions;
(2b) in commands.
The verb is also first in conditional clauses if the conjunction *wenn* is left out, cf **4.5.3.**

Type 3: **finite verb last**	The opening bracket is a conjunction or preposition and the closing bracket is formed by all parts of the verb. This type is found:

(3a) in subordinate clauses: here the opening bracket is a conjunction;
(3b) in infinitive phrases: the opening bracket may be one of the prepositions *ohne, (an)statt* or *um* but it is often absent entirely.

This basic framework covers all German sentences in all registers; the only exception is that, especially in R1, some element may follow the closing bracket (see **5.1.6**).

5.1.2 The closing bracket

The closing bracket may be formed by more than one element. The order is then as follows:

	Closing bracket	
	Full verb	**Auxiliary**
Er hat es mir nicht	sagen	wollen
Das ist mir doch	gesagt	worden
Er wird es bald	geschrieben	haben
. . . , ohne es mir	gesagt	zu haben

In type 3a the finite verb usually follows all infinitives and participles:

	Closing bracket		
	Full verb	**Auxiliary**	**Finite verb**
. . . , weil er es mir nicht	gesagt		hat
. . . , weil er es mir nicht	sagen		will
. . . , weil es mir nicht	gesagt	worden	ist
. . . , weil es mir nicht	gesagt	werden	kann
. . . , weil er es bald	geschrieben	haben	wird

R1* = vulgar
R1 = informal
    colloquial
R2 = neutral
R3 = formal
R3a = literary
R3b = non-literary
(see 1.1.5)

N = North
C = Central
S = South
SW = South West
SE = South East
AU = Austria
CH = Switzerland
(see 1.2.3)

There is one exception to this rule. If there are two infinitives at the end of the clause (eg in the compound tenses of modal verbs), then the finite verb comes before them:

	Closing bracket		
	Finite verb	Full verb	Auxiliary
. . . , weil er es mir	hat	sagen	wollen
. . . , weil er es mir	wird	sagen	müssen

5.1.3   Initial element

It is an invariable rule of German that in type 1a clauses (ie main clause statements) *one* and *only one* element can occur before the finite verb which forms the opening bracket. This initial element can be a single word, a phrase or a subordinate clause:

	Finite verb		
Initial element	[	Central elements	]
Gestern	haben	wir hitzefrei	gehabt
Vor drei Tagen	sind	wir nach Ulm	gefahren
Als ich klein war,	habe	ich in Berlin	gewohnt

We sometimes find an interjection or a name or certain adverbs preceding the initial element, usually separated by a comma. These are not really exceptions to the basic rule of 'verb second', as they are too loosely linked to the rest of the sentence to be thought of as part of it. The most common of these apparent exceptions are:

(a)   Interjections, exclamations, names, etc, eg *ach, ja, nein, du liebe Zeit, Herr Kollege.*
> **Ach**, dort kommt sie!
> **Mensch**, das ist doch nicht wahr!
> **Karl**, du spielst auch, oder?
> **Gut**, das machen wir!

(b)   Some linking adverbs or phrases, eg *das heißt, weißt du, kurz (gesagt), mit anderen Worten.*
> **Kurzum**, er hat unrecht
> **Wissen Sie**, das hätt' er mir doch gestern sagen können

(c)   A few adverbs can occur initially with another element *or* be placed in their usual position in the clause. The commonest are: *aber, also, allerdings, freilich, höchstens, immerhin, sozusagen, übrigens, wenigstens,* eg:
> Sonntag **also** kannst du nicht kommen
> OR
> **Also** kannst du Sonntag nicht kommen
> OR
> Sonntag kannst du **also** nicht kommen

(d) Two elements can precede the verb if one simply extends the other. This is commonest with adverbs of time or place, eg:

Dort in der kleinen Dorfschule hat der Junge wenig gelernt
Morgen um zwei Uhr kommt ihr Zug an

(e) Main clauses which begin with two or more elements are common in English. Apart from the few cases explained above, in the corresponding German sentences all but one of these elements will be shifted into a position between the brackets, eg:

Then, however, he went to sleep

Dann ist **er jedoch** eingeschlafen
Er ist **dann jedoch** eingeschlafen
Jedoch ist **er dann** eingeschlafen

5.1.4 The use of initial position in German

In type 1a main clauses in German almost any element may occupy initial position. It is then given prominence as the 'topic' of the clause, about which some new information is given later on. Very often it refers back to something just mentioned or is something well known to both speaker and listener. Time phrases are particularly common in this role. This facility in German of using the initial position whilst keeping the basic bracket construction of the clause intact is not shared by English, where the subject must come before the verb. As a result, things are often put in a different way in English; we have to use complicated constructions in order to manœuvre an element into initial position to make it the topic of the clause if it is not the subject of the verb. The following examples show how German can cope with such things within the basic bracket construction and has no need for the complexities of English.

(a) Subject *there/es*

In both English and German the subject can be moved out of initial position to give it more emphasis later in the clause, in which case it is replaced by *there* in English and *es* (or in R1, *da*) in German, eg:

There was no–one waiting for her
Es **hat niemand auf sie gewartet**
Da **hat niemand auf sie gewartet** (R1)

On the other hand, German does not need to use this construction if there is another element which can be placed in initial position, eg:

There was no–one waiting for her
Auf sie **hat niemand gewartet**

There are some pages missing in this book
In diesem Buch **fehlen ein paar Seiten**

There's no–one there, though
Da **ist doch niemand**

(b) *have* + participle

In English we can shift something into initial position by making it the subject of *to have*; the 'real' verb of the sentence then becomes a participle. There is no need for this construction in German, where the elements are merely shifted within the basic construction, eg:

> *This book has* some pages missing
> **In diesem Buch fehlen ein paar Seiten**

> *They've had* their windows smashed
> **Ihnen wurden die Fenster eingeworfen**

> *The room next door has* a student living in it
> **Im Zimmer nebenan wohnt ein Student**

(c) Passive

A common reason for preferring a passive in English is to put what would normally be the object of the verb into initial position. This is usually unnecessary in German, where we can simply move the object and the subject round within the basic construction, eg:

> These words must now be followed by deeds
> **Auf diese Worte müssen nun Taten folgen**

> They were being helped by the gipsies
> **Ihnen haben die Zigeuner geholfen**

(d) Cleft sentences

An element can be shifted into initial position in English by putting it into a clause of its own, usually with *it* and the verb *to be*. These so-called 'cleft sentence' constructions are unnecessary in German; the relevant element simply goes into the initial position of the basic construction, eg:

> *It was only yesterday* that I saw him
> **Erst gestern habe ich ihn gesehen**

> *It's that television* I wanted to complain about
> **Über diesen Fernseher habe ich mich beschweren wollen**

> *It's what you do* that counts
> **Was man tut, zählt**

There are many variations on this construction, all of which have simpler equivalents in German, eg:

> *That's the book* I'm supposed to read
> **Das Buch da soll ich lesen**

> *This is where* she lives
> **Dort wohnt sie**

> *That's the sort of man* he is
> **So einer ist er**

> *Autumn is when* it's lovely here
> **Im Herbst ist es hier schön**

5.1.5 Central elements

Except for the initial element in type 1 clauses, all the words in a German clause come inside the bracket explained in **5.1.1**. The relative order of these central elements is exactly the same for all clause types. The table overleaf gives a rough preliminary guide to the order of the most important of these elements. A more detailed explanation is given in points (a) – (e) below.

(a) Pronouns

We must distinguish:
(i) personal pronouns: *ich, dir, Ihnen, ihm, man*, etc
(ii) demonstratives: *der, dieser, jener* (R3) used without a noun following. Some unstressed adverbs are counted as demonstratives and share their place in the clause, the most common being *da, dort, hier, gestern, heute, morgen, dann, damals, daher, also*.

The order is then:
(i) Personal pronouns come before demonstratives, eg:

	[	**pronoun**	**demon**		]
Gestern	hat	**mich**	**der**	nicht	erkannt
	Möchten	**Sie**	**diese**	gleich	mitnehmen?
	Hat	**er**	**da**	lange	gewohnt?

(ii) Personal pronouns have the order: nominative – accusative – dative, eg:

	[	**nom**	**acc**	**dat**	]
Wann	werden	**Sie**	es	**ihm**	geben?
Wenn	Wenn	**er**	sie	**Ihnen**	bringt, …
…,	statt		es	**mir**	zu sagen

However, in R1 an unstressed *'s* may follow a dative pronoun, eg:
 Er will **mir's** nicht sagen

The only exception to the rule that pronouns are always found immediately after the opening bracket is that a subject noun in the nominative *may* come before a pronoun, eg:
 EITHER: Gestern hat **mein Mann ihn** in der Stadt gesehen
 OR: Gestern hat **ihn mein Mann** in der Stadt gesehen

However, it is more usual in all registers for the pronoun to come first.

(b) Adverbs and subject/object noun phrases

Within the bracket, adverbs and subject/object noun phrases come immediately after the pronouns and before the complements; the table on page 234 shows the order in which they most commonly

Initial element	Opening bracket [	Pronouns	Subject noun phrase	Indirect object noun phrase (dat)	Most adverbs	Direct object noun phrase (acc)	Manner adverbs	Complement	Closing bracket]
Heute	sind		die Kinder		mit dem Zug			nach Trier	gefahren
Leider	ist		Jürgen		in der Kurve		zu schnell		gefahren
Warum	hat	sie			vor kurzem	ihren Onkel		um Geld	gebeten?
Wann	soll		das Wetter		endlich			besser	werden?
	Haben		die Kinder		bei ihm	Englisch			gelernt?
	Hat		dein Freund	dem Lehrer	am Freitag	das Buch			gegeben?
	Hören	Sie		dem Bericht	doch bitte		gut		zu!
	Halt	ihr			aber	die Tür	weiter		auf!
...;	daß		die Bayern		in Hamburg		schlecht		spielen
...;	weil	ich			in zwei Tagen	den Brief			kriege
...;	um			dem Freund			herzlich	für den Brief	zu danken
...;	um			dem Kerl	plötzlich	den Ball			zuzuwerfen

occur relative to one another. It must be stressed, though, that this order is not an absolute rule of German grammar; much variation is permitted for reasons of emphasis. Basically, the more we want to stress one of these elements, the later it will come. Conversely, an element may be given less prominence by being placed earlier, eg:

Das hat er dann seinem Vorgesetzten *nach langem Zögern* **mitgeteilt** **Das hat er dann nach langem Zögern** *seinem Vorgesetzten* **mitgeteilt**	In the second sentence *who* he told is seen as more important than the hesitation, and the dative object follows the adverb.
Der Lehrer hat nach der Pause dem Jungen *das Heft* **gegeben**	*When* the action took place is less important, and the adverb precedes both objects.
Die Tatsache, daß der EG unausweichlich 1984 *das Geld* **ausgeht**	*What* will run out is by far the most important piece of new information, and thus the subject comes last.
Ich habe mir diesen neuen Anzug *im Herbst* **gekauft** **Ich habe mir im Herbst** *diesen neuen Anzug* **gekauft**	In each case it is the second phrase which is given the greater emphasis.

(c) Adverbs

An adverb is an optional element giving additional information about the circumstances of an action, ie how, when, where, etc. It is not dependent on the verb in the way that complements are.

Adverbs can be:

(i) single words: *schlecht, trotzdem, vorhin, gründlich*, etc
(ii) noun phrases: *den ganzen Tag, eines Abends, eine Weile*, etc
(iii) preposition phrases: *in der Kirche, zum Glück, ohne Zögern, am Ende*, etc.

These differences in form do not affect word order in any way. It should be noted, though, that the same form may vary in function, and its position will change accordingly, eg:

Verb complement dependent on the verb and not deletable – always the last element before the closing bracket (see (e) below)	**Er wohnt seit drei Jahren** *in Frankfurt*
Phrase qualifying the previous noun	**Im Römer** *in Frankfurt* **wurden die deutschen Kaiser gekrönt**
Adverb giving extra information	**Er möchte** *in Frankfurt* **Jura studieren**

The table opposite shows that most adverbs – with the exception of adverbs of manner, which invariably come immediately before the complements – tend to come between the dative object and the

	Attitude	Time	Reason	*mit/ohne* phrases	Place	Manner	
Er ist	vielleicht	seit Montag	wegen des Unfalls		auf dem Hof		verreist
Sie mußte	leider	vor zwei Tagen	jedoch	mit dieser Maschine	im Park		operiert werden
Er wird es		morgen	aus diesem Grunde	mit einer Kettensäge	in Mailand		mähen
Er will sie				ohne ihre Mutter	in Erbach		zerschneiden
Sie haben						lustig	gespielt
Er hat	wohl	am Mittwoch	trotz des Wetters	mit seinem Bruder		schön	gesungen
Er hat						tüchtig	gearbeitet

In this table, the various types of adverbs have been grouped into six broad categories as follows:

Attitude: ie modal particles (see **2.6**) and others which express an attitude on the part of the speaker to what is being said, eg *angeblich, hoffentlich, sicher, wahrscheinlich, vielleicht.*

Time: giving information about *when* an action or event occurs.

Reason: adverbs expressing conditions, eg *bei schlechtem Wetter*; reasons, eg phrases with *trotz* and *wegen*; consequences, eg *folglich*; purpose, eg *zur Durchsicht*; concession, eg *dennoch*; and passive agents with *von* or *durch*, eg *von meinem Bruder.*

mit/ohne **phrases**: these also include adverbs expressing a 'point of view', eg *finanziell* 'from a financial point of view'.

Place: giving information about *where* an action or event occurs.

Manner: denoting *how* an action is carried out, eg *ausführlich, merkwürdigerweise, gern.*

accusative object, whether the adverb is a single word such as *trotzdem* or a phrase such as *voriges Jahr* or *in der Stadt*. If there is more than one adverb, they will most often appear in the order given in the table opposite.

However, this order, too, can be varied for emphasis; an adverb can be stressed more or less by being placed later or earlier, eg:

Das Schloß ist von Ulm aus **in einer knappen Stunde** zu erreichen

Das Schloß ist in einer knappen Stunde **von Ulm aus** zu erreichen

Er hat ihr trotzdem **gestern** geschrieben

Er hat ihr gestern **trotzdem** geschrieben

Sie hat sehr lange **dort** gewartet

Sie hat dort **sehr lange** gewartet

NOTE: as the examples above show, the traditional *Time – Manner – Place* order for adverbs is quite misleading.

(d) The position of *nicht*

In general, *nicht* (and all other negatives, such as *nie* and *kaum*) comes after all adverbs *except* those of manner and after the accusative object, but before adverbs of manner and all complements, eg:

- *after* place and time adverbs but *before* manner adverbs

  Die Berliner haben gestern in Frankfurt *nicht* schlecht gespielt
  Sie haben sich seit langem *nicht* mehr ausführlich unterhalten

- *after* the accusative object

  Er will mir das Kleid *nicht* kaufen
  Sie hat die Vase *nicht* zerbrochen

- *before all* complements

  Wir fahren morgen *nicht* ans Meer
  Er ist sicher *nicht* groß

The above guideline applies if *nicht* is understood to refer to the whole clause. With a change in emphasis, though, ie if a particular element in the sentence is to be negated, then *nicht* precedes it. In such instances there is usually an implied contrast with *sondern*, eg:

Er will mir nicht 'das Buch geben	not *that* book, but a different one
Ich war nicht am 'Sonntag in der Stadt	not on *Sunday*, but some other time
Ich fahre nicht mit meinen 'Eltern nach Italien	not with *my parents*, but perhaps with someone else

(e) Complements

Complements are those elements which are most closely linked with the verb in a sentence (or 'governed' by it, see **4.1**) and 'complete' its action in some way. With the exception of the subject and the accusative and dative objects, which have their own place in the clause (see above), they invariably come last, immediately before the closing bracket. The following list gives all the types of complement to which this rule applies:

(i)   Genitive object (restricted to R3, see **4.1.3**), eg:
      Das Gericht hat den Hausierer zu Unrecht **des Diebstahls**
        beschuldigt
(ii) Prepositional object (see **4.1.4**), eg:
      . . . , weil sich die Mutter nun **um ihre beiden Kinder**
        kümmern wird
(iii) Place phrases after verbs expressing position, eg *bleiben, wohnen,*
      sitzen, stehen, liegen, sich befinden (R3), *sich aufhalten* (R3), eg:
      Warum willst du unter keinen Umständen **in Würzburg**
        wohnen?
(iv) Direction phrases after verbs of motion, eg:
      Dann hat Peter den Stein **in den Bach** geworfen
      Ich will schnell mit dem Audi **in die Stadt** fahren
(v)   Nominative noun phrases and adjectives after the verbs *sein,*
      werden, bleiben, scheinen, heißen, eg:
      Immerhin ist Hans-Jürgen längere Zeit **der beste Schüler**
        gewesen
      Hedwig ist in den letzten Jahren **sehr groß** geworden
(vi) The noun portion of phrasal verbs, eg:
      Der Betriebsrat hat uns gestern davon **in Kenntnis** gesetzt

5.1.6 Can anything follow the closing bracket?

It is by no means an absolute rule of German that the sentence (or clause) *must* end with the closing bracket. This has never been the case in R1, but in recent times so-called '*Ausklammerung*' (ie putting some element after the closing bracket) has become common in R2 and R3. Nevertheless, there are strict limitations on what can follow the closing bracket, as follows.

(a)   Certain elements are rarely enclosed within the bracket in any register. These include:

      (i) Subordinate clauses. In particular, constructions where a number of clauses are enclosed within one another (the so-called '*Schachtelsatz*'), with a cluster of verbs at the end, are now avoided, even in R3a, where they were common in the 19th century:
      NOT: Mein Vater, der selten, obwohl er immer zeitig aufstand, frühstückte, aß an dem Tag vier Butterbrote
      RATHER: Mein Vater, der selten frühstückte, obwohl er immer zeitig aufstand, aß an dem Tag vier Butterbrote

To achieve this, even relative clauses can be separated from their antecedents:

NOT: Else hatte dem Fremden, dem sie am Tag vorher mittellos auf dem Paradeplatz begegnet war, geholfen

RATHER: Else hatte dem Fremden geholfen, dem sie am Tag vorher mittellos auf dem Paradeplatz begegnet war

(ii) Infinitive phrases. These will not be enclosed unless they consist merely of the simple *zu* + infinitive, and even then only in R3:

Er fing zu weinen an (R3)
Er fing an zu weinen

NOT: Er hat eine kleine Atempause zu machen beschlossen
RATHER: Er hat beschlossen, eine kleine Atempause zu machen

(iii) Comparative phrases with *als* or *wie*. These are never enclosed, eg:

..., wo wir uns bewegten wie Tiere auf der Wildbahn
Gestern hat es mehr geschneit als heute

(b) Less regular, but still common, is the postponement of prepositional phrases of any kind or, in R1 only, of any adverb.

(i) In R1, a prepositional phrase or an adverb may follow the closing bracket, either as an afterthought or to emphasize it, eg:

Du hast ihn doch gestern gesehen **in der Stadt** (R1)
Der wird doch nix lernen **bei dem Lehrer da** (R1)

(ii) Especially in written R3, a lengthy prepositional phrase may be postponed in order not to overstretch the bracket construction, or if a further clause depends on it, eg:

Diese Aufgabe kann nun gelöst werden **auf der Grundlage eines einheitlichen Systems des Bildungswesens** (R3b)
Von dieser Höhe aus konnte er wenig sehen **von der kleinen Stadt**, die am anderen Ufer im Dunst lag (R3a)

5.2 Alternatives to subordinate clauses

A very characteristic feature of modern German is a tendency not to use subordinating constructions (clauses or infinitive phrases) if alternatives are available. The extent to which this is so varies from register to register, ie:

R1: main clauses used predominantly.
R2: some subordination, but each main clause will rarely have more than one subordinate clause dependent on it.
R3a: fairly free use of subordinate clauses, but complex sentences with numerous such clauses are still less frequent than in English.
R3b: little subordination and a clear preference for phrases with verbal nouns instead.

The texts in **1.6** illustrate how the extent of subordination varies with register. It is vital to realize that, in all registers, English uses

R1* = vulgar
R1 = informal
      colloquial
R2 = neutral
R3 = formal
R3a = literary
R3b = non-literary
(see 1.1.5)

N = North
C = Central
S = South
SW = South West
SE = South East
AU = Austria
CH = Switzerland
(see 1.2.3)

subordinate clauses much more readily than German. This means that, if an English learner of German expresses himself in German using the main and subordinate clause constructions which sound most natural to him in English, his German will sound rather forced, artificial and foreign. Unfortunately, it is difficult to give any hard and fast rules. Subordinate clauses are not ungrammatical in German; they are simply used less, and other constructions often sound much more natural.

It is therefore important for English-speaking learners to be aware of possibilities of expressing themselves in German through main clauses or noun phrases – rather than through the subordinate clauses which may often appear to be the nearest equivalent to the corresponding English sentence.

Examples of these possibilities are given in the following sections. However, the possibilities are endless and the list cannot hope to be exhaustive.

5.2.1   Alternatives to relative clauses

Major alternatives to relative clauses include the use of extended epithets (esp R3b), compounds (esp R3b) and simple main clauses (esp R1).

Subordinate clause construction	Alternative
das Gebiet, das an Bodenschätzen reich ist, . . .	**das an Bodenschätzen reiche Gebiet . . .** (R3b) **das Gebiet, an Bodenschätzen reich, . . .** (R3)
ein Ereignis, das das Leben bedroht, . . .	**ein lebensbedrohendes Ereignis . . .** (R3b)
Die Stahlarbeiter, die um ihre eigenen Arbeitsplätze fürchten, wollen nicht streiken	**Die um ihre eigenen Arbeitsplätze fürchtenden Stahlarbeiter wollen nicht streiken** (R3b)
Ich bemerkte den Mann, der neben meiner Frau saß	**Ich habe den Mann bemerkt, der hat neben meiner Frau gesessen** (R1)
Techniken, durch die Abgase gereinigt werden, . . .	**Abgasreinigungstechniken . . .** (R3b) **Techniken zur Reinigung von Abgasen . . .** (R3b)
ein Formular, in dem ein Auftrag bestätigt wird, . . .	**ein Auftragsbestätigungs-formular** (R3b)

5.2.2 Alternatives to noun clauses with *daß* or *wie* and infinitive phrases

Especially in R3b, verbal nouns (often compounded) are used as an alternative to noun clauses with *daß* or *wie* and infinitive phrases; R1 often uses main clause constructions if possible.

Subordinate clause construction	Alternative
Vorschläge, wie das herkömmliche Jurastudium neu gestaltet werden kann	**Vorschläge zur Neugestaltung des herkömmlichen Jurastudiums** (R3b)
Sie haben dagegen protestiert, daß zwanzig Zechen stillgelegt werden sollen	**Sie haben gegen die geplante Stillegung von zwanzig Zechen protestiert** (R3b)
	Zwanzig Zechen sollen stillgelegt werden, und dagegen haben sie protestiert (R1)
Er bestreitet, an dieser Demonstration teilgenommen zu haben	**Er bestreitet die Teilnahme an dieser Demonstration** (R3b)
Er bestreitet, daß er an dieser Demonstration teilgenommen habe	

5.2.3 Alternatives to other subordinate clauses

It is worth being aware of some common alternatives, using other conjunctions, to subordinating constructions:

	Subordinate clause construction	Alternative
als	Als sie hinausging, bemerkte sie einen roten Schein in der Ferne	**Beim Hinausgehen bemerkte sie einen roten Schein in der Ferne** (R3)
		Sie ging hinaus, und da bemerkte sie einen roten Schein in der Ferne
als daß	Das Wasser ist zu kalt, als daß man da baden könnte (R3)	**Das Wasser ist zu kalt, da kann man nicht baden**

⫸→

	Subordinate clause construction *contd*	Alternative *contd*
als ob/wenn (see **4.5.4**)	Es sieht aus, als ob es in der Nacht geschneit hätte	**Es sieht aus, als hätte es in der Nacht geschneit** (R2/R3)
außer wenn	Ich gehe spazieren, außer wenn es regnet	**Ich gehe spazieren, außer es regnet** (R1)
bevor	Bevor er einschlief, hat er den Brief gelesen	**Er hat den Brief vor dem Einschlafen gelesen**
		Er schlief ein, aber vorher hatte er noch den Brief gelesen
damit/um . . . zu	Wir machen es immer so, damit Mißverständnisse vermieden werden	**Zur Vermeidung von Mißverständnissen machen wir es immer so** (R3b)
	Wir machen es immer so, um Mißverständnisse zu vermeiden	**Wir machen es immer so; so können wir auch Mißverständnisse vermeiden**
indem/dadurch, . . . daß	Sie verrieten ihre Ziele dadurch, daß sie die demokratischen Institutionen mißachteten (R3)	**Sie verrieten ihre Ziele durch die Mißachtung der demokratischen Institutionen** (R3b)
	Sie verrieten ihre Ziele, indem sie die demokratischen Institutionen mißachteten (R3)	
nachdem	Nachdem er Monate lang gewartet hatte, erhielt er die Nachricht von seinem Erfolg	**Nach monatelangem Warten erhielt er die Nachricht von seinem Erfolg (R3)**
	Nachdem ich den Brief geschrieben hatte, ging ich im Park spazieren	**Ich schrieb den Brief und ging dann im Park spazieren**
obwohl	Obwohl er alt ist, geht er jeden Sonntag im Wald spazieren	**Trotz seines Alters geht er jeden Sonntag im Wald spazieren** (R3)
		Er ist zwar alt, aber er geht jeden Sonntag im Wald spazieren
		Er ist schon alt, trotzdem geht er jeden Sonntag im Wald spazieren

	Subordinate clause construction *contd*	Alternative *contd*
ohne daß/ ohne ... zu	Er hat jahrelang studiert, ohne daß er jemals ein Hauptseminar belegt hätte (R3)	**Er hat jahrelang studiert und hat nie ein Hauptseminar belegt** (R1)
	Er hat jahrelang studiert, ohne jemals ein Hauptseminar belegt zu haben	
	Sie ging in die Stadt, ohne daß er es wüßte (R3)	**Sie ging ohne sein Wissen in die Stadt**
		Sie ist in die Stadt gegangen, und er hat nichts davon gewußt (R1)
seit(dem)	Er hinkt, seitdem er vom Fahrrad gestürzt ist	**Er hinkt seit seinem Sturz vom Fahrrad**
		Er ist vom Fahrrad gestürzt, und seitdem hinkt er (R1)
so daß	Er stand mitten im Gang, so daß keiner vorbeikommen konnte	**Er stand mitten im Gang, also konnte keiner vorbeikommen** (R1)
während	Während er in Marburg studierte, hat er immer den evangelischen Gottesdienst besucht	**Während seines Studiums in Marburg hat er immer den evangelischen Gottesdienst besucht** (R3)
weil	Hier gibt es eine Umleitung, weil die Marienkirche restauriert wird	**Hier gibt es eine Umleitung, die Marienkirche wird restauriert** (R1)
		Wegen der Restaurierung der Marienkirche gibt es hier eine Umleitung (R3b)
		Hier gibt es eine Umleitung, die Marienkirche wird nämlich restauriert
		Hier gibt es eine Umleitung, denn die Marienkirche wird restauriert (R3a)
		Die Marienkirche wird restauriert, deshalb gibt es hier eine Umleitung

》》》→

	Subordinate clause construction *contd*	**Alternative** *contd*
wenn	Wenn man diese Zeitschrift regelmäßig bezieht, erhält man viele Sonderangebote	**Beim regelmäßigen Bezug dieser Zeitschrift erhält man viele Sonderangebote** (R3b)
		Bezieht man diese Zeitschrift regelmäßig, dann erhält man viele Sonderangebote (R3)
	Wenn der Dollar nochmals aufgewertet würde, so würde das zu einer schweren Krise führen	**Eine nochmalige Aufwertung des Dollars würde zu einer schweren Krise führen** (R3b)
	Wir werden es schon schaffen, wenn wir auch wenig Hilfe erwarten können	**Wir werden es schon schaffen, allerdings können wir wenig Hilfe erwarten** (R1)
		Wir werden es zwar schaffen, aber wir können wenig Hilfe erwarten
		Wir können wenig Hilfe erwarten, aber wir werden es trotzdem schaffen

5.2.4 Adverbs rather than clauses

(a) In many cases German may use an adverb construction *or* a subordinate clause where English uses a clause. By and large the German constructions on the left, with adverbs, sound more idiomatic.

Das ist **allerdings** richtig	Ich muß zugeben, daß das richtig ist
	I have to admit that this is correct
Er wird **allmählich** (R1 **langsam**) ungeduldig	Er beginnt ungeduldig zu werden
	He is beginning to get impatient
Er ist **angeblich** krank	Er behauptet, daß er krank ist
	He claims to be ill
Er ist **anscheinend** nicht gekommen	Es scheint, daß er nicht gekommen ist
	He seems not to have come
Hast du **auch** deine Socken eingepackt?	Bist du sicher, daß du deine Socken eingepackt hast?
	Are you sure you've packed your socks?

Wir können Ihnen **bedauerlicherweise** nicht weiter behilflich sein (R3b)	Wir bedauern, daß wir Ihnen nicht weiter behilflich sein können

We regret that we can be of no further assistance to you

Er ist **bekanntlich** ein hervorragender Physiker	Es ist bekannt, daß er ein hervorragender Physiker ist

Everyone knows that he is an outstanding physicist

Hier können Sie **beliebig** lange bleiben	Hier können Sie so lange bleiben, wie Sie wollen

You can stay here as long as you wish

Thomas kommt **bestimmt** mit	Ich bin sicher, daß Thomas mitkommt

I'm sure Thomas is coming with us

Es ist **freilich** nicht einfach	Man muß zugeben, daß es nicht einfach ist

It must be admitted that it isn't easy

Gegebenenfalls kann man auch eine andere Taste wählen	Wenn es nötig sein sollte, kann man auch eine andere Taste wählen

If the need should arise, another key may be chosen

Hoffentlich erreicht er die Hütte vor Sonnenuntergang	Ich hoffe, daß er die Hütte vor Sonnenuntergang erreicht

I hope he reaches the cabin before sunset

Sie kann **leider** nicht kommen	Ich fürchte, daß sie nicht kommen kann

I'm afraid she can't come

Meiner Meinung nach ist er dazu kaum fähig	Ich meine, daß er dazu kaum fähig ist

I hardly think that he is capable of it

Er kommt **möglicherweise** noch vor dem Abendessen	Es ist möglich, daß er noch vor dem Abendessen kommt

It is possible that he will come before dinner

Die Firma stellt diese Ersatzteile **nicht mehr** her	Die Firma hat aufgehört, diese Ersatzteile herzustellen

The firm has ceased/stopped making these spare parts

Alle Passagiere sind **vermutlich** ums Leben gekommen	Man vermutet, daß alle Passagiere ums Leben gekommen sind

It is presumed that all the passengers lost their lives

Er hat **wohl** keine Lust dazu	Ich nehme an, daß er keine Lust dazu hat

I imagine/suppose he doesn't want to

Zweifellos ist dieses Jahr die Ernte besser als letztes Jahr	Es besteht keinen Zweifel darüber, daß dieses Jahr die Ernte besser als letztes Jahr ist

There is no doubt that the harvest is better this year than last

(b) In some cases a German adverb is the only natural idiomatic equivalent for an English verb.

Er hat **andauernd** gelacht	*He **kept on** laughing*
Es wird **bestimmt** regnen	*It **is sure** to rain*
Sie stört mich **dauernd**	*She **keeps (on)** disturbing me*
Im Sommer spielt er **gern** Tennis	*He **likes** playing tennis in the summer*
Sind Sie mit dem Lesen **fertig**?	*Have you **finished** reading?*
Er hat **früher** im Garten gearbeitet	*He **used to** work in the garden*
Sie zieht sich **gern/oft** extravagant an	*She **tends to** dress extravagantly*
Er arbeitet abends **gewöhnlich** im Garten	*He **tends to** work in the garden in the evenings*
Jetzt sehe ich ein, daß ich mich geirrt habe	*I have **come to** realize I was wrong*
Im Winter spielt er **lieber** Handball	*He **prefers** playing handball in the winter*
Er kam **nicht** rechtzeitig an	*He **failed** to arrive on time*
Sei **ja/nur** pünktlich!	***Mind** you're on time!*
Nimm dir **ruhig** noch etwas zu trinken	***Don't be afraid** to help yourself to another drink*
Er las **weiter**	*He **continued** to read*
Ich habe sie **zufällig** in der Straßenbahn gesehen	*I **happened/chanced** to see her in the tram*

5.2.5 Other alternatives to subordinate clauses

(a) Some modal verb constructions correspond to more elaborate constructions in English (see also **4.6**), eg:

Wir **dürfen** hier nicht so viel Lärm machen	*We're not **allowed to** make so much noise here*
Man **muß** nicht so fest ziehen	*It **is** not **necessary** to pull so hard*
Ich **soll** den Brief morgen schreiben	*I'm **supposed to** write the letter tomorrow*
Er **soll** bleich geworden sein	*People **say** that he went quite pale*
Dieses Zeugnis **soll** uns helfen	*This certificate **is intended to** help us*
Sie **soll** eine Fünf in Latein gekriegt haben	*I've **heard** that she got a five in Latin*

Du **sollst** das Licht ausmachen	*I **want you to** switch off the light*
Es **sollte** ein Geschenk sein	*It was **meant** to be a present*
Er **will** es ihr erzählt haben	*He **claims** to have told her*

(b)   Especially in R3, German often uses adjectives and participles as nouns where a full clause is needed in English.

Die Farbe dieser Vögel war **das für mich Interessante**	*The colour of these birds was **what interested me***
Er hat sich über **das Gesagte** aufgeregt	*He got annoyed about **what had been said***
Sie hat **das Übrige** kaum beachtet	*She hardly paid attention to **what remained***
Er wollte **die Ankommenden** begrüßen	*He wanted to welcome **the people who were arriving***
Das Erschreckende an diesem Vorfall war seine scheinbare Unabwendbarkeit	***What was terrifying** about this occurrence was its apparent inevitability*

(c)   Where emphasis can be given in English by the use of cleft sentences with two clauses, German almost always prefers a single main clause construction, using the initial position to give emphasis (see **5.1.4(d)** for further details), eg:

Dort sind wir uns begegnet	***It was there that** we met*
In diesem Haus wohnt sie	***This is the house which** she lives in*
Klar will er nicht mitmachen	***It's obvious that** he won't join in*

(d)   English often uses *to do* to repeat the idea of a previous verb. German does not use *tun* in this way but prefers constructions without a verb at all.

Ein Gebiet, das alle Tiere meiden, nur die Vögel nicht	*An area which all animals avoid, only birds **do not***
Ich schreibe genau wie meine Mutter	*I write just like my mother **does***
Er fühlt sich jetzt besser als gestern	*He feels better now than he **did** yesterday*

5.3 The present participle in German and English

The English *ing*-form (sometimes called 'present participle' or 'gerund') appears to correspond to the German present participle in *-end*, eg *lachend, lesend, sterbend*, etc. However, this is used far less often than the English *ing*-form, and the English-speaking learner of German must be aware of when present participles can occur in German – and when German prefers to use other constructions.

5.3.1 The use of the German present participle

- The German present participle is used most often simply as an adjective or an adverb; this is found in all registers, eg:

  die **schreienden** Vögel   das **kochende** Wasser
  die **streikenden** Arbeiter   das **laufende** Jahr
  überraschend schnell   **überzeugend** dargestellt

- Like all adjectives, it can be used as a noun (mainly R3), eg:

  der **Hinkende**
  etwas **Erschreckendes**

- It can be used with *zu* to make an adjective from an infinitive (typically R3b), eg:

  das **abzufertigende** Gepäck
  die **zu schreibenden** Briefe

- It can be compounded with a noun (most often in R3), eg:

  von **atemberaubender** Schönheit
  die **fußballspielenden** Jungen
  die **Arbeitssuchenden**

- The use of extended adjectives with a present participle is very characteristic of R3b, eg:

  diese **von den vorgeschriebenen Normen abweichende**
    Aufmachung

- A few present participles have become true adjectives and can even be used after *sein*, sometimes with a change in meaning. The most common are:

abstoßend	beruhigend	rührend
abwesend	dringend	spannend
anstechend	drückend	überzeugend
anstrengend	einleuchtend	umfassend
anwesend	empörend	verblüffend
auffallend	entscheidend	verlockend
aufregend	glühend	zwingend
bedeutend	reizend	

Note that there are very few of these. English speakers must beware of confusing them with the *ing*-forms of the progressive tenses, cf:

ein **überzeugendes** Argument   *a convincing argument*
das Argument ist **überzeugend**   *the argument is convincing*

Compare:

die **fehlenden** Seiten   *the missing pages*
die Seiten **fehlen**   *the pages are missing*
NOT: die Seiten sind **fehlend**

A present participle can be used in isolation, most commonly in R3:
Er antwortete mir **lachend**
Die Kinder strömten **singend** durch die Gassen

Phrases with present participles are sometimes to be found, eg:
Ich saß, **meine Puppe auf den Knien haltend**, zwischen meinen
    Eltern am großen Tisch
This use is limited to R3a and, although it is not uncommon there,
there are complex restrictions on when it may be used, and English
students are best advised not to imitate it but instead to use one of the
alternative constructions detailed in **5.3.2**.

5.3.2 German equivalents of English *ing*-form constructions

As the German present participle is used almost exclusively as an
adjective or an adverb, the German equivalents for the many
constructions possible with the English *ing*-form need to be
mastered. The possibilities are almost endless, and only some of the
most common are given below. In many instances, some registers of
German may prefer alternatives without subordinate clauses, the
details of which are given in **5.2**.

(a) *ing*-form qualifying a noun

German usually uses a relative clause or, especially in R3b, an
extended adjective:

The passengers *waiting to be admitted* were becoming impatient	**Die Reisenden, *die auf Einlaß warteten*, wurden ungeduldig**
The steel-workers, *fearing for their own jobs*, did not want to strike	**Die *um ihre eigenen Arbeitsplätze fürchtenden* Stahlarbeiter wollten nicht streiken** (R3b)

(b) *ing*-form expressing simultaneous actions or attendant circumstances

The commonest German equivalent in all registers is simple main
clauses joined by *und*, possibly with *dabei* to stress the link. Note that
in modern German a clause with *indem* is not found in these
instances.

He gazed into the book, *biting his lip*	**Er starrte in das Buch *und biß sich (dabei) auf die Lippe***

                                                             ≫→

He would sit *watching her* for hours	**Er saß oft stundenlang da *und sah ihr zu***
She turned round, *her heart beating with joy*	**Sie drehte sich um, *und dabei klopfte ihr das Herz vor Freude***

If the English sentence begins with a phrase with an *ing*-form, a clause with *als* or *wenn* may be possible in German if the actions are simultaneous.

Looking out of the window, we saw the policeman	**Als wir zum Fenster hinausschauten, sahen wir den Polizisten**
	Wir schauten zum Fenster hinaus *und* sahen den Polizisten

Depending on the sense of the English phrase, other conjunctions may be appropriate in German.

It being late, they decided to take a taxi	**Da es schon spät war, beschlossen sie, ein Taxi zu nehmen**
Standing on top of the tower you can see both the streets	**Wenn man oben auf dem Turm steht, kann man die beiden Straßen sehen**
Having changed the wheel, he set off	**Nachdem er das Rad gewechselt hatte, fuhr er los**
Finding the door open, I nevertheless rang the bell	**Obwohl ich die Tür offen fand, klingelte ich**

(c)   *ing*-forms used as nouns

The German equivalent for these is most commonly a *daß*-clause, an infinitive phrase with *zu* or, especially in R3b (see **5.2**), a verbal noun.

Attentive listening is important	**Es ist wichtig, *aufmerksam zuzuhören***
	Es ist wichtig, *daß man aufmerksam* zuhört
	Aufmerksames Zuhören ist wichtig (R3b)
He admitted *having broken the window*	**Er gab zu, *daß er das Fenster zerbrochen hatte***
	Er gab zu, *das Fenster zerbrochen zu haben*

Entering the operating-theatre is forbidden	**Das Betreten des Operationsaals ist verboten** (R3b)
I can't imagine *her selling her ring*	**Ich kann es mir nicht vorstellen, *daß sie ihren Ring verkauft***
the *art of writing*	**die *Kunst des Schreibens***

Where a verb (or noun or adjective) takes a preposition, the same options are available in German, but the *daß*–clause or infinitive phrase will usually be anticipated by the adverb *da(r)* + preposition. (For instances where this is optional see **4.1.5.**)

I don't remember *having met her*	**Ich erinnere mich nicht (daran), *ihr begegnet zu sein***
	Ich erinnere mich nicht (daran), *daß ich ihr begegnet bin*
their objection to *entering the hall of the temple*	**ihr Einwand dagegen, *die Tempelhalle zu betreten***
	ihr Einwand gegen *das Betreten der Tempelhalle*

(d)   *ing*-form after prepositions

by   **by** + *ing*-form: a clause with *dadurch, daß* or *indem*, or *durch* followed by a verbal noun, eg:

We were able to help her *by postponing the deadline*	**Wir konnten ihr dadurch helfen, *daß wir den Termin verschoben***
	Wir konnten ihr helfen, *indem wir den Termin verschoben*
	Wir konnten ihr *durch eine Verschiebung des Termins* helfen

on   **on** + *ing*-form: a clause with *als* or *wenn*, or *beim* followed by a verbal noun, eg:

On reading the letter, she blushed	***Als sie den Brief las*, wurde sie rot**
	***Beim Lesen des Briefes* wurde sie rot**

⋙→

for	**for** + *ing*-form: *(um)* . . . *zu*, or *zu* followed by a verbal noun, eg:	
	She no longer has any time *for practising*	**Sie hat keine Zeit mehr,** *(um)* **zu üben**
		Sie hat keine Zeit mehr *zum* **Üben**
	They use them *for drinking beer out of*	**Sie benutzen sie,** *um daraus Bier zu trinken*

with	**with** + *ing*-form: various possibilities, eg:	
	She stood in the hall *with tears streaming down her face*	**Sie stand im Flur,** *und Tränen liefen ihr (dabei) über das Gesicht*
	The proposal was rejected *with the Soviet Union voting against*	**Der Vorschlag wurde zurückgewiesen,** *wobei die Sowjetunion dagegen stimmte*
	We could see the old town *with the castle towering over it*	**Wir sahen die alte Stadt,** *über die das Schloß emporragte*
	With unemployment increasing even in Germany, we can expect little improvement in the other European countries	*Mit dem Anstieg der Arbeitslosigkeit* **sogar in Deutschland können wir wenig Verbesserung in den übrigen europäischen Ländern erwarten** (R3b)
		Da die Arbeitslosigkeit **sogar in Deutschland** *gestiegen ist,* . . .
	It's lovely here in autumn, *with the leaves turning*	**Es ist hier im Herbst schön,** *wenn die Blätter sich verfärben*
	With German troops approaching from the East, the position is hopeless	**Jetzt,** *wo sich deutsche Truppen von Osten nähern,* **ist die Lage hoffnungslos**

(e)   Other miscellaneous instances with verbs

see, **hear**, **feel**	We saw *them approaching*	**Wir sahen, wie sie näher kamen**
		Wir sahen sie näher kommen (R3)
	He felt *his heart beating wildly*	**Er fühlte, wie sein Herz heftig schlug**
		Er fühlte sein Herz heftig schlagen (R3)

	They heard *the boys crying for help*	**Sie hörten, wie die Jungen um Hilfe schrieen**
		Sie hörten die Jungen um Hilfe schreien (R3)
keep	We were kept *waiting*	**Man ließ uns warten**
leave	She left her things *lying about*	**Sie ließ ihre Sachen herumliegen**
have	I have a coat *hanging* in the closet	**Ich habe einen Mantel im Schrank hängen**
go	We went *sailing*	**Wir sind segeln gegangen**
come	They came *running* towards us	**Sie kamen auf uns zu gelaufen**

5.4 Spelling and punctuation

5.4.1 Capitals

The basic rule in German is that every noun begins with a capital letter. However, there are a number of areas of uncertainty.

(a) Other parts of speech used as nouns normally have a capital letter, eg:

das Warten	**eine Fünf**
das Ich	**das Für und Wider**
das Zögern	**das Entweder-Oder**

This is in particular the case with adjectives used as nouns (see **3.4.4**), eg:

der Alte	**nichts Schlimmes**
etwas Neues	**das schon Gesagte**
ein Bekannter	**alles Angenehme**

However, there are a number of exceptions to this rule:

(i) A small letter is used if a preceding or following noun is understood, eg:

Die grüne Bluse gefällt mir nicht, ich nehme die **rote**

Es ist sicher das **schnellste** von diesen drei Autos

(ii) The following adjectives normally have a small letter:

ähnlich[†]	**derartig**[†]	**nächst**
ander	**einzeln**	**übrig**
beide	**folgend**	**verschieden**
beliebig	**gewiß**[†]	**weiter**[†]
bestimmt[†]	**gleich**	

NOTE: those marked [†] *do* have a capital after *alles* and *nichts*, eg:

alles Weitere   **nichts Derartiges**

R1* = vulgar
R1 = informal colloquial
R2 = neutral
R3 = formal
R3a = literary
R3b = non-literary
(see 1.1.5)

N = North
C = Central
S = South
SW = South West
SE = South East
AU = Austria
CH = Switzerland
(see 1.2.3)

(iii) Small letters are used in some common phrases, eg:

im allgemeinen	**alles mögliche**
beim alten bleiben	**aufs neue**
jdn zum besten haben	**von neuem**
durch dick und dünn	**des öfteren**
im großen und ganzen	**im stillen**
von klein auf	**im voraus**
vor/seit kurzem	**im wesentlichen**
seit langem	

(iv) Superlatives with *am* or *aufs* have a small letter, eg:

am schnellsten   **aufs genaueste**   **aufs herzlichste**

(b) Some nouns in set phrases have small letters, eg:

etw außer acht lassen	**recht haben**
sich in acht nehmen	**jdm recht geben**
mir ist angst	**das ist schade**
ein bißchen	**er ist schuld daran**
es tut mir leid	**unrecht haben**
es tut not	**es tut weh**
ein paar (see **2.2.1**)	

(c) Nouns used as time adverbs generally have small letters, eg:

**abends   anfangs   morgens   vormittags   sonntags
tagsüber   von morgens bis abends
beizeiten   derzeit   zuzeiten   zurzeit** (AU, CH)

NOTE: usage in phrases with *Mal* is variable, and one finds the following alternatives:

diesmal	**dieses Mal**
das erstemal	**das erste Mal**
zum erstenmal	**zum ersten Mal**
jedesmal	**jedes Mal**
einigemal	**einige Male**
das letztemal	**das letzte Mal**
ein andermal	**ein anderes Mal**

The one-word forms are usually preferred unless the individual words need to be particularly emphasized, eg:

Ich bin nun das erstemal in London
BUT: **das erste Mal, als ich in London war**

In many instances, only one-word forms are used, eg:

**einmal   zweimal   hundertmal   manchmal
allemal   keinmal** (BUT **kein einziges Mal**)
ein paarmal   zigmal (R1)

However, there are also a few instances where separate words are the norm:

beide Male   viele Male   das eine Mal   nächstes Mal

(d)   Many nouns which have become prepositions have small letters:

angesichts	**auf seiten**	**mittels**
anhand[†]	**in bezug auf**	**von seiten**
anstelle[†]	**infolge**	**zufolge**
aufgrund[†]	**inmitten**	**zugunsten**

NOTE: those marked [†] may be written separately and with a capital in older style R3, ie:

an Hand   **an Stelle**   **auf Grund**

(e)   Nouns used as separable verb prefixes normally have small letters:

achtgeben	**haushalten**	**teilnehmen**
wundernehmen	**radfahren**	**skifahren**

NOTE: for the last two verbs only: *Ich fahre Rad, Ich fahre Ski.*

(f)   As in English, capitals are used for titles and proper names, eg:

das Schwarze Meer	**der Rote Milan**
Karl der Fünfte	**die Lange Gasse**
das Deutsche Eck	**die Olympischen Spiele**

NOTE: unlike English, adjectives of nationality have small letters unless they are part of a proper name, eg:

die italienische Sprache   **die schottischen Clans**

(g)   The pronoun *Sie* and its forms (*Ihr, Ihnen*, etc) always have capitals. In letters, the pronouns *Du, Ihr* and their forms (*Dich, Euch, Dein*, etc) are also usually written with capitals (see **2.8**).

5.4.2   The use of *ß* and *ss*

The letter *ß* (usually called *scharfes s*) is currently used universally, both in handwriting and printing, throughout Germany and Austria. Only in Switzerland is *ss* used in its place. It is advisable for foreign learners to follow the majority practice and use *ß* where appropriate. Note that *ß* is not normally used in capitals, eg *groß*, but *GROSS*.

(a)   *ß* is used:

(i)   before consonants, eg:

du läßt, ich wußte, sie müßte

(ii)   at the end of a word or part of a compound, eg:

Fuß, gewiß, Maß, haßerfüllt

(iii)   between vowels *if* the preceding vowel is long, eg:

einigermaßen, größer, beißen, Maße

(b)   *ss* is used between vowels *if* the preceding vowel is short, eg:

wissen, lassen, Wasser

NOTE: these rules are applied automatically and *ß* and *ss* may therefore alternate in the declension of many words with a short vowel, eg:

gewiß	**ein gewisser Herr**
Fluß	**die Flüsse**
er läßt	**wir lassen**
ich muß	**sie müssen**

⟫⟫→

By contrast, words with long vowels will have *ß* throughout, eg:

groß	**ein großer Mann**
Fuß	**die Füße**
Gruß	**die Grüße**
reißen	**es reißt**

The only exception to these rules is that some personal names are conventionally spelt with *ss*, eg:

Günther Grass   **Theodor Heuss**   **Richard Strauss**

5.4.3   The use of the comma

The comma in German is not used to mark a pause in speaking but to show the beginning and end of a grammatical unit (especially clauses or infinitive phrases). The basic rules are very simple, but prove difficult for English learners. Only these are given here, ignoring the many peripheral and special cases (which even many Germans are unfamiliar with).

The basic rule is that *all* clauses (main or subordinate) and infinitive phrases within a sentence should begin and end with a comma, eg:

> Der Bauer, der dabei war, seinen dicken Wintermantel anzuziehen, war der Meinung, daß man in den nächsten Tagen Schnee erwarten dürfte

NOTE: this means that, unlike normal English usage, adverbs within a sentence are *never* surrounded by commas, eg:

> Sie hat jedoch recht gehabt
> *She was, however, correct*
> Nach dem Krieg ging er nach Ulm zurück
> *After the war, he returned to Ulm*

There are then some exceptions to this basic rule:

(a)   No comma is used between main clauses joined by *und* or *oder if* the subject of the second clauses is understood, eg:

> Er kam nach Dresden und ließ sich dort nieder

(b)   There is no comma between parallel subordinate clauses joined by *und*, eg:

> Sie sagte, daß ihr Vater krank sei und daß er ein paar Tage im Bett bleiben müsse

(c)   There is no comma before a simple infinitive + *zu*, eg:

> Wir hatten beschlossen zu warten

However, if there is anything besides the simple infinitive + *zu*, then a comma is normally used, following the basic rule, eg:

> Wir hatten beschlossen, noch dreißig Minuten zu warten

After certain verbs, though, a comma is not used, even if there is more than the simple infinitive + *zu*. This is so:

(i) always with the following verbs:

brauchen   haben   pflegen   scheinen   sein   vermögen

eg:

> Er scheint krank geworden zu sein
> Ich habe mich morgen beim Chef zu melden

(ii) optionally with the following verbs

anfangen	**drohen**	**verstehen**
aufhören	**fürchten**	**versuchen**
beginnen	**glauben**	**wagen**
bitten	**hoffen**	**wissen**
denken	**versprechen**	**wünschen**

if these verbs themselves have no adverbs or objects with them, eg:

Sie versuchte(,) den Korken herauszuziehen

Ich wünschte(,) diese Frau etwas näher kennenzulernen

(d) Insertions, exclamations, explanatory phrases, phrases in apposition and the like usually have commas, eg:

Fleisch, insbesondere Rindfleisch, war jetzt sehr knapp geworden

Er war, wie schon gesagt, durch den Tod seines Freundes bestürzt

Wir wurden durch Herrn Meißner, den Direktor des Instituts, in der Eingangshalle empfangen

Petra, komm bitte schnell in die Küche!

However, comparative phrases with *als* and *wie* do not have commas, eg:

Bis jetzt ist weniger Schnee gefallen als vor einem Jahr

Diese Jacke ist nicht so teuer wie die anderen

5.4.4 Other punctuation marks

(a) Quotation marks are used much as in English, though it is normal practice to place the first set *on* the line rather than above it, and foreign learners should follow this, eg:

Er sagte: „ Vater will, daß ich Jura studiere. "

NOTE: a colon is used to introduce direct speech.

(b) The exclamation mark is used with commands, eg:

Komm bitte sofort in den Garten!

Geben Sie mir diese beiden Schachteln!

However, this rule is applied less strictly than formerly, and a full stop is now sometimes preferred.

For the use of the exclamation mark in letters, see **2.8(c)**.

Abbreviations

acc	accusative case	nom	nominative case
adj	adjective	occ	occasionally
AU	Austria, see **1.2.3**	perf	perfect tense
C	Central German, see **1.2.3**	pl	plural
CH	Switzerland, see **1.2.3**	pluperf	pluperfect tense
conj	conjunction	prep	preposition
dat	dative case	pres	present tense
demon	demonstrative	pron	pronounced, pronunciation
Engl	English	R1	colloquial register, see **1.1.5**
esp	especially	R1*	vulgar, see **1.1.5**
etw	*etwas*	R2	neutral register, see **1.1.5**
fem	feminine gender	R3	formal register, see **1.1.5**
Fr	French	R3a	literary register, see **1.1.5**
fut	future tense	R3b	non–literary written register, see **1.1.5**
gen	genitive case	S	South German, see **1.2.3**
Ger	German	sb	somebody
itr	intransitive verb	SE	Southeast German, see **1.2.3**
jd	*jemand*	sing	singular
jdm	*jemandem*	sth	something
jdn	*jemanden*	subj	subjunctive mood
jds	*jemandes*	SW	Southwest German, see **1.2.3**
masc	masculine gender	tr	transitive verb
N	North German, see **1.2.3**	/	or
neut	neuter gender		

Where necessary a stressed syllable is indicated by ' before it, eg:
der Ma'jor, das Konti'nent

In appropriate instances the plural of a noun is indicated in brackets after the noun, eg:
der Vater (¨), die Frau (–en), der Lehrer (–), der Stuhl (¨e)

In addition, if the genitive singular of a masculine noun does not end in –*(e)s* it is given as follows (see **3.2**):
der Bube (–n,–n), der Mensch (–en,–en), der Name (–ns,–n)

Adjectives used as nouns (see **3.4.4**) are indicated in the following way:
der Beamte(r), das Äußere(s), der Fremde(r)

German word index

This index includes words on which specific information is given on points of usage in the chapters (ie Chapters 2–5) which deal with vocabulary and grammar.

Topic index